CONTRARIAN INVESTING

ANTHONY M. GALLEA

WILLIAM PATALON III

NEW YORK INSTITUTE OF FINANCE

NEW YORK • TORONTO • SYDNEY • TOKYO • SINGAPORE

Library of Congress Cataloging-in-Publication Data

Gallea, Anthony.
   Contrarian investing / Anthony M. Gallea, William Patalon III.
      p.   cm.
   Includes index.
   ISBN 0-7352-0000-9
   1. Investments. I. Patalon, William. II. Title.
   HG4521.G184 1998
   332.6—dc21   97-44720
                                              CIP

Foreword "Selling Hysteria and Buying Panic" reprinted from an article by Jim Rogers, author of *Investment Biker.*

Interior Design: Robyn Beckerman

This publication is designed to provide accurate and authoritative information in regard to the subject matter covered. It is sold with the understanding that the publisher is not engaged in rendering legal, accounting, or other professional service. If legal advice or other expert assistance is required, the services of a competent professional person should be sought.

From a Declaration of Principles Jointly Adapted by a Committee of the American Bar Association and a Committee of Publishers and Associations

Printed in the United States of America

10 9 8 7 6 5 4 3 2 1   10 9 8 7 6 5 4 3 2 1

ISBN 0-7352-0000-9   ISBN 0-7352-0078-5

ATTENTION: CORPORATIONS AND SCHOOLS

NYIF books are available at quantity discounts with bulk purchase for educational, business, or sales promotional use. For information, please write to: Prentice Hall Press/Special Sales, 240 Frisch Court, Paramus, NJ 07652. Please supply: title of book, ISBN number, quantity, how the book will be used, date needed.

 NEW YORK INSTITUTE OF FINANCE
New York, NY 10004-2207
A Simon & Schuster Company

On the World Wide Web at http://www.phdirect.com

Prentice Hall International (UK) Limited, *London*
Prentice Hall of Australia Pty. Limited, *Sydney*
Prentice Hall Canada Inc., *Toronto*
Prentice Hall Hispanoamericana, S.A., *Mexico*
Prentice Hall of India Private Limited, *New Delhi*
Prentice Hall of Japan, Inc., *Tokyo*
Simon & Schuster Asia Pte. Ltd., *Singapore*
Editora Prentice Hall do Brasil, Ltda., *Rio de Janeiro*

From Tony
To my wife, Bonnie, with all my love

From Bill
To my parents, William and Kathleen, the two finest
people I ever have known

CONTENTS

PART I
CONTRARIAN OVERVIEW

CHAPTER 1
WHAT IS A CONTRARIAN?   9

CHAPTER 2
THE CONTRARIAN ADVANTAGE   23

CHAPTER 3
INVESTING AGAINST THE GRAIN: THE PSYCHOLOGY OF THE CONTRARIAN STRATEGY   39

CHAPTER 4
MARKET MANIA: CONTRARIAN LESSONS   55

PART II
CONTRARIAN BUY SIGNALS

CHAPTER 5
TECHNICAL ANALYSIS:
A KEY CONTRARIAN STRATEGY   81

CHAPTER 6
RIDING THE PRICE TREND:
LOOKING FOR VALUE   93

CHAPTER 7
INSIGHTS ON INSIDERS: BUYING WITH
THE SMART MONEY   113

FOREWORD

SELL EUPHORIA, BUY PANIC

In 1980 the price of a barrel of oil had risen alarmingly and long lines of frustrated American motorists sat fuming at every gas pump.

Newspaper articles appeared daily that bemoaned the permanent shortages in nonrenewable fuels, and every learned expert on Wall Street and in academia was certain oil would rise from $40 to $100 a barrel. Headlines in mid-1979 shouted, "Chaos in the Gas Lines," "Nationalize Big Oil?" and "Recession Looms."

Interest rates had risen alarmingly, and investors were hysterical over high inflation and labor unrest. There was a sense that the United States was slipping as a world power and that shortages in all sorts of goods were permanent—that the world was running out of everything. The stock market had been stagnant for years, and now it was clear why.

It was true that for a while in the 1970s the supply of oil was smaller than the demand, but with the rise in prices had come the inevitable rise in production. There were more drilling rigs, more money pouring into holes in the ground under the Gulf of Mexico, the North Sea, and South America, and more young people going into geology. Yet in 1980, while the popular press might not have gotten it right, the petroleum trade journals were clear: Rising prices had brought out enough oil to exceed the demand. Supply continued to increase, and yet the price was still rising, fueled by a media hysteria. This led to inventory building and hoarding.

Consumers turned down their thermostats and bought sweaters. They bought smaller, more efficient cars and household appliances— changes in the public consciousness that would push down demand and hold it down for years to come.

It made a thoughtful person wonder what was going on. The iron law of supply and demand makes perfect common sense: If there is more of an item for sale than there are buyers, the price goes down.

If there is less, the price goes up. There may be time lags, but it has always held true. If, say, the stock market is at new heights, there are 500 co-op apartments for sale in Manhattan and 2,000 Wall Street yuppie buyers ready, willing, and able to buy one, then co-op prices will go up. If the stock market has crashed and only 250 yuppies want those 500 co-ops, the price will fall. Not even a Marxist economist will debate this conclusion.

In fact, the thoughtful investor would read the newspapers and absorb what television reports had to say, and come to the conclusion that he should buy or sell the oil or the co-op. He would not need fancy charts or an MBA or economic advisors. He would think for himself, and gauge his timing on the extremes he found in public thinking.

This oil panic seemed strange to me. I thought back to a visit I had made to a Tulsa drilling rig company in 1971. During the 1940s and 1950s, Tulsa had been the oil rig capital of the world and, since in 1971 I was bullish on oil, I had in mind investing in oil rigs, a "pick and pan" strategy. That is, rather than betting on prospectors' finding gold, I would invest in the less risky business of selling pick-axes and sluicing pans to prospectors. In this case, I would invest in the rigs needed by those who were going to drill for oil.

The chairman of the oil rig company told me, "Oh Lord, Jim, I know I should not say it, since we need all the support we can get, but you seem like a nice young fellow, even if you are from New York. Don't buy our stock. It would be a big mistake. If only I weren't 55 years old but 28, I'd get out of this business in a minute. I'd start over in anything rather than oil. Drilling is a dying business."

Ten years later every pundit who appeared in print was telling the world that oil was going from $40 to $100 a barrel. It was enough to make a thoughtful investor do some hard thinking. In 1971 everybody with any sense wanted out of the oil business, and in 1981 everybody with any sense wanted to be in it—and both were utterly wrong. By the mid 1980s the bottom had dropped out of the price of oil once more.

What is a smart investor to do?

Well, one thing he can do is learn to listen to the popular press with an ear tuned for these extremes. At market tops, the refrain will run, "This time it's different from all other times. Trees will continue to grow and grow and grow. Buy yourself a tree and watch it reach 50 feet, 100 feet, a thousand feet. This is an investment you put money in and forget."

At market bottoms, the song will go (as we can now hear in the melody for lead, the metal, which has become a pariah), "We've lost our chief markets, paint and gasoline. Lead is a poison and kills people. Prices are severely depressed. Every company with any sense is getting out of lead. It has only a marginal future." Phrases such as "disaster," "doomed," and "dead" will be used to describe such a market, and the alert investor will hear them clearly without a newsletter or a call from his stockbroker to advise him.

At this point everybody in the investment world "knows" that lead is dead. But, the savvy investor always examines the other side of what everybody knows. Am I telling you to buy a lead mine? Not necessarily, but you might consider the use of lead in batteries, which continues unabated. The world press tells me the sale of cars and motorscooters to the Chinese, Indians, and other developing countries is growing steadily; won't every car and scooter need a battery?

Another example of what everyone "knows," and what could be a current bottom, is the production of tea. Prices are down over a 15-year period. Tea plantations have been plowed under to make way for palm oil, rubber, and soybean production. I am bullish on tea: supply is down, demand is up, and the tea- drinking Far Eastern nations are becoming richer. But, when I chatted with the chairman of a major tea company recently, he told me he was selling off his tea assets.

"But why?" I asked. "You of all people must know that you're not doing your shareholders any good by selling them off. Tea is so low now it has to come back."

"I know that, but my shareholders say it might be another ten to fifteen years to big profits, and they can't wait."

If enough companies sell off their tea assets, their loss can be the shrewd investor's gain.

It is an old story in the stock market. Today's news articles trumpet the stock market as the ideal place to increase wealth long term, that nowhere else can parents provide so well for their children's college educations. And it is so easy, too. Put your nest egg in a mutual fund company, and it will do all the work.

This is when my mother calls and asks what mutual fund she should invest in. When I tell her none, she becomes exasperated. "But Jim," she says in her most waspish voice, the one reserved for reminding me I have not learned anything since I was seven, "the stock market's gone up eight times in the past 15 years."

"Momma, I know that. You're supposed to buy stocks before they go up, not after."

She is right about the market rising. The Dow Jones index today is around 8,000, but 15 to 20 years ago when the index was under 1,000 and there were only 400 mutual funds, the newspapers put it: "Recession Looms" and "Surge in Interest Rates Puts Squeeze on Already Ailing Economic Sectors." *Business Week* ran a cover declaring "Stocks are Dead." (Some investors claim they are able to profit by taking the opposite tack to *Business Week's* covers. They sell when the magazine declares something is a good investment and buy on the "something-is-dead" covers.)

In all markets, supply and demand are constantly rising and falling, hurtling from one extreme to the other. To an investor with the right ear and eye, fortunes are waiting to be made. Is it easy? No. Does it take work? Yes.

When oil did drop in price from $40 a barrel in the early 1980s to $10 in the mid 1980s, it took with it the real estate market in Texas. It became hard to give away real estate there. Texans invented the phrase "see-through buildings" for partially completed buildings without tenants or the prospects of tenants. Why build an office building when the Resolution Trust Commission, the folks who had taken over the assets of the S & Ls, would sell you two for the same price? Predictions were as gloomy as you can imagine: Texas had enough real estate to last it for the next two to three decades.

Well, that turned out to be the time to buy. Today, buildings are again being erected in Texas. Those who bought buildings there for a few dollars a square foot are able to sell them for ten and twenty times as much.

There is an old adage in investment lore that says, "Buy when blood is in the streets." Actually, it is sometimes best to wait a while. An investor did not have to buy during the riots in the streets of Watts; a year later was time enough to catch the lowest prices and make a fortune. On the sell side, back at the end of the 1970s, when gold was on its way to $875 an ounce, I sold short at $675 on the way up and watched it promptly rise another 30 percent. Gold, of course, later fell sharply and has never made it back to $675. The lesson here is that timing is important. You can be right—but early—and suffer badly.

The other pitfall of buying after the bottom is to sell your position too soon. The best way is to buy once the move is underway, and sell before the top. When no less an investor than Baron Rothschild was asked how he got rich, he responded that he always sold too soon.

Long-term tops and bottoms are similar in that they usually go to extremes. In a bear-market panic driven by fear, as well as a bull mania driven by greed, the mob almost always goes too far. The wise investor expects such a run, gets out too soon, and is better off.

So, the all-important questions become when to buy and when to sell. Timing is difficult. Note, however, that all major market bottoms are alike, whether they are in the corn, stock, or real estate markets. The same is true for tops. Pick any previous top or bottom, anywhere, any time, from the beginning of time until now. When you study it, you'll see that the conviction of certainty of all the participants at the extreme top and the extreme bottom is startling.

Learning to listen to the gloom and doom at bottoms and question it, and to the exultation at tops and question it, makes a sharp investor. It does not take esoteric knowledge or an MBA or some mystical skill. Read the newspapers, watch the television, and think. It did not take a financial genius to see that when the farmers were going broke in the 1980s and Willie Nelson was conducting Farm Aid concerts that some sort of bottom was establishing itself. After all, the world was not going to stop eating.

Tops and bottoms are creatures of extremes. They rise above all rational expectation and then go higher, and they fall farther than common sense suggests.

In a way, buying any security on the public market is like having a crotchety old uncle as a partner. When things are tough, all you hear from him is that the two of you should get out of the business; it never was any good; only a fool would have gone into it in the first place. Let things turn around, however; let a few years of profits roll in and his tune changes: This is the greatest business in the world; things will go well forever; let's not ever give this up. In fact, now that our shares have tripled, let's buy out everybody else.

Your partner is utterly wrong in both his opinions. The trick is to study and think, think and study. When that crotchety old uncle wants to sell, that is when you should be thinking of buying. Not actually buying, perhaps, but giving it strong consideration. Then you have to figure out when to pull the trigger, and when to actually commit funds.

At market tops, greed and hysteria always get the best of the crotchety old uncle, and at bottoms fear and panic buffalo him. The smart investor—the one who does not consider himself a financial genius, but trains himself to analyze the magazines and television, and to pick tops and bottoms by the extremes in the public's attitudes—learns to buy fear and panic and to sell greed and euphoria.

The wise citizen keeps his head and watches for these extremes. But knowing the propensity of his fellows to form mobs, he himself is not caught up in their destructive force.*

---

*Reprinted from an article by Jim Rogers, author of *Investment Biker*.

ACKNOWLEDGMENTS

Contemplating a book about contrarian investing is like thinking about climbing Mt. Everest. You're excited by the challenge, but overwhelmed by the difficulty. Fortunately, many great investors and thinkers have climbed that mountain before and in the process, developed a basic approach we were able to build on. This book, and the strategies it outlines, would not have been possible without the countless contributions found in the work of others. The authors freely acknowledge that we stand on their shoulders.

We wish to thank our families and friends for their patience, encouragement, help, and (thankfully) good humor during this project. While son, boyfriend, father, or husband was distracted from the daily flow of family life, they carried on with kindness and we are deeply grateful to them.

Many individuals were crucial to the creation of this work, and without them, it simply would not have come to life.

Gratitude is due, as always, to Tony's partners on The Gallea Team who once again shouldered the daily workload so he could play author—Richard DiMarzo, Bonnie Lane, Paul Beck, Tara Nemergut, Donna Caufield, Darren Moran, Tom Teall, Sue Monnat, Valerie Adams, Jo Gallea, and Patty Davis. You are the best.

A special thanks to Toni Elliott, Jennifer Hartmann, and Eila Baron, who worked relentlessly to help bring this project to life.

Marge Whitney worked tirelessly on all the endless details for a successful launch and thereby earned our deep appreciation.

We were blessed with interns who lent enthusiasm and hard work to the task of verifying sources, finding research, and reconstructing market histories: Jaime D'Amico from Cornell University spent a summer in the depths of the University of Rochester and Cornell libraries chasing down research; David Cheikin from Tony's alma mater, the University of Rochester, assisted in screening stocks and applying our contrarian criteria to real world problems; and Darryl

Porter from St. John Fisher College went to the original sources to help piece together the Crash of 1929.

Thanks to Dr. Nancy Norment McCabe at Georgetown University Hospital for her critique and guidance on anxiety and loss in our discussion of investor psychology. Kudos also to Marshall Kaplan for his encouragement and leadership; to Chris Bicek at Imageview for his input into graphics design, to Jeff Newman once again for his excellent work as our attorney, and to Harry Sealfon, CPA, for his explanation of the taxation of stock options. Appreciation also to James Liddle of Legg Mason Wood Walker Inc. in York, Pennsylvania, Bill's friend and advisor, for serving as his sounding board for some of the strategies we would eventually craft. We are grateful, too, to Bill's friend, Robin Ritter, for her encouragement and feedback on the manuscript.

To all the professors, academics, investment managers, analysts, and government offices whose published research was so impressive, whether or not it agreed with the contrarian case (and their institutions at the time of research publication): William Brock and Blake LeBaron at the University of Wisconsin; Josef Lakonishok at the University of Illinois; R. Richardson Pettit at the University of Houston (who was kind enough to clarify his research on insider transactions); P. C. Venkatesh at the Office of the Comptroller of the Currency; Yulong Ma at Alabama A&M; Jia He at the University of Houston; Andrei Shleifer at Harvard University; Robert Vishny at the University of Chicago; John S. Howe at the University of Kansas; Tweedy, Browne Co. L.P.; Value Line Inc.; Jack Schwager at Prudential Securities; Alan Shaw at Smith Barney; David Dreman; Werner De Bondt at the University of Wisconsin; Richard Thaler at Cornell; Torben Anderson; Vic Sperandero; Roger Ibbotson; the Public Affairs Office of The Securities and Exchange Commission; Wilbert McKeachie at the University of Michigan, Charlotte Doyle at Cornell, Henry Oppenheimer, William F. Sharpe, W. Scott Bauman, Richard Dowen, Julie Rohrer, John R. Chisholm, Sanjoy Basu, Mario Levis, and James Rea. If we have omitted anyone, it is by error and not by design.

We wish to thank the good people at Equis International for their excellent charting program MetaStock, whose charts are found throughout this text. Also, to the people of Bloomberg L.P. who have, in "the Bloomberg," created the investment world's truly great research tool.

To our editor at Prentice Hall, Ellen Schneid Coleman, our thanks, our respect, and our gratitude for carrying the flag for this project to its successful conclusion.

Finally, we wish to thank in Tony's case, his clients; and in Bill's case, his editors and—most importantly—his readers. It is the stimulation provided by their endless curiosity and their need for proven and common-sense investment advice that formed the true inspiration for this book and our desire to see it through to completion.

INTRODUCTION

---

*A*chetez aux canons, vendez aux clairons.
(Buy on the cannons, sell on the trumpets.)

—Old French Proverb

Investing is a strange business. It's the only one we know of where the more expensive the products get, the more customers want to buy them. That doesn't happen with a car, a house, or a VCR. Usually, people shop for bargains. They haggle for good deals. They wait for a sale, when prices are marked down.

It's not that way with the stock market. The higher prices go, it seems, the more the people want to buy. Of course, that's just the opposite of what investors should be doing. We have watched, on a daily basis, how people manage their money and how they make their investment decisions. Their thought processes, and their emotional responses to changes in the market, go a long way toward explaining their investment results, which all too often are disappointing.

When the stock market starts rising, most people are, at first, afraid to step aboard. It's not until stocks have gone up a long way for a very long time that most investors become interested and start buying. Conversely, when stocks begin to drop, most investors are not afraid. Their courage has been bolstered by the persistently rising tide. Just because the market has gone up a long way, investors believe it will keep going up. It's almost a gold-rush mentality.

Contrarians buy on bad news, and sell on good news. "Buy low, sell high" is a well-worn cliché. But it's well-worn for a good reason: That's how an investor must think in order to profit.

Both authors have had excellent seats from which to watch the markets and individual investors. As a business reporter for Gannett, Bill Patalon has written on business topics too numerous to mention.

1

In following the difficulties and resurgence of Eastman Kodak as his primary beat, he's been able to see firsthand what can cause a company (and its stock) to falter, and also to see what is needed for a turnaround. Writing every day for the typical investor has given Bill the chance to see how these investors approach the market, and how the news media helps forge the mass opinion that contrarians try to bet against. Time spent reporting overseas from China and Japan underscored for him how investors the world over can abandon sound strategies and fall under the spell of an overheated stock market.

Tony Gallea, as a Senior Portfolio Management Director for Smith Barney, one of the country's largest financial services firms, has been investing for, and working with, individual and institutional investors for nearly 20 years. He and his team are directly responsible for more than $600 million in client investments. He uses many contrarian techniques and strategies in his daily work managing portfolios for individuals and institutions. Those strategies are outlined for you in this book.

Bill used to attend Tony's monthly seminars, sometimes for story ideas, and sometimes simply to listen and learn. Over the years, a friendship developed as they each came to appreciate the contrarian in the other. This book is the result of that friendship.

Contrarian investing is not new. In fact, it has a long history. But a review of the most recent literature on contrarian investing revealed that a gap existed. Since contrarian investing can be a difficult strategy to follow, and requires commitment and discipline to make it work, many of the books on the subject are too complex or convoluted for the interested investor to follow.

Too often, financial seers get caught up in highly technical discussions on such arcane points as what adjustments to make on some company's restated second-quarter earnings. Such debates are not only incomprehensible to most people, they can scare off the individual investor.

We saw the need for a book, written in plain English, showing investors how to assemble a stock portfolio that's very profitable, has a chance to beat the market, and lowers their overall risk—all by betting against popular opinion. The book would not only include the latest research, it would boil it down into a simple-to-use set of guidelines.

Much of what passes for contrarian investing is actually "value" investing, a less-extreme discipline that shares some contrarian characteristics. The rest falls into the realm of gut instinct or market folklore. For instance, in an attempt to gauge market sentiment, contrarians might survey magazine covers at the local newsstand to discern when the crowd has reached an extreme opinion worth betting against in the stock market. A neat strategy, but how do investors translate that folklore into a disciplined investment strategy that can be used profitably time after time?*

In our search for information we were delighted to find that there's been considerable research during the past fifteen years that validates the contrarian approach. However, much of this research was written by academics, for an academic audience, and is, frankly, indecipherable to nearly all investors. It took considerable time to unlock the message. But we believe the effort was worthwhile and hope you will, too.

During our journey, we made many new and exciting discoveries. One of the most important: Success as a contrarian demands a long-term view, and a willingness to hold many of the stocks for two to three years. Many strategies and academic studies call for more active trading, which for the typical investor can result in high transaction costs and disappointing results. We also found, to our surprise, academic research validating some technical analysis techniques, and research that poked a few fair-sized holes in the "Random Walk Theory."†

But most important, we found many studies that validate contrarian investing as a viable and, indeed, a *preferred* investment strategy.

We wish to mention a word about criticism. Being a contrarian means betting against the crowd, and against the prognosticators and pundits who, as highly visible experts, are the makers of mass opinion. A discussion of contrarian investing, by necessity, requires us to use specific examples of how individuals, organizations, and

---

*In late 1995, Bill Gates' picture was on the cover of nearly every magazine of note. What's more, media hype of Microsoft's new Windows95 operating system was so great that Wall Street's lofty forecasts for sales could easily be missed. If ever a contrarian signal to sell a stock short existed, this was it! During the following year, Microsoft rose 40 percent, illustrating the pitfalls of using such subjective indicators as magazine covers as the basis for an investment strategy.

†The Random Walk Theory, or Efficient Market Hypothesis, in various forms all come to the same conclusion: Stock prices can't be predicted because prices conform to a random—and therefore unpredictable—wandering through time. This is one of the most hotly contested areas in investment theory today.

groups have been incorrect or have blundered along the way. We do not intend these discussions to be arrogant or cruel. Our society expends too much energy trying to make others look foolish or ridiculous in order to win a point or an argument. The fact that we are all capable of foolishness does not necessarily make us fools. Those of us who have spent any time at all in the investing game are nothing if not humbled by our own occasional lack of skill. The authors, too, have been humbled many times through the years.

In today's society, people often feel a need to brand entire groups as out of touch, wrongheaded, or just plain stupid. The investment arena is no exception. Fundamentalists will ridicule technicians, contrarians will point the finger at momentum investors, and growth managers will argue with the disciples of value. In a book that shows how to profit by betting against majority opinion, we would be remiss in not warning of the danger of assuming a superior state of mind. This arrogance leads to disaster, and must studiously be avoided. Indeed, we should point out that the crowd is most often correct. It's only when contrarians are buying or selling stocks that we want to be different (a point we must really emphasize).

With these cautions in mind, we have tried to avoid personifying the techniques and studies presented in this book. If an analyst got an earnings report wrong, we didn't have the space to discuss all the things he got right. We leave it to the reader's sense of fairness to avoid this pitfall.

This brings us to the essence of contrarian investing: Buying and selling when others won't.* In buying, you've already bought your ticket and have the best seat in the house when the investment hordes start bidding for their own spots in line. In selling, you are out the door before the others, and won't be trampled in the stampede when the crowd rushes to get out of a stock. That doorway can be pretty narrow!

Liquidity drives markets. By getting in early, you are in a position to let other investors drive up the price of the shares you already own. Likewise, it's when those same investors start taking money off the table (and out of a particular stock) that the price of those shares start to fall. Let us say it again: It's only when buying or selling that

---

* Of course, this is exactly the function of the specialist on the New York Stock Exchange, an excellent example of successful contrarian investing.

the contrarian wants to be different. Once we've made our moves, buying or selling, we *want* other investors to come around to our point of view.

You will also find that out-of-favor stocks often pose less risk, since the bad news has already been built into their prices. In a falling market, that means stocks that already were trading near their lows will frequently drop a lot less than shares that had been trading near their highs.

In this book, we show you how to make money on stocks by investing as a contrarian. We discuss some of the classic contrarian tools and show you a few new ones, too. We'll help you find and recognize contrarian stock plays, and leave you with a workable strategy with specific rules for buying and selling that takes a lot of the guesswork out of investing in stocks.

This is not a get-rich-quick book. It's not financial alchemy. It's not magic. It's about basic, sound investment strategies that offer the prospect of excellent returns, with less downside risk than a portfolio stuffed with the latest "hot" ideas. We'll teach you to think like a contrarian, to recognize and avoid the mass-mania speculation that accompanies a market top. And we'll show you how to assemble the kind of investment portfolio that year after year will leave you feeling happy and prosperous.

The contrarian path is not always an easy one to travel. Thinking and acting like a contrarian has never been—and never will be—without challenges. We are conditioned from birth to go along, to think in a socially acceptable way. This conditioning makes true independent thought difficult. We're all more comfortable with lots of company than we are taking a solitary walk. Later on, we discuss the psychological reasons for this crowd mentality.

Have you ever wondered why investors become more enthusiastic about a stock as its price goes higher? Why people don't sell when the market begins to decline? And why people hold on during a stock's long decline only to give up, sell at the bottom, and then watch with clenched fists as the stock rebounds and climbs to new highs? Contrarians can answer all three questions.

We live in an enlightened, capitalist democracy. For capitalism to flourish, it needs large and active groups of buyers and sellers, all competing independently to set the proper price on an infinite variety of goods and services. It is dangerous for a capitalist system to operate with a heavy preponderance of either buyers or sellers.

When this happens, markets can soar or crash, and economies can sicken and die from too much of a good thing.

We have seen too many instances of speculation-turned-frenzy throughout history not to be enlightened by these lessons. In this book, we show how the Dutch literally ran to ruin over, of all things, tulip bulbs and how the Crash of 1929 began and why it became investment legend.

In short, we examine why people act the way they do, and show you how to profit from the crowd's mistakes.

That, in the final analysis, is the art of the contrarian.

PART I

CONTRARIAN OVERVIEW

CHAPTER 1

WHAT IS A CONTRARIAN?

*I have a trading rule I call the "Alligator Principle."
It's based on the way an alligator eats; the more the victim tries to
struggle, the more the alligator gets. Imagine an alligator has you by the
leg; it clamps your leg in its mouth and waits while you struggle. If you
put one of your arms in the vicinity of its mouth while fighting to get your
leg free, it lunges and then has your arm and leg in its clutches. The
more you struggle, the more the alligator takes you in.*

—Vic Sperandeo, *Methods of a
Wall Street Master*

Have you ever found yourself in the alligator's clutches? Have you ever had your investment position move against you and, the more you struggle to extricate yourself from loss, the tighter the 'gator's jaws clamp down? You double up on a losing position, only to have that position slide deeper into the muck. You finally throw in the towel on a stock and then watch with disgust as it turns and heads higher. You struggle, you thrash about, but it only gets worse. The alligator slowly and painfully gobbles you up.

If you wish to avoid the alligator's clutches, if your investment performance has been mediocre—or downright disastrous—you need a clean break from your old stock-picking strategy. You need to start thinking like a contrarian.

What exactly is contrarian investing? Who uses it, and why? When does it make sense? Why don't more people practice it? How can you train yourself to be a contrarian? In this book, we answer all those questions and leave you with a disciplined approach to

9

investing that will boost your returns even as it whittles down your risk.

The Contrarian Philosophy

A contrarian investor measures the opinion of the investing public, and when that opinion reaches an unreasonable extreme, invests against it. Jack Schwager, in his excellent book, *Market Wizards: Interviews With Top Traders*, explains why we can profit from contrary opinion:

> "(It is) the general theory that one can profit by doing the opposite of the majority of traders. The basic concept is that if a large majority of traders are bullish, it implies that most market participants who believe prices are going higher are already long, and hence the path of least resistance is down. An analogous line of reasoning would apply when most traders are bearish."[1]

Professional trader Mark Lively has, well, a livelier interpretation:

> "The old saying 'a million Frenchmen can't be wrong' would send a chill through the blood of those dedicated to the use of market sentiment indicators. Proponents of market sentiment would argue that if, indeed, the day arrives when a million Frenchmen are in agreement about any one thing, it is more likely that they will be wrong than right. Why? Because market sentiment theories take the view that strong agreement by a majority of individuals about a given situation or topic is likely to mean that the situation is, in fact, the opposite of what it is perceived to be."[2]

We begin with a very simple premise. If everyone believes something, and believes in it strongly enough to have *acted* on it, there is profit to be made in taking the opposite position. If everyone has bought into the bullish prospects for a particular stock, who is left to buy the stock and push it higher? The path of least resistance is now down. This path of least resistance is fertile ground for contrarian investors.

■ *NOTES FROM A CONTRARIAN PORTFOLIO MANAGER*

In 1996, a major tobacco company's agreement to reach a settlement relating to its liability to a smoker sparked a sell-off in tobacco stocks. You could sense the fear in the air, could actually feel it. Philip Morris dropped 10 percent on the news. Was Philip Morris a contrarian buy? Would the contrarian pick up the stock because most people were afraid? No. The fact was that, at the time, most investors had chosen to hold the stock, and analysts were sharply divided over what the settlement would mean. Buying simply because most people were afraid wouldn't have been a true contrarian play. What was needed was a real consensus, an extreme of opinion. ■

Let's assume that there are 1,000 commodity traders who trade coffee, and that their outlook for coffee is neutral. Supply and demand are in fair balance. About 550 are long coffee, and 450 have sold it short to the other 550. Opinions aren't very strong in either direction and, with the price at 80 cents per pound, trading is described in the press as "listless" and "quiet."

But then rumors of a ruinous freeze in South America galvanize traders into action. One hundred of the bear traders move into the bullish camp, and the 350 remaining bears continue to sell coffee to them, albeit at higher prices now running around 90 cents per pound. Then rumors of the freeze are confirmed and now nearly everyone is bullish. There are only about 50 bears left, and the 950 bullish traders are buying all the coffee they can because they believe the freeze will "eliminate" nearly all supplies by September, when the big coffee-drinking season begins in the Northern Hemisphere.

Traders from outside the coffee market are drawn to the fray and provide a new source of buying power to overwhelm the bears. The price crosses $2.50 per pound as a buying frenzy develops.

News of the bankruptcy of two notable coffee traders (they bet the wrong way) persuades everyone that a bet against this market is not only foolhardy, it's suicidal. At this precise moment, everyone who was going to buy coffee on speculation has done so. There are no more buyers left.

The next day, coffee opens higher by 20 cents at $2.70 per pound. But this proves to be the ultimate peak. Breathless and bullish pronouncements from coffee commentators—perhaps coffee will go to $4.00?—have pulled everyone in. With the last buyer now in, the price reverses and falls below $2.20. Since there is no news to explain the drop, most bulls hold. Margin calls the following day are met by more selling, and then growers—not wanting to miss a good price for their crop—enter the trading as strong sellers. Coffee plunges. The Brazilian government, in a surprise move, announces that it will release additional coffee to the market, dooming the bulls. Now, there are 400 bulls and 600 bears. As the market descends, more and more traders throw in the bull hand and step aside, or turn outright bearish. At the bottom, the bulls are exhausted and most traders are bearish. If not exhausted or bearish, others are apathetic. Coffee meanders listlessly around 90 cents a pound for the next few months.

■ *NOTES FROM A CONTRARIAN PORTFOLIO MANAGER*

Investors are attracted by action, by the potential for profit. When a stock has been rising for a long time, and then really accelerates to the upside, it can suddenly attract a whole new group of investors who will strongly bid for the stock. People have a way of projecting, into the future, a straight line based on the past. Unfortunately for them, that run rarely continues. Just when you think the future will be the same as the past, a reversal occurs. ■

Let's consider a few cases where contrarian thinking would have led to big profits.

In 1991, in the depths of a recession, the shares of Citicorp were trading at about $9 each. Analysts were giving last rites to the nation's biggest bank. Its capital base was below federal minimums, the result of bad loans made on real estate and to Third World countries. Its dividend would be eliminated to preserve cash. America's biggest bank seemed ready to fail. Not only did few rate Citi's shares a "buy," most experts said to avoid it.

As we write in mid-1997, Citi shares are trading at close to $130, and some analysts still rate it a buy because of the bank's strong consumer franchise, global reach, and solid financial position. It's paying a dividend again and is buying back shares. Many on Wall Street believe the stock still has room to run.*

For the investor who bought 100 shares of Citi in 1991, a $1,000 outlay for the stock and brokerage fees has grown to nearly $13,000, not including dividends. How many investors made this move? Probably very few. (We'll look more closely at Citibank in a case study at the end of Chapter 7.)

Capitalizing on such "extreme" opinion is the core of contrarian investing. If you're a buyer, look for opportunities in stocks, industries, or even overseas markets that are out of favor, situations usually punctuated by widely accepted bad news and "calls for new lows." If you are a seller, seek out the consensus "good news" situations: Such rampantly bullish outlooks often ignore looming problems.

Contrarian investing doesn't demand as strong a stomach as you might think. In fact, by using the tools we outline in this book to assemble a diversified portfolio of out-of-favor stocks, research shows you can enjoy market-beating returns, while actually taking on less risk than most other investors.

To better understand the contrarian mindset, let's consider a few other cases where a bet against the consensus would have led to big gains.

Take Xerox Corp. In early 1991, its stock was lingering under $10 per share (adjusted for a three-for-one split) and paid a $1 dividend. At this price the dividend alone meant an investor who bought the stock would be getting an annual 10 percent return on the original investment into perpetuity, even with no rise in the stock price.

Xerox had made a disastrous foray into real estate and its diversification into the insurance and investment-management businesses was turning out to be more of a drag, than a boost, to its earnings. Plus, the economy was in the dumper in several of Xerox's major markets—companies weren't shelling out big bucks for new copiers and printers.

By mid-1997, however, Xerox shares had eclipsed $80, analysts considered it a "buy," and some even viewed it as their best idea. Make no mistake, it's a good company, even today. But investors

---

*Citi is so instructive to the contrarian that we've included it as a complete case study later on in the book.

who bought in at $9 have seen their $1,000 investment turn into $8,000—and that doesn't include the 10-percent annual dividend stream that could have been used to finance other contrarian plays. (For more on Xerox, see the case study at the end of Chapter 11.)

Other examples come to mind: Chrysler Corp. not once, but twice (at the end of the 1970s and again in the early 1990s); Union Carbide after the Bhopal disaster; and General Public Utilities after the accident at the Three Mile Island nuclear power plant. These are the "Big Uglies," well-known companies that fall on tough times and need fixing. Often, they are companies that are too big to fail.

This concept of buying during the depths of despair isn't limited to big-company stocks. Many small companies experience the same kinds of problems. Indeed, entire asset classes sometimes qualify as contrarian investments. In the early 1990s, gold was widely viewed as a dead-money investment. When gold trended down to $330 per ounce—and stalled there—commentary at the time suggested the next move would be for gold to fall below $300 per ounce. Instead, $330 proved to be the bottom, and gold prices rallied to over $400 per ounce.

Entire markets, too, can be contrarian plays. Throughout the 1990s, many in the investment world knew Japan was hiding serious banking system problems. When Japan's "bubble economy" collapsed, so did its stock market: The Nikkei dropped 68 percent from its 39,000 high. When the Japanese government decided to force that country's banks to recognize their losses and purge them, the Tokyo markets began to revive. Despite the obvious parallels to the American banking crisis of the late 1980s (remember Citibank), many investors avoided Japan, citing as their reason the losses the banks were now publicly recognizing. The upshot: They missed a rebound that saw the Nikkei jump over 50 percent within months.

Even commodities warrant some study in a search for contrarian ideas. In the early 1980s, with oil at $40 a barrel or more, it was widely believed that oil would rise to $100 per barrel by the end of the century. Instead, those bullish forecasts signaled the peak in oil prices. When prices eventually slipped to $12, some were calling for a new drop to $10 or even $8 per barrel! As we know, those "calls for new lows" signaled the bottom in oil prices, which reversed and began to rise.

Let us give you one more example.

■ *NOTES FROM A CONTRARIAN PORTFOLIO MANAGER*

In 1992, I noticed a small Wall Street Journal *item saying that a major insurance company was closing its gold mutual fund. It seemed investor interest had dwindled so much that the company could no longer keep the fund operating profitably. An exodus of investors had pulled the fund down to an unprofitable size. That aroused my contrarian nature. If they couldn't keep a gold fund open, perhaps a turn in the price was at hand. A look at the gold market showed gold at $329 per ounce. Recent commentary was sparse, reflecting the lack of interest in a market that had been in decline for a decade. Better still, the smattering of commentary we could find was either apathetic or downright bearish. New calls for new lows could be found predicting a price drop to $280 per ounce. When I read an article that pondered the potential for gold to fall to $190, it became pretty clear that the market was washed out.*

We began buying gold funds, gold stocks, and some bullion. Eventually, we had several million dollars invested in these positions. Why I saw that small notice and why I paid attention to it, I originally attributed to luck. Only later did I realize that my "luck" actually stemmed from my daily habit of reading as much as possible (no matter how obscure), and being constantly aware; thinking like a contrarian; and looking for new opportunities all the time. ■

Succeeding as a contrarian investor is more than just differing with the popular view. If that were all there was to it, everyone would embrace this approach to investing. Being a contrarian means not only disagreeing with the crowd, but knowing when to *act* on that disagreement. That means looking for extremes: specifically, buying when a stock has been beaten down below its fair value, or selling short when the price of a stock has been pushed up above its actual worth.

But as our gold example shows, gauging extreme sentiment can be quite subjective. In fact, it's the point at which many people go wrong in contrarian thinking. You need a real extreme in order to act. If gold goes from a high of $875 per ounce and a decade later, after 10 straight years of inflation, gold is at $329 per ounce and people believe it is going to $190, you've got an extreme point of view. Just because it drops to $329 doesn't mean a thing. Maybe it is going to $190. But when people are willing to openly predict that kind of decline, and when companies are closing gold funds, and you can't seem to find *anybody* who owns a gold stock or is bullish on the prospects for gold, you have yourself an extreme opinion. (Were *you* bullish on gold in 1992?)

CONTRARIAN INDICATORS

Our contrarian stock-picking strategy removes much of that subjectivity from the investment equation. We've created a set of easy-to-use indicators that serve as *proxies* for investor sentiment. Our indicators will help you identify contrarian stocks, and let you know when to buy them. The rules we've built into this strategy also tell you how long to hold onto your stocks to give you the biggest gains, and to limit the downside risk to your money. Each part of this approach is backed by substantial research by academics, brokerage firms, and other investment experts. We've simply pulled it all together for you.

We highlight these rules right here at the start so you can keep them in mind as you read the book. At this juncture, many will seem strange or out-of-whack. Don't worry. As we travel together through the history of contrarian investing, the psychology of investment, and the research backing these ideas, it will all fall into place.

The Buy Signals

We begin with what we like to call the "down-by-half rule." *To qualify as a contrarian play, a stock must be down at least 50 percent from its highest closing price during the past 12 months.* In other words, a $40 stock has to fall to $20 to even be considered a contrarian play. But that's just a starting point; the stock has to meet at least one of several additional criteria:

1. Significant stock purchases by insiders, or by outsiders one might deem as "knowledgeable investors"—experts such as Warren Buffett. Significant insider purchases are defined as at least $120,000, which is twice the average insider purchase. Insider purchases on a stock down 50 percent make it a virtually automatic buy. Or,

2. Any two of the following four criteria:
   - A price/earnings (P/E) ratio of less than 12.
   - A price/free cash flow (P/FCF) ratio of less than 10.
   - A price/sales (P/S) ratio of less than 1.0.
   - A price/book value (P/BV) ratio of less than 1.0.

Although it is not one of our formal criteria, a change in top management or stock buybacks in concert with the other indicators may be viewed as additional bullish indicators.

The Sell Signals

Sell once the stock rises 50 percent from its purchase price, or after three years, whichever comes first. The exception is when a once-troubled company's prospects are clearly improving, or when the stock price seems to be climbing a "wall of worry."

Risk Management

1. Place a good-until-canceled, stop-loss order to sell the shares automatically should they fall 25 percent from the purchase price. If the stop loss is triggered, you can buy the stock again later, but only at a price higher than you paid when you bought it the first time.
2. Diversify by holding a portfolio of 20–35 different stocks, with no one stock comprising more than 5 percent of your portfolio (3 percent is recommended).
3. Don't concentrate any more than 15 percent of your portfolio in any one idea or theme (such as gold or utility stocks). Less than 10 percent is preferable.
4. Consider having dividends paid in cash, and not reinvested, to build a stake for other contrarian plays.

Used together, these guidelines form a disciplined approach to buying and selling contrarian stocks. Our "buy" indicators are actually a way to quantify, or measure, an extreme opinion held by investors toward a particular stock. In other words, these indicators are a *proxy* for the extreme sentiment we are seeking.

Research shows that each piece of our strategy, by itself over time, generates returns greater than those of the overall market. We've woven them together to create a consistent and disciplined approach to stock picking.

- The buy indicators should provide market-beating returns in the long run.
- Our sell indicators make the always-tough selling decision easier.
- The risk-management rules help you keep the gains you have earned and limit your losses.

The rules we've highlighted quickly here are not the entire strategy, but illustrate an important point: *Contrarians don't buy at the top, and they don't sell at the bottom.* Quite the opposite. While all investors *intend* to buy low and sell high, it's the contrarians who actually do it consistently.

Since a contrarian acts against the crowd, all the other investors already will have pushed the individual stock, industry sector, market index, or commodity to an extreme price. That, by definition, allows the contrarian to buy low and sell high. Consider our coffee and gold examples. Contrarians wouldn't buy coffee at the steep price of $2.50 per pound, because investor opinion at that point was obviously bullish. Nor would the contrarian buy gold when it was $875 because sentiment also was rampantly bullish.

In short, by using these guidelines, the contrarian will rarely buy a stock unless nearly everyone else hates it. It's not enough to have many investors saying bad things about a company's shares. Their disdain for the stock has to be reflected by a pummeled price and its relative value as measured by the four key price ratios.

Having an opinion and *acting* on that opinion are two entirely different things. The investors we wish to bet against may express an opinion in support of—or even against—some investment theme, but if they haven't acted on that belief, it isn't extreme enough to interest the contrarian.

This is true for both market tops and market bottoms. At the top, investors have committed all their reserves to the market, meaning there is no more money available to push it higher. At the bottom, these investors have taken all their money off the table, and typically will refuse to wade in until a market resurgence is clearly under way.

It seems irrational to believe everyone can be wrong about something. But you can look back into history and see that this happens all the time. Later on, we will talk more about some of the truly remarkable manias that have seized whole countries. For now, we'll list a few notable "they got it wrong" examples from history:

1. Harry Truman would lose the 1948 presidential election.
2. Iraq would be a formidable foe against the Coalition in its occupation of Kuwait.*
3. The ragtag American colonists couldn't possibly beat the greatest military power in the world and secure independence.
4. The Allied invasion would not be at Normandy.
5. Even when told the Germans were pouring across the Russian border, Josef Stalin didn't believe that Germany would attack.

In a military conquest, or in other forms of warfare (calling a political endeavor a "campaign" underscores the warlike nature of the affair), the majority are often surprised at the turn of events. Gerald Loeb, a great market tactician from another era, called one of his books, *The Battle For Investment Survival*, making clear his view of the nature of the investment quest. Successful investing, like a successful military campaign, has its potential for surprise and miscalculation. Contrarians understand this fact, and use it to their own advantage.

It's true the contrarian might buy gold at $329, after its long slide, only to watch as it plunges to $250 or even $200. That's a risk inherent in any investment, and there's no way to eliminate that kind of miscalculation. But it's equally true that contrarians put the odds in their favor by not getting caught up in all the hoopla. Indeed, they use that euphoria, or that funk, to their advantage.

Because of this go-against-the-crowd mentality, contrarians reduce their investment risk. Even if they're wrong, they usually don't see the devastating drops that can decimate a portfolio. They use strategies that limit their downside risk.

---

* It was widely believed that the stock market was going to fall at the beginning of the war. Quite the contrary . . .

THE DIFFICULTIES OF CONTRARIAN THINKING

Thinking like a contrarian will be difficult (at least at first) because you are bucking prevailing opinion. When everyone around you is bullish on the stock market, it takes a steely nerve and an independent mind to be on the lookout for the chance to bet the other way. We all want to fit in. But as a contrarian, you must become a detached thinker and learn to be comfortable as a loner. Indeed, being alone is reassurance to the dedicated contrarian.

Contrarians can often pull the trigger too early. Doing so means they are not only alone in their opinion but, for a time, are wrong as well. That solitude can be disconcerting when nearly everyone you talk with has a viewpoint that's opposite yours. Picture yourself at a cocktail party where all your business associates are rampantly bullish on the stock market. When your view is sought, you cause discomfort when you predict the market will soon roll over like a dead whale. Think of the stony stares, the silent reaction, the ice melting in your drink. The role of the contrarian can be lonely indeed. But, for contrarians to profit, all the other investors have to be wrong when you are buying or selling your shares.

■ *NOTES FROM A CONTRARIAN PORTFOLIO MANAGER*

I remember very well when we began investing in the gold market. One of our clients, a retired pharmaceutical-company executive, called to question if we really were on the right track with our gold position. He had played golf just that Saturday with his regular foursome, and when he told his friends about his gold investments, they laughed at him. He felt humiliated. I, of course, felt something quite different: Reassurance. We were on the right track indeed.*   ■

You need to make the contrarian point of view part of your very being, practicing until it's second nature. Being a part-time contrarian is more dangerous than not being one at all. If you are constantly shifting between the majority and minority opinion, you're not nurturing and honing those contrarian instincts. Success requires commitment.

---

* We sold his position about a year later at a 30-percent profit. He reminds them about it to this day.

Contrarians are natural skeptics. They learn to question everything they hear, everything they read, and everything they see. It is not that contrarians *mistrust* what people are saying and doing. They don't believe there is some secret cabal to disseminate misinformation. They simply weigh things on the contrarian scale, asking repeatedly: "Does this piece of information point to an extreme in opinion?"

Many misunderstand the contrarian's nature. They view him as a gloom-and-doomer, a crank, or a dyspeptic curmudgeon who will never be happy. We're not sure how that started. But if you go to a party and speak like a bear when everyone is bullish, don't expect flattering remarks. And when times are gloomiest, and the contrarian is optimistic and bullish, people might view him as "loony" or "out of touch with reality." Of course, we know the opposite is true. Remember the old folk saying, "It's always darkest before the dawn"? A contrarian said it first.

Don't feel completely alone. Contrarian thinking has a long and illustrious history. In 1841, Charles MacKay wrote the seminal work on the subject of mass behavior, *Extraordinary Popular Delusions and the Madness of Crowds*, showing how the masses can be whipped into a speculative frenzy over things like tulip bulbs and stock in companies with no real businesses.* *Reminiscences of a Stock Operator*, by Edwin Lefevre, was first published in 1923 and is a treasure trove of contrarian thinking.[3] In 1954, Humphrey B. Neill, considered by many to be the guiding light and original thinker about contrary opinion in the modern era, wrote *The Art of Contrary Thinking*.[4] Twenty-five years later, David Dreman's two books on contrary thinking, *Contrarian Investment Strategy*, and *New Contrarian Investment Strategy*, outlined contrarian investment strategies using the low price/earnings ratio method.[5]

During the past few years, *Barron's*, under the guidance of Alan Abelson, has carried the contrarian banner with insightful analysis that exhibits a clear contrarian bent.

Today, the contrarian philosophy is respected, although often misunderstood. For every true contrarian, there are 100 investors who falsely claim the contrarian mantle. Many are value investors, who often choose the same beaten-up stocks contrarians are buying. But the value investor is merely looking for bargain stocks—

---

* This work is still in print and is published by Crown Trade Paperback, New York, NY.

those selling at discount to their actual value—and isn't as interested in extreme opinion. Just because an investor takes an unpopular stance, disagrees with the crowd, or buys stocks trading at their lows doesn't make him a contrarian. A contrarian is interested in extremes in market sentiment, not just disagreement with the majority.

It is also crucial to remember that a contrarian point of view is merely an entry and exit technique. You are looking for the right time to buy and to sell, and are using the crowd's opinion to tell you when the time is right. But once you've taken a position, you want the majority to come around to your point of view. Then, you can stay with them for most of the ride. Only the majority can push the price of an investment up or down enough to create the kinds of profits you want to earn. After you buy a stock, you want other investors to see the bargain you spotted—and you want them to pile in, to drive the share price higher.

Most of the time the majority will come around and see what you saw. Once you've purchased that stock, you need to be able to flip your thinking and go along for the ride. That's the great irony of contrarian investing: Most of the time, you're actually going along with the crowd. The crowd is wrong at the tops and bottoms, when you're buying and selling, but in between the group actually sees things your way. You're just trying to get in before the crowd when you're buying, and out before the crowd when you're selling.

We have found contrarian investing to be a profitable, intellectually stimulating, and enjoyable approach to picking stocks. It's liberating because you strike out on your own and explore new thoughts and new ideas using original thinking. It frees you from that tiring dependence on others. You can stop your endless search for a guru to take you to the promised land. What you'll find, to your endless delight, is that *you* are the answer to your search.

Endnotes

1. Schwager, Jack, *Market Wizards, Interviews With Top Traders*; New York Institute of Finance, New York, 1989, p. 448.

2. Robbins, Joel, *High Performance Futures Trading*; Probus Publishing Co., Chicago, 1990, p. 291.

3. *Reminiscences of a Stock Operator* is currently in print by the Fraser Publishing Company, Burlington, VT.

4. The Caxton Printers, Caldwell, OH, 1954.

5. Respectively: Random House, New York, NY, 1979 and 1982.

CHAPTER 2

THE CONTRARIAN ADVANTAGE

*A man is to go about his own business as if he
had not a friend in the world to help him in it.*

—George Savile, Marquess of Halifax

Contrarian investing is a lonely journey. But there are profits at the end of the path. As we will see a bit later when we study a few of history's more notable speculative manias, the crowd has a tendency to latch on to an idea and carry it to an unjustified extreme. The masses repeat and reinforce the notion until what began as a mere opinion on a stock's prospects is ultimately accepted as an immutable law of the universe. We are conditioned to behave this way. Absent a strong belief independently conceived, we embrace the crowd's opinion as our own. But contrarians can profit from those extremes.

Your advantage as a contrarian is that you never pay the high price for an investment and never succumb to a ruinous mania. A high price is the visible evidence of a strong majority opinion. If a stock rockets from $24 to $60, contrarians won't pay $40, $50, or $60 for the stock. The essence of the contrarian discipline makes this impossible, since contrarians don't follow the crowd. But we do get the chance to buy the stock at $20, $22, or $25—after it has plunged from $40 or $50.

Of course, buying that stock after it's had a big drop doesn't guarantee the carnage is complete. You can buy it at $24, and believe you've bought at the bottom, only to see it plunge to $16. In that case, $24 was a pretty high price indeed.

Except for that kind of miscalculation, it's fair to say that contrarians—in their quest for bargains—avoid the over-hyped, over-extended investments that are ripe for the devastating falls that catch so many investors. And because contrarians buy only after such big drops, their portfolios tend to fall less in a bad market. These stocks have already had their bear market before contrarians bought them.

Contrarians have an advantage because they buy after a price decline. They don't pay the higher price.

INVESTING AGAINST THE CROWD

While betting against the masses may at first seem foolish, think about the crowd's behavior. Most people have success in a rising market. The rising tide lifts all boats, as the saying goes, and a lot of investors see their stocks rise along with that tide.* But it's the bear market that really tests an investor's mettle, and the longer the bear-market decline, the bigger the test. We have seen that investors tend to buy at tops and sell at bottoms, the opposite of what they should be doing. These investors feel comfortable with the crowd—even when the crowd is losing money.

Theoretically, most investors could be big winners; they have the tools they need. Some will actually go on to beat the market, and will see their portfolios rise in value. But about three-quarters of the group—or more—won't even match the market's performance. Think about your own friends or coworkers. Most have money in stocks. But how many are making an acceptable return? If the crowd holds an opinion, *and everyone has acted on that opinion*, there is no new money available to keep propelling that stock in the same direction.

Example: Assume three investors make up an entire market. Investor A believes XYZ is cheap at $20 and buys the stock. Investor B now joins in and buys at $22. Finally, Investor C is persuaded and she, too, buys the stock, this time at $23. XYZ will rise no further,

---

* Another bit of market wisdom fits well here: "Never confuse brains with a bull market."

since there is no more money left to buy the stock and push the price higher. Everyone is bullish and, therefore, everyone is set up to be wrong. The potential now is for a drop in price.

Many studies bear this out. Why do investors bid up the price of stocks to ridiculous levels? And why do they become so pessimistic at market bottoms? Research points the way.

Good News, Bad News and the "Down-by-Half Rule"

John S. Howe, an assistant professor of business at the University of Kansas, published findings that help us understand the contrarian advantage.[1] Howe studied the price movements of stocks that experience "good news" and those that see "bad news."

He defined a "good news" stock as one experiencing a 50-percent price increase, and a "bad news" stock as one that had a 50-percent drop. Looking at stock-price movements on both the American and New York Stock Exchanges between 1963 and 1981, Howe examined the price movements in the year after the "good news" or "bad news" surfaced.* His findings are illuminating:

"Specifically, stocks that experienced large positive returns (good news) performed poorly in the 52-week period following that event, with returns averaging about 30 percent below the market. This poor performance was not concentrated in the period immediately following the event, but was spread out over a period of almost a year."[2]

Translated: Howe found that once a stock experienced a great return, which he defined as a 50-percent price increase, it performed substantially worse than the overall stock market the following year.

There is a flip side. Howe also found that "bad news" stocks did, indeed, perform better than the general market averages in the short run. Once a stock experienced poor performance, defined as a drop of 50 percent, it tended to outperform the market in the year afterwards. Yet this outperformance was of a different nature:

"The bulk of this rebound . . . occurred in the five weeks following the event, with most of the impact concentrated in the first week."[3]

---

* For instance, the performance of a stock experiencing a 50-percent price increase during the period of Jan. 15, 1976 to Jan. 15, 1977 was measured for the subsequent 52-week period—in this case, Jan. 15, 1977 to Jan. 15, 1978.

What Howe's work shows us is that contrarian investing—buying on bad news and selling on good news—has a foundation in fact. However, a contrarian hoping to profit using Howe's findings would have to strike quickly to capture that gain. That's not really how we want to operate.

Howe does make two observations that point us in the right direction:

- Once a stock experiences a big return, investors should reduce the number of shares they hold, or eliminate it altogether from their portfolios.

- Investors may wish to buy for the "rebound," after a stock experiences a major decline.[4]

Buying for a quick bounce is not what the contrarian is after. Such hair-trigger, in-and-out trading allows little time for reflection and can eat into profits by running up transaction costs. Contrarians want the long-term profits there for the picking after the crowd unfairly decimates a stock. To get those profits, we need to tip the odds in our favor. That leads to our first contrarian rule:

> **H**owe found that a 50-percent drop in stock price was a valid buy signal. A stock cannot be purchased unless it has fallen at least 50 percent from its high of the past 12 months.

Howe's work shows that investors can put the odds decisively in their favor by following this rule, since stocks down 50 percent have a tendency to rise.

Contrarians seek to measure investor opinion to find an extreme they can bet against. Since we can't go out and survey each investor in the market, we look for something to serve as a *proxy* for that sentiment. A stock that loses half its value clearly has fallen into disfavor with the masses. And the "down-by-half rule" gives us a quantifiable starting point for contrarian analysis. Since contrarian investors seek to profit by betting against the majority opinion, when a stock tumbles 50 percent on investor disappointment, it merits a look. Conversely, we want to avoid the current "hot" stocks, since the shares that have already notched large gains are the most prone to a fall.

This strategy of buying bad-news stocks and avoiding good-news stocks has a psychological basis. Professor Howe found that investors "tend to put too much emphasis on the most recent information. In a financial setting, this finding suggests that investors might overweight recent bad news and drive the price of the affected stock too low."[5] Underscoring this point is a comment from Dean LeBaron, a respected money manager with Batterymarch, who says that "in the aggregate, spot news is likely to be overreacted to."[6] Now we see why investors become more bullish about the stocks that are going up. The most recent news, in those cases, is positive.

These observations underscore the appeal of our contrarian strategy, as well as its core value. Investors overreact to recent news and lose sight of the longer-term, more-compelling reasons for owning—or selling short—a company's shares. The more this overreaction runs counter to the company's actual long-term prospects, the more quickly it is corrected. When, for instance, bad news knocks down the price of a sound stock, the long-term tendency for the stock price to rise asserts itself more quickly.

This may also help explain why bear markets are shorter in duration than bull markets.

Professors Werner De Bondt and Richard Thaler agree.* In a seminal work, "Does The Stock Market Overreact?" the two researchers arrived at the same conclusion as Howe and LeBaron: Investors tend to overweight the most recent information and underweight the information that came before.[7] If the most recent news is bad, for instance, we forget the good information that preceded it. If that recent information is good, we tend to downplay the bad news that came before.

This investment myopia isn't limited to amateur investors. The researchers also found "considerable evidence that the actual expectations of professional security analysts and economic forecasters display the same overreaction bias."[8]

The findings of De Bondt and Thaler support anecdotal evidence that professional money managers and the analysts they rely

---

*In 1985, Werner De Bondt was teaching at the University of Wisconsin at Madison and Richard Thaler at Cornell.

on are nearly as likely as amateur investors to overreact. After the stock-market collapse of 1969, market-watchers generally agreed that professionals showed poor judgment in the white-hot market of 1967–1968: They paid too much and analyzed too little. They were seduced by the bull market. But did the bloody bear market that followed serve as a lesson?

History says no. By 1973, these investors were mesmerized by the "Nifty Fifty." They believed that if you owned a few highly regarded growth stocks (such as instant-film-maker Polaroid), your future would be secure. A subsequent market drop of nearly 50 percent broke the Nifty Fifty's spell.

Have we finally learned? We need only consider the concept stocks of 1995 to see the answer is once again, "No." Anything dealing with the Internet, with semiconductors, or with technology in general had a wide following and meteoric price increases. A true speculative frenzy developed and, as the decline set in, the stocks of many good companies were unfairly punished along with all the "story stocks." Look at money manager David Dreman's description of the 1969–1970 debacle and think of it in terms of the 1995 technology frenzy:

> "Money managers indicated they would not repeat the critical mistakes of attempting to outperform, loading up with thinly traded stocks, buying 'stories' before they were carefully researched, and buying 'concept' stocks . . . a roaring speculative inferno would break out in a matter of months."[9]

Clearly, nothing has changed. In the pressure-cooker performance race, managers of mutual funds and professional money managers all believe they must take on additional risk in order to beat the market averages—and outperform their peers. We don't have to do the same. If, as other research shows, it takes from one to three years for a beaten-down stock to return to higher levels, that helps explain why true contrarian investing doesn't have a big following in the professional ranks: It can take too long to play out in a high-profile arena where performance is gauged in terms of weeks, not years.*

---

* More about our three-year investment horizon later in this chapter.

As we worked on this book and outlined our contrarian strategy to investors, we often were asked: "If contrarian stock picks sometimes don't show their biggest returns until the second or third year after their share prices are pounded, why not just wait a year to buy them?"

That's a fair question. There are several important pieces to our answer:

- We are long-term investors, willing to hold stocks for two, three or even five years if need be. And while the returns on an individual stock may vary from year to year, research shows that our strategies can generate average annual returns that soundly beat the market averages.

- While returns on contrarian stocks often accelerate in the second or third year after we buy them, there are often some very nice gains in that first year, too. Remember, the more investors overreact to bad news, the more quickly the stock price recovers. The degree of overreaction is not easily measured, and it's not worth missing that initial jump. It's the cumulative return we're concerned with; that is, that our average annual return at the end of the holding period beats the broader market.

- The essence of contrarian investing is buying when others won't. Waiting until the price of a share recovers would essentially mean you are buying along with the masses—which contrarians don't do. Howe's work demonstrates that our "down-by-half rule" is a legitimate starting point.

- And finally, as contrarians, we're not just concerned with the returns we can earn. We also want to lower our risk. Contrarian stocks tend to be more volatile than the market; that is, their price movements tend to be more pronounced than stocks in general. But since so much bad news is already built into the prices of such shares, that volatility tends to be focused to the upside. *In short, since contrarian stocks have already undergone a major decline, when they do move, that movement tends to be up.* Waiting to buy until after the stocks have started to move up, may actually increase your risk.

Together, our rules are designed to help you become a disciplined, long-term investor.

■ *NOTES FROM A CONTRARIAN PORTFOLIO MANAGER*

We all elevate our risk when we start measuring our performance over short periods. Consider the fund manager who runs flat for two years, and then earns 32 percent in the third year as his particular sector or specialty (emerging markets, growth, or healthcare, for instance) catches fire. His average return is about 10 percent, but odds are that his fund has dropped in size as whipsawed shareholders voted with their feet and cashed out of the mutual fund—in favor of one with a more pre-dictable return.

Compare that with the manager who earns 15 percent the first year, 15 percent the second year, and finally, falls 20 percent in the third year. Her annualized return is closer to 8 percent. But I'd bet she has a much larger client base when her fund takes the hit.

We really should measure performance over a three- to five-year pe-riod. The problem is, most investors are too impatient.   ■

THE DIVIDEND AND EARNINGS PROBLEM

The price of a share of stock is determined by the future earnings and dividends expected to accrue to that share. At least, that's the theory. When earnings and dividends are projected to rise, you would expect the stock price to do the same. Stock prices should therefore be fairly predictable, and their movements fairly tame.

One researcher who studied how this actually played out in the market found something quite different: "In spite of the observed trendiness of dividends, investors seem to attach disproportionate importance to short-run economic developments."[10]

A stock showing clear and persistent dividend increases over many years should, theoretically, exhibit low volatility if investors were focused on that important, long-term predictability. That investors do not is of interest to contrarians since short-term dips away from this longer upward march in price can be exploited for profit. This tendency to ignore the long-term prospects in favor of short-term news also buttresses the argument that investor overreaction is a fact of market life.

Like Howe, professors De Bondt and Thaler studied a long pe-riod of market history: All New York Stock Exchange securities from 1926–1982. They divided securities into portfolios based on performance, using 36-month spans. They reached conclusions startlingly similar to Howe: Investors overreact to news. But unlike Howe, who looked at one-year holding periods, De Bondt and Thaler took a longer-term view. The two researchers created portfolios of "loser" stocks (those that had performed worse than the market), and "winner" stocks (those that had beaten the market). Their finding: You're better served buying losers than winners:

"Over the last half-century, 'loser portfolios' of 35 stocks outperformed the market by, on average, 19.6 percent, 36 months after portfolio formation."[11]

Not only did "winners" earn less on average than "losers" over these three-year periods, they even earned 5 percent less than the overall stock market:

"Winner portfolios, on the other hand, earn about 5.0 percent less than the market, so that the difference in cumulative average residual between the extreme portfolios equals 24.6 percent."[12]

The "residual" of 24.6 percent measures the difference between the "good news" stocks and "bad news" stocks after backing out the movement of the general market. For instance, if the market average rises by 5 percent, and a stock increases 9 percent, the "residual" is 4 percent (9 percent stock return − 5 percent market return = "residual" performance of 4 percent).

Portfolios of "loser" stocks that were held for three years beat the general stock market by a cumulative average of 19.6 percent, while portfolios of "winner" stocks actually lagged the market by 5 percent. The upshot of this experiment: *An investor who put together a portfolio of loser stocks and held it for three years would beat an investor who assembled a portfolio of so-called winner stocks by nearly 25 percent.*

Quite clearly, De Bondt and Thaler found great value investing in stocks with poor prior performance. Their emphasis on a three-year holding period echoes the approach of Ben Graham, the noted value investor whom Warren Buffett regards as his teacher. Graham concluded that it took 18 to 36 months for the market to correct an overreaction on a stock. Dr. James Rea, who collaborated with Graham prior to the value investor's death in 1976, said Graham later refined his holding period to two years.[13]

Like Howe, the De Bondt and Thaler study pointed to January as a period of higher returns for contrarian stock strategies. Just as important was their discovery that contrarian stocks really picked up steam in the second and third year after they were purchased.

Indeed, after the first year, the cumulative performance difference between the winners and losers was only 5.4 percent. This helps us put a realistic time frame on our contrarian strategy, and may help explain why many believe this approach doesn't work: They have too short a view. De Bondt and Thaler's work also validates Howe's finding, showing that "bad news" stocks often rebounded quickly after a negative event, with that rebound resonating through the following three years.

Harry Oppenheimer tested Ben Graham's stock-selection rules and found that a 50-percent profit, or a two-year holding period (whichever came first), was a strategy that generated a mean annual return of 38 percent between 1974–1981. Oppenheimer looked at stocks on the NYSE and AMEX exchanges.[14]

It appears that stocks, once selected for a contrarian portfolio, require 12 to 36 months to generate satisfactory returns. Put another way, it seems to take one to three years to unwind the overly pessimistic hammering of a stock, for the "healing process" to occur. Success demands patience and a stick-to-it resolve. Those are rare qualities in investors, especially when the stock they buy could be dead money for a year. Many won't give the contrarian strategy enough time to work.* Investors who do will be rewarded for their patience, since as we noted before, our research shows that the returns on contrarian stocks tend to accelerate in the second or third year after purchase.

We have shown how a unanimity of crowd opinion, and the actual act of investing based on that opinion, creates investment opportunities for contrarians. In the real world, however, this unanimity is difficult to gauge. It was easy in our three-investor example. But in today's complex and interrelated financial markets, understanding the crowd's opinion is much more difficult. We can't poll everyone, analyze the money they can bring to bear, and conclude how far a crowd's particular belief has been extended. For this reason, our contrarian trading rules include other techniques on which you can rely;

---

*This raises an interesting hypothetical for a mutual- or private-fund money manager: For a contrarian manager to be evaluated fairly, does this mean a six-year history must be studied? It would take a period that long to develop a three-year track record for investment results: Stocks bought in years 1, 2, and 3 would show their cumulative results in years 4, 5, and 6.

strategies that are effective indicators of how investors feel about a particular stock. Remember, our goal is to buy stocks when others won't. However, once we've bought those stocks, we want the other investors to see what we spotted.

■ *NOTES FROM A CONTRARIAN BUSINESS REPORTER*

Underscoring this last point is the case of Paxson Communications Corp., a Florida-based broadcaster. Tony bought the stock March 6, 1997 at $8.687, when it was down 57 percent from its 52-week high of $20.25. The company's shares had been pounded partly over concerns the U.S. Supreme Court might overturn a law requiring cable TV broadcasters to carry programming from independent broadcasters like Paxson.

However, even as analysts said the pending decision made the stock "risky," seven executives were using company loans to buy $2 million worth of Paxson shares.[15] The big price decline, insider buying, and a strong fourth quarter had combined to pique Tony's interest. Paxson shares would later get a jump on news of the insider buying, and from a favorable Supreme Court decision. That August, Fortune *magazine ran a very favorable profile of the company and its 62-year-old maverick CEO, Lowell "Bud" Paxson.[16]*

Five months after it was spotted, Paxson's turnaround was in the mainstream and the stock was up more than 35 percent to just over $12.   ■

THE IMPACT OF THE NEWS ON CONTRARIAN STRATEGY

Contrarian investing works because we can get the information we need to make a judgment on a particular stock. It is beamed to us via print, the Internet, voice, and cable. Nevertheless, many investors are too scared, or too lazy, to think for themselves. They prefer to watch the market, and let the market (and hence other investors) lead them on. If a particular sector of the market is hot, they jump in. They give little thought to the movement in prices: how the price movement started, how long it could run, or why it is running. The knowledge that the market, or a particular stock, is rising is enough to make them invest. They ignore the research showing that hot stocks tend to cool off and that cold stocks tend to get hot. All this gives the contrarian a true investing advantage.

If stocks are falling, the crowd won't buy, believing the shares are something to avoid. This is probably due to a combination of factors: desire to go with the crowd, to be comfortable, to avoid the difficulty of original thought, and the general lack of confidence to bet against the flow.

■ NOTES FROM A CONTRARIAN BUSINESS REPORTER

The news media—newspapers, financial news services, magazines, and network and cable television—play a huge role in shaping mass-investor opinion, merely by reporting the news of the day. In today's era of "sound-bite" journalism, the day's events (a big company such as Intel having a product problem, changes in interest rates, the latest jobs report, a 100-point fall in the Dow) are presented with little long-term perspective, which is probably a key reason investors tend to focus on the most recent news and forget about the events that came before. This is particularly true when a stock is on a hot streak; the intense coverage of the stock's escalating price rise serves to hype the shares (Microsoft's Bill Gates or Intel's Andy Grove on magazine covers as their company shares hit new highs). It's also true that the news teams pile on when a company falls on hard times, which prompts investors to avoid the shares at the very time they should consider buying them. Little wonder that investors view good news as an opportunity, and bad news as a cautionary message.

Let me give you a humorous, but sobering, example of what I mean:

Remember Alan Greenspan's "irrational exuberance" warning in December 1996? It was meant as a cautionary comment about stock-market speculation, but roiled the markets for a day. A few months later, the newspaper I was writing for ran a news service story about the success of some Russia funds benefiting from a torrid rise in that country's stock market. Within a week, we received two letters from inmates at separate area correctional facilities who wanted more information on those funds—so that they might invest the few hundred dollars they earned a year as prison laborers.

My colleagues and I joked about this "correctional exuberance." Wry newsroom humor, yes, but a story that underscores how news coverage helps forge, and then reinforce, mass opinion. ■

We believe that the media, just by reporting news as it happens, help extend popular opinion, driving it to extremes in both directions. When the markets are rising, talk of "hot stocks" and "hot funds" fills the air, grabbing the attention of readers and listeners. Investors are portrayed as "anxiously awaiting" some insignificant news announcement. A stock may drop $3 to $80 and be characterized as "plunging." Minor announcements are hyped as major.

However, contrarians must understand that this focus on the news of the day reinforces the individual investor's tendency to overemphasize the short term.* As we have seen from available research, this short-term focus causes investors to bid up shares more than is justified, and drive shares down below their true value. Contrarians invest for the long term and capitalize on these temporary extremes. Some market news is truly important to heed (a change in interest rates by the Fed for instance), but most is transitory and should not form the basis of any contrarian strategy.

For instance, a bellwether stock may post headline-grabbing earnings that move the market. Such movements tend to be fleeting, and whatever impact on the contrarian's portfolio, it will not be lasting. It's not worth worrying about what economic report will come out tomorrow.

■ *NOTES FROM A CONTRARIAN PORTFOLIO MANAGER*

Whenever the market sits on pins and needles, it seems everyone waits for the latest economic number to "clarify" the situation. It is maddening to have that number released, only to find everyone already waiting for the next number the next day or next week. What do most of these numbers really mean, anyway? Most are adjusted several times, some require footnote reading to have the proper perspective, and the rest are either ignored or given more importance than warranted. In my experience, when

---

*In Chapter 12 we discuss the proper media to include in the contrarian's research arsenal. Often, the decision needs to be made based on the timeframe of the media source.

the Fed raises or lowers interest rates, it is very significant for the stock and bond markets. But all the rest seems to blend into a constantly changing kaleidoscope that is of limited value when you're buying beaten-down stocks that you expect to hold for as long as three years. This isn't to say that all of this news and commentary isn't important. It just depends on your focus. But if you have a long-term view, you can sit comfortably above it all. ■

SUMMARY

Contrarians need to understand that most investors follow trends, instead of anticipating them. The crowd puts too much emphasis on short-term market events and other news, instead of embracing a long-term strategy. The more a rising price trend confirms the collective belief of the investment masses, the more willing those investors are to pony up still more money to further confirm that belief. And when prices are falling, those investors are just as quick to pull money out of stocks, which exacerbates the decline. In either case, at some point, investors have pushed a price to an unreasonable extreme, and that creates the opportunity for the contrarian to either buy or sell. Since independent analysis is the key ingredient to successful contrarian investing, contrarians must keep their bearings by studying what the majority is saying and doing.

Our first contrarian trading rule, the "down-by-half rule," makes this much easier: When a stock is down at least 50 percent from its 52-week high, it merits a look. The fact that a stock has fallen by half is a proxy for negative sentiment among investors. Naturally, we have other rules or "screens" to help us weed out poor investment opportunities. But the "down-by-half rule" is the first trigger, and is the mainstay of our contrarian approach.

Endnotes

1. Howe, John S., "Evidence on Stock Market Overreaction," *Financial Analyst's Journal*, July/August 1986, pp. 74–77.
2. Ibid, p. 76.
3. Ibid.
4. Ibid.

5. Ibid, p. 74.

6. Ibid.

7. De Bondt, Werner F. M., and Thaler, Richard, "Does the Stock Market Overreact?" *Journal of Finance*, July 1985, pp. 793–805.

8. Ibid.

9. Dreman, David, *Psychology and the Stock Market*, AMACOM, 1977, p. 157.

10. Anderson, Torben M., "Some Implications of the Efficient Markets Hypothesis," *Journal of Post-Keynesian Economics*, Winter 1983–84, pp. 281–294.

11. De Bondt and Thaler, p. 799.

12. Ibid.

13. "Ben Graham's Last Will and Testament," *Forbes*, Aug. 1, 1977, p. 43.

14. "A Test of Ben Graham's Stock Selection Criteria," *Financial Analyst's Journal*, September/October 1984, p. 72.

15. Matthews, Steve, "Paxson Executives Buy $2 Million in Stock Near Lows: Insider Focus," Bloomberg News wire report, March 17, 1997.

16. Gunther, Marc, "Will Uncle Bud Sell Hollywood?" *Fortune*, Aug. 18, 1997, pp. 185–88.

CHAPTER 3

INVESTING AGAINST THE GRAIN: THE PSYCHOLOGY OF THE CONTRARIAN STRATEGY

Worry is interest paid on trouble before it falls due.

—William Ralph Inge

There is a scientific, psychological basis for the success enjoyed by contrarian investors. By studying the psychology of the individual, as well as the psychology of the group, we can better understand how the contrarian can profit by investing against the crowd. Although this discussion could become quite technical, we'll explore some basic concepts related to both individual and group psychology, see how they fit in with investing, and show how contrarians can exploit them for profit *(The Practical Effect).*

GOING ALONG TO GET ALONG

From our earliest years, we are conditioned to act in the best interests of our society. For a society to exist and thrive, individuals within that society must conform and follow accepted conventions.*

---

*This urge to conform is not universal. The French, for instance, score much higher in independent behavior than, say, the Norwegians, who value a cohesive and mutually

For instance, we have all agreed to stop our cars at red lights. We do so because we understand that failing to stop will cause injuries and property damage.

A big part of raising children is teaching them society's conventions and instilling behaviors that will allow them to function as members of the group. Acceptable behavior is rewarded, and unacceptable behavior punished.

> ***The Practical Effect:*** From an early age, people (and future investors) are taught to conform. This makes them susceptible to "groupthink," where members of a group all perceive things the same way. In the investment arena, this makes it extremely likely that most investors are going to think alike—the "mass opinion" contrarians strive to exploit.

Without realizing it, we use many strategies to make sure others conform to social norms. We encourage team play; for instance, it's a high compliment to characterize someone as a "real team player." When someone in a group expresses an opinion not held by the other members, the group works collectively to change that opinion. If it becomes clear that the person won't change, he or she can simply be ignored as the group moves on. The threat or fear of being left behind is a powerful motivator in getting people to conform to a group's opinion or point of view.*

Our language contains many phrases that articulate this desire for conformity:

- Let me run it by you.
- What do you think of this?
- Reality check.
- Get with the program.
- Teamwork.

---

responsible society (Milgram, S., "Behavioral Study of Obedience," *Journal of Abnormal Psychology*, 67, 4, pp. 371–378).

*Nevertheless, we recognize the importance of not going along. The greatest accolades given to Winston Churchill resulted from his almost solitary view in the 1930s that the Nazis were a serious threat.

- To get along you've got to go along.
- Conventional wisdom.
- The consensus.
- Team player.

When we don't conform, or when our viewpoint is out of the mainstream, we have words to describe the pain, awkwardness, and difficulty of the conflict we cause in others, and feel ourselves:

- You're by yourself on this one.
- You don't understand.
- He's lost touch with reality.
- They're misreading the data.
- She's a loner (also anything that expresses isolation).
- He's uncooperative.
- Shouldn't you run it by them?

Over time, we are conditioned to conform, to think in a way that earns us society's approval. While we are rewarded for these positive traits, we also pay a price for this conformity: This conditioning stifles independent and creative thought, and can foster mental lethargy. Since we instinctively know what the group (society) believes, we feel we're on firmer ground if we simply adopt the majority view.

As psychologists Wilbert McKeachie and Charlotte Doyle said: "Many people generalized obedience and conformity to such an extent that they failed to act on their own thinking. There lies a very serious problem: To distinguish between situations in which compliance is appropriate and those in which it is not."[1]

Being able to see when independence is warranted is a skill the contrarian must master to profit in the investing game. McKeachie and Doyle also said that such ". . . independence was possible only if the individual trusted his own ability to perceive, to interpret, and to evaluate *independently of his peers and his superiors* (emphasis added)."[2]

That's exactly what contrarians strive for.

> ***The Practical Effect:*** People have a tough time deciding when they should go along with the crowd, and when they shouldn't. That's particularly true when it comes to investing. Most investors fear taking a solitary stand on a stock—even when they know they should—and instead act on majority opinion, for comfort's sake.

For investors to profit, however, they must break free of the flawed thinking and inherent irrationality of the crowd that comprises most of the market. They have to be contrarians, questioning the assumptions that form the basis for the crowd's opinion. When these contrarians see the crowd acting in a way that clearly represents an extreme and irrational opinion, they must be willing to bet against it by putting money at risk in the stock market.

Making the transition won't be easy. People simply find it difficult to form and express independent beliefs. In the absence of independent belief, they will embrace the view of the group as their own.

Think of your own experiences at work, at school, or as a volunteer with some civic group. How often have you had an interesting (or even radical) thought but, before you voiced it, dismissed it as "a stupid idea"? Even if someone prods you to share your thought, you resist. The idea really wasn't "stupid"; you were afraid of the ridicule it might elicit because it was so far out of the mainstream. You quickly went through the following thought process:

- Here's an interesting idea!
- This idea would run counter to the group's thinking.
- If I express it, I may embarrass myself.
- They won't go along with it anyway.
- I'll bury the thought.

We self-censor our thinking to avoid the pain of rejection. This process is so pervasive that there is now an entire industry of consultants to help people open up and express ideas. These brainstorming sessions are often held at weekend retreats in isolated settings. They are marked by a staccato barrage of ideas; some useful, others not. To encourage this free flow, criticism is strictly forbidden. That professional consultants have to be hired to change behavior underscores how difficult it is for people to express their new and creative thoughts without fear.

When we actually are willing to make the leap, and have the courage to express original or "dangerous" thoughts, we couch them in language that signals the listener that rejection is acceptable:

- Let's throw it on the wall and see if it sticks.
- Let's brainstorm.
- Let's offer all ideas, no matter how silly.

Even the word "brainstorm" conjures an image of a chaotic—and potentially destructive—whirlwind of ideas. But to you as an investor, it is even more destructive to adopt the crowd's view as your own. You will *never* make a lot of money that way.

Each of us is a cauldron of fears and anxieties. So we find comfort when we're in agreement with others. We test our thoughts and impressions with friends or family—a "safe" audience—to see if we are on "the right track." If we find reassurance there, only then will we venture out in search of support in a more public forum.

THE CREATIVE CONTRARIAN

Much of the time, our desire to conform is beneficial to society, allowing it to function and thrive. However, there are some settings in which nonconformity, or contrary opinion, is important. For instance, a research and development scientist strives for original thoughts. Scientific breakthroughs demand that researchers be free of the shackles of conventional, expert, accepted opinion. Indeed, if you want to win a Nobel Prize, you better get the work done while you're young. By the time middle age sets in, your thinking may become too rigid for the spectacular insights that change the scientific world. Albert Einstein, for example, was a young man when he formulated his Theory of Relativity.

Artists build on the past, but also push for breakthroughs. The history of art is punctuated by violent quarrels as new artists struggled to bring their vision to life. When *Le Sacre du Printemps* was debuted by Stravinsky in Paris, a riot erupted. The work was too revolutionary to gain acceptance without first destroying some existing

notions about music. Conventional society felt the threat and re-
acted. "Starving artists" labor financially and emotionally; but the
true pain comes when their advancements are rejected time and
again by the established art community before finally finding acceptance. Little wonder contrary thinking is so difficult.

> ***The Practical Effect:*** Contrarians are not easily bred. There-
> fore, they represent a minority of opinion. That means there's
> a mass of opinion contrarian investors can act against.

Contrarians think differently. They are independent, ask questions others don't, and approach problems in a fresh way—rejecting
the "herd mentality." That's never an easy position to take. We all
want to be accepted, even loved. Voicing opinions that run against
popularly held beliefs is not the way to gain that acceptance.

Even the word "contrary" has a derogatory flavor. If you don't
believe us, just look the word up in any thesaurus. Synonyms listed
in *Rodale's Synonym Finder* include "opposite, counter, contradictory,
contrapositive, converse, antiethical, incompatible, incongruous,
irreconcilable."[3]

Stings a bit, doesn't it? Why does society cast contrary thinking in this negative light? Again, because we seek conformity with
our views. When an individual expresses doubt, we use many strategies to force agreement, including branding dissenters as outsiders or
even troublemakers.

HOW AN ATTITUDE IS FORMED

By understanding how attitudes are formed, contrarians can avoid
the pitfalls of groupthink. When we see a situation unfolding, we
develop an expectancy about that course of events, and form an attitude.* This attitude is shaped by all the knowledge, experience, and
beliefs we bring to bear in analyzing the event we're studying. We
view something like the stock market as an object, and form beliefs
and expectations about that object.

---

*This follows an excellent discussion of attitude in *Psychology*, pp. 560–595, by Wilbert
McKeachie and Charlotte Lackner Doyle, Addison Wesley Publishing Co., Inc., New
York, New York, 1966.

Attitudes vary in many ways. The strength of the attitude, or its *intensity*, and the expectation of either pleasure or pain, called the *position* of the attitude, are the two defining axes. For instance, if you believe intensely that a particular stock is going to rise, your intensity is strong and the position of the attitude is highly positive. In addition, your attitude can vary depending on your level of acquaintance with the object. A major league baseball player has a much different attitude about a 92-mile-per-hour beanball than the fan in the bleachers or the sportswriter high up in the press box.*

Attitudes do not always prompt action. When you express a viewpoint, you reveal your attitude, but you are not actually taking an action based on that attitude. It is one thing to say that the market is going to rise, but quite another to actually put money at risk by buying stock. If a gap exists between an attitude and an action, it is this: People will often say one thing and yet do another. Remember that the next time someone gives you a market prediction or a tip on a "hot" stock.

What helps people form an attitude? Attitudes are formed based on four forces:

1. Utilitarian

2. Value-expressive

3. Ego-defensive

4. Knowledge[†]

Sometimes, one of the four forces is overriding; at other times several are at play. Of the four, *knowledge* is the one that we'll emphasize, because it has the greatest relevance to the contrarian. A knowledge-based attitude is one defined by facts and experiences.

An attitude based on knowledge is part of a person's attempt to form a consistent, clear, and stable view of the world. When people are in a situation where their knowledge or experience is limited (like investing in the stock market), they will usually seek guidance in order to form an attitude they believe has a sound basis. Investors search for the missing pieces in three ways:

---

* Why else would players characterize such pitches as "headhunting" while sportswriters refer to them as "chin music"?

[†] An attitude with a *utilitarian* basis is one based on survival or safety; *value-expressive* on the need for self-esteem or self-actualization; *ego-defensive* deals with defense mechanisms. All can be related to investing.

1. By looking for more information.
2. By adopting the attitudes of other people around them.
3. By adopting an attitude consistent with their other beliefs or knowledge.

We begin to see how the thought process of most investors can lead to group behavior and even a frenzy among the masses.

> *The Practical Effect:* Investors approach the market with a high expectation they will make money. The pleasure of pulling down profits is great, so the investor puts a lot on the line from a psychological standpoint.

As an example of how attitudes are formed, consider Arthur, who wants to buy some stock with money he just inherited. Since he's never invested before, and is faced with almost limitless choices, he seeks to simplify the problem by finding a couple of stocks or ideas on which to focus. His attitude toward any particular stock is not yet formed. He has no strong opinion, no deep base of knowledge on which to act. However, he does believe that Internet technology is a great growth area, and is predisposed to stocks in that niche. Now we'll see how the three steps we mentioned apply to the investment process.

Initially, Arthur lacks a deep information base, so he will have to seek information (step number 1). Though he is generally aware of the thirst for high-tech stocks, no particular stocks are on his buy list.

One Saturday, while sitting at the barber shop waiting his turn, Arthur picks up a copy of a national computer magazine and catches a headline about a new mass-memory storage device for computers. The story explains in a breathless tone how this revolution in computer storage means big things for Alley Oop Digital. Intrigued, he makes a note to explore this further. Now, he is actively seeking information.

Arthur goes to the library, and finds several other stories about the Alley Oop storage device that parrot the first article he read. He is unaware that all three articles were generated from the same Alley Oop press release and, therefore, are essentially three renderings of the same information.* Intrigued by—but not yet sold on—Alley Oop, Arthur vows to chat with a coworker, Tom, who is his company's information-systems director. (He is still at step number 1, seeking more information.)

Monday comes. Tom is enthusiastic about Alley Oop's product and says, yes, it seems to be the real thing. Tom's excitement is contagious and Arthur is now growing bullish on Alley Oop. (He is at step number 2, beginning to adopt the attitude of others.) He calls his broker who also knows Alley Oop and is quite high on the stock. The broker faxes Arthur the brokerage firm's most recent research report on the company (step number 2, more reinforcement from others).

Arthur reviews what he has heard and read, and, since it fits in neatly with his other beliefs and knowledge (number 3, consistency with his bullish view of technology stocks), he buys Alley Oop stock.

Does Arthur's thought process sound familiar? After starting with a vague awareness, Arthur progressed to a firm attitude about Alley Oop. But his attitude had to reach a high enough level of intensity to spur him from mere verbal acceptance into action (actually buying the stock). Arthur's broker endorsed the stock, labeling it "a compelling value." Since Arthur places his broker in the expert-information camp, that, plus coworker Tom's positive response, created a level of intensity high enough to trigger action. Alone, neither Tom nor Arthur's broker could create the intensity level needed for Arthur to actually take action and buy the stock.

Taken together, however, the concurring opinions of Tom and the broker were enough to cross Arthur's intensity threshold. And since the *position* of the attitude is highly positive (the thought of making money), Arthur bought the stock.

If his broker had nixed the idea, Arthur would not have bought the stock. If Tom had been negative on the company, Arthur might not have asked his broker. Faced with conflicting opinions, and without a strong knowledge base that would have allowed him to make a

---

* For investors who like to go beyond the mainstream business newspapers and magazines and burrow into trade journals for investment ideas, this statement has more validity than most might suspect. Bill knows of one very sharp trade-journal writer who writes under 15 different bylines. While that certainly spreads the writer's work around among many different trade publications, it also means those many articles pretty much contain only one point of view.

decision on his own, Arthur would not have made the investment. Our illustration helps explain why naive investors tend to buy at the top. *The less investors know, the stronger confirmation they need before they'll risk their money.* Now we see why it's the roaring bull market near its end that draws in the most inexperienced of investors.

The way most investors approach the market closely mirrors our hypothetical scenario. Investors seek expert opinion, try to confirm it, and then invest based on that knowledge.

Where the Analysts Stand

As we'll see when we study several of history's speculative financial manias, it is this quest for knowledge that lets mass hysteria take hold. We might assume that experts are immune from investment hysteria: After all, don't they already have a strong knowledge base to draw from? You'd think so, but a close examination of the expert's world shows how even highly skilled professionals often throw in their lot with the crowd. What we'll discover is that the investment experts we so often depend on for guidance are not the independent thinkers we believed them to be.

Let's go back to Alley Oop Digital. All securities analysts are looking at Alley Oop using the same base of information. Financial reports, industry press releases, newspaper and magazine stories, interviews on network and cable TV personal finance shows, and the opinions of rival analysts all contribute to the expert's opinion. Analysts don't suffer from a lack of knowledge. But other forces sometimes push aside that knowledge and play a bigger role than they should, as analysts try to form attitudes (recommendations) about a particular stock or the market in general. One factor that's probably the biggest influence on Wall Street analysts is their need to survive in a highly competitive—and unforgiving—atmosphere. Attitude formation constantly wars with survival.

Analysts' utilitarian basis (the practical aspects of seeking reasonable security in life), along with their focus on survival and safety, both play a role in their tendency to conform with the crowd's opinion. Securities analysts, or mutual fund managers, know if their opinions are too far off the mark, and if clients lose money on their picks, their credibility will be damaged. They could even lose their jobs. Therefore, the judgment of analysts is clouded by their need to survive. It is okay to be wrong, but to be *grossly* wrong is unacceptable.

For instance, the fund manager who buys the same stocks as all the other fund managers, and is proved wrong, can survive, because all the competitors were wrong, too.* What is not acceptable is to buy stocks no one else is buying, only to be proved wrong and lose money for the client. Then you look stupid (remember the ribbing Tony's client took from his golfing buddies about gold stocks?).

Little wonder that analysts, pension-fund and mutual-fund managers are so susceptible to group bias. It is the exceptional analyst who exhibits free-thinking and an independent point of view.

Since an analyst's work is generally organized around specific industries, sectors, or markets, analysts fall prey to *value-expressive* bias. A value-expressive bias is the tendency of people to view favorably the things they like, skewing their opinions. For example, if an analyst enjoys covering the pharmaceutical industry, there inevitably will be some positive bias toward the stocks he covers.

Finally, when an estimate proves incorrect, analysts may understandably find it hard to admit the error. Their attitude is colored by *ego-defensive* behavior. Together, all these factors can cause analysts to be conformists, meaning their work might reflect that bias. Since so many people like Arthur rely on an analyst's forecasts, the biases of the analyst, combined with the knowledge basis that forms the individual's attitude, can create a "follow-the-leader" mentality. The analyst publishes a bullish report, which feeds into the knowledge base of investors' attitudes, which causes further bullishness on the stock, which elicits still more bullish comments on the stock. It's a cycle that feeds on itself, moving faster and faster.

The prophecy becomes self-fulfilling. The stock rises more and more, reinforcing a positive bias, prompting investors to pay higher and higher prices, until the stock trades at a lofty level not warranted by the prospects of the underlying company. A mania has taken hold.

The Practical Effect: While most—if not all—analysts are bright, hard-working, and knowledgeable, psychological pressures can subtly bias their judgment. That's why it's important for investors to think for themselves, and not base their buying and selling on one-size-fits-all stock recommendations.

---

* This reminds us of the old stock-picker's saw: "No one ever got fired for buying IBM"—even when IBM shares were falling from $175 down to around $40.

Changes in Attitude, Changes in Latitude

In a study done during World War II, soldiers who believed that war with Japan would continue for a long time after Germany's surrender were exposed to an expert who delivered a one-sided speech supporting their view. This resulted in a marked increase in the intensity of their attitude.[4] So, too, the intensity of a bullish market view will increase when expert opinion is presented supporting that bullish attitude. Bullishness begets more bullishness.

In the stock market, when everyone is making money, the positive feelings ratchet up the intensity of investors' attitudes toward stocks. Those investors continue to clear new intensity "hurdles," which spurs them to buy still more stocks. Some buy on margin. Others beat the bushes looking for "the next" Alley Oop.* Greed takes hold and fear is forgotten.

> **The Practical Effect:** As a stock or a market gathers momentum, new investors are drawn into the fray. That, in turn, reassures the original investors, and encourages that first group to pony up more money. That cycle continues until something happens that's dramatic enough to bring about a change.

What, then, will produce an attitude change? As a stock, or a market, runs higher and higher, what causes it to fall? What causes a change in investors' behavior? You would think an increase in fear would do the trick. After all, fear and greed rule the market and increased fear of losses should be enough to change behavior. Surprisingly, this may not be true. Research shows that when people are presented with messages designed to produce more or less anxiety, they tend to ignore the messages creating the greatest amount of fear.[5] Put another way, people become hostile to the message-giver who arouses anxiety, and ignore the message. By shooting the messenger, investors very often put a bullet into themselves.

---

*In Rochester, where both Tony and Bill work, investment types would often talk about "the next Xerox." Xerox, which invented the office copier, had been founded and based in Rochester for many years. Its explosive growth during the 1960s and part of the 1970s made many workaday people very wealthy. It was an effective analogy that was, sadly, most of the time, misplaced.

This helps explain why people are so critical of doomsayers. If the market is rising, or even if it is starting to fall, people who are bullish tend to ignore those calling for a market decline. During each of the manias we will discuss, someone of prominence always warned that a frenzy had taken hold. But those cautions were always countered with the predictable response—"things are different this time"—and were ignored.

Indeed, other research shows that people selectively read newspapers and magazines or watch TV, looking for those commentators or programs that reinforce attitudes they already hold—and shunning those that might change their opinion.[6] A number of studies have shown that the theory of "dissonance," as expressed by psychologist Leon Festinger, points to a solution.*

Festinger theorized that when people are confronted with viewpoints contrary to their own attitudes and beliefs, they fall into a state of *dissonance*. That is, their world view has been shaken and they must reconcile the new, opposing information in order to get back into their comfortable state of equilibrium and contentment. There are three circumstances in which people will change their attitude:

1. When there is no simple way to disregard the inconsistency.

2. If events prove the new information rewarding.

3. If the person feels that the new attitude is already his, or uses his ideas.

The Practical Effect: As people struggle with new information, they tend to reject it in favor of beliefs they already hold. This is inherently irrational. But as we know, the market is, at times, irrational.

Why don't people sell all their stocks when the market turns ugly? They hold on because they find it difficult to reconcile their bullish attitude with the new bearish environment. They're in a state of dissonance. However, if they sell a stock short and reap a reward

---

* Festinger, a distinguished academic, received the 1959 Distinguished Scientist Award, given by the American Psychological Association.

for doing so (because the price falls as they predicted), selling more stock is not at all difficult to do. Proceeds from stock sales are put into a money-market fund and earn interest, making impossible further losses. Outright short sales provide positive reinforcement. Thus, the investor begins to feel this negative outlook is *his* idea. Since the new feedback (profits from short sales) proves rewarding, his attitude changes. Finally, after the market bottoms, a new bull trend will cause the same dissonance and inconsistency as the previous bearish trend. The reason: This new bull trend runs counter to the investor's now-bearish belief.

This helps explain why investors are slow to sell in a downtrend, and slow to buy in an uptrend. It takes time to reconcile this new environment with their existing notions. All the forces that help build an attitude, while positive in most social circumstances, are usually deadly when applied to investing. There seems to be a diabolical scheme afoot to fool most of the people most of the time. For investors who aren't contrarians, there is.

How often have you bought a stock near the top of its run, watched as it changed course, and ridden it all the way to the bottom? How often have you sold that stock, only to watch with fists clenched in frustration as it reverses course and explodes toward new highs? After taking such big losses, you have a tough time dealing with this new, bullish trend. The rising share price is inconsistent with your attitude that the stock is a loser. You ignore it, instead of admitting you were wrong and buying the stock back to profit from this new trend.

Perhaps you are being ego-defensive and don't want to admit you were wrong. In any case, your attitude-forming mechanisms are firing on the wrong cylinders. No wonder it is difficult for people to make the right choice!

> *The Practical Effect:* It is this psychology that is behind the bull and bear runs in a typical stock.

Most investors do not invest rationally, even if they think they do. They believe that rational thought is behind their decisions to buy or sell stocks. Actually, these decisions are driven by the need to be in step with the group. They are acting out an emotional process that they have fooled themselves into believing is rational. In reality, they are held captive by irrational needs, wants, and desires.

Further research shows it is not a good practice for investors to share their market opinions with others. This is especially true for contrarians. The contrarian view is rejected by the masses, if not held in downright contempt. When people publicly express their attitude about a topic, research shows it becomes much more difficult for them to later change course—even when changing course is clearly the right thing to do.[7] By expressing their views, investors saddle themselves with the additional burden of *being shown wrong.* Since so few of us are willing to admit error, we'll go to unusual ends to stand by our positions.

This is why the analyst, who must constantly present and defend his case to the investing public, can get hung up defending an indefensible position. The analyst (or other investor) stubbornly clings to the wrong point of view, and only admits the error after a prolonged and painful decline.

Bucking the Trend

Investors have a tough time deciding when they should go along with the crowd, and when they shouldn't. Investing increases anxiety and, in that arena, people have a bias to seek and hold onto majority opinion for comfort.

Once we understand the fragile base on which the majority opinion is built, we find it easier to buck that opinion. A stock may rise, and that rise may persist for many months, but it is fair to say that of the thousands who may have purchased it, only a few did so from an independently framed opinion. The majority are simply going along for the ride, unaware they did not make that investment based on independently conceived beliefs.

If all investors did the necessary and difficult work that should go into formulating their own beliefs, would we get the seemingly irrational and wild swings in prices that are a daily market occurrence? Would people be so quick to buy on a whim? Isn't it reasonable to believe that, just as investors jump aboard based on the flimsy reasoning that a rising stock must continue to rise, they will bail out when insignificant downturns occur?

> *The Practical Effect:* As people struggle with new information, they tend to reject it in favor of beliefs they already hold. This is inherently irrational. But as we know, the market is, at times, irrational.

The Practical Effect: Markets and stocks can turn quickly—and for the most insignificant reasons. Attempts to divine a single cause for events like the Crash of 1987 can be fruitless. Sometimes, there is no clear answer because the truth may actually lie in an irrational, crowd-induced frenzy that has no rational basis.

This is precisely what the contrarian struggles to learn: how to identify this frenzy, recognize it as the impostor that it is, and go the other way.

Conclusion: To invest successfully, we must develop an independent attitude, and be fresh, clear thinkers. We cannot be swayed inordinately by expert opinion, by the musings of celebrity sources, or by the opinions of others. It is the solitary walk that gets us to our destination.

Endnotes

1. McKeachie, Wilbert J., and Doyle, Charlotte L., *Psychology*, Addison-Wesley Publishing Co., Reading, Mass., p. 593, 1966.
2. Ibid.
3. *Rodale Synonym Finder*, Warner Books/Rodale Press, p. 26, 1978.
4. Hovland, C. I., Lumsdaine, A. A., and Sheffield, F. D., "Experiments on Mass Communication," *Studies in Social Psychology in World War II*, Vol. III, Princeton University Press, Princeton, N.J., 1949.
5. Janis, I. L., and Feshbach, S., "Effects of Fear-Arousing Communications," *The Journal of Abnormal Psychology*, 48, pp. 78–93, 1953.
6. Katz, E., and Lazarsfeld, P. F., *Personal Influence: The Part Played by People in the Flow of Mass Communication*, Free Press, Glencoe, Illinois, 1955.
7. Bennett, E. B., "Discussions, Decision and Consensus in 'Group Decision'," *Human Relations*, 8, pp. 251–273.

CHAPTER 4

MARKET MANIA: CONTRARIAN LESSONS

History repeats itself all the time in Wall Street.

—*Reminiscences of a Stock Operator,*
Edwin Lefevre

Lefevre was right: History does repeat itself all the time in Wall Street. In fact, when it comes to investing in general, history has repeated itself with great regularity through the years. Unfortunately, as some of history's great financial manias show, investors have had to re-learn that lesson—again and again—the hard way.

So far, we've devoted a lot of space describing just what a contrarian is. But it's just as important to understand what a contrarian is not. It's worth spending some time looking at some of the spectacular, and destructive, speculative manias that have played out through history.

UNDERSTANDING MANIAS: A CONTRARIAN PERSPECTIVE

A mania is a period of insanity marked by incredible excitement, delusional speculation, and a violent, and usually ruinous, climax.

The insanity infects everyone. Trading is aggressive, frenetic, and euphoric. The crowd loses all concern for the intrinsic value of their investments.

These manias show how easy it is to be seduced by greed and to succumb to the psychology of the crowd. Understanding crowd psychology, and knowing when to bet against it, are the paths to profit for the contrarian.

Just as the seeds of a hurricane are sown in tropical storms, the seeds of mania are sown in market speculation. Most tropical storms do not become hurricanes, most speculative frenzies do not develop into full-blown manias. The difference between a frenzy and a mania is a matter of degree. A true mania crosses all sectors, engulfing entire markets.

For instance, market-watchers were stunned by the appetite investors showed for technology stocks—and Internet stocks in particular—during the summer of 1995. Often, the prices paid for the stocks were higher than could be justified by any investing yardstick. Many companies were startups with no profits. Some had no sales. But even this whirlwind of speculation does not qualify as a true mania, since there was always a fair-sized group standing on the sidelines preaching caution. In a true mania, even that caution gets tossed away as investors believe they are invincible.

In a mania, anyone with the audacity to point out that prices are too high, or to predict a terrible crash, is ridiculed. Warnings are cavalierly dismissed.

Consider what John Kenneth Galbraith wrote about the stock market crash of 1929: "The striking thing about the stock market speculation of 1929 was not the massiveness of the participation. Rather it was the way it became central to the culture."[1]

In a true mania, speculation becomes "central to the culture." Everyone is doing it, and everyone accepts the reasons why everyone is doing it. We read about manias like the Dutch tulip madness of the 1600s, shake our heads and maybe even laugh. We wonder how a whole nation could be whipped into speculative madness over tulip bulbs.

A mania illustrates, in an extreme way, just how wrong the crowd can be. By understanding the mania, contrarians better understand the crowd. Even with the benefit of hindsight, speculative manias occur with some regularity. Among them:

- Great Britain's South Sea Company in the early 1700s
- Stocks and Florida land in the United States. in the 1920s
- The "Nifty Fifty" stocks in the late 1960s and early 1970s
- Gold in the late 1970s
- Baseball cards and "muscle cars" in the 1980s

We will explore two manias, beginning with the great tulip bulb mania in 17th century Holland. It's a good example to start with since the whole idea is ludicrous beyond belief: The Dutch fervently believed the path to world domination was paved with tulip bulbs. Then, we'll look at the Crash of 1929.

TULIP MADNESS: THE FLOWERING INFERNO

Tulip Madness was not a springtime fraternity event, nor a 50-percent-off sale at your local lawn and garden center. In the mid-1600s, The Netherlands was swept by a financial mania so severe that the subsequent crash smashed the Dutch economy and transformed the country from a world power into an economic backwater.

Tulip Madness, Tulipomania, or *Tulpewoerde*, is the most celebrated mania in history for two reasons: It was the first financial frenzy to be thoroughly chronicled; and the frugal and practical Dutch were such unlikely victims that it perfectly illustrates the precipitousness of groupthink and greed.*

At the mania's height, a sailor was imprisoned on felony charges because he mistook a valuable tulip bulb sitting on a countertop in a merchant's office for an onion—and ate it for lunch along with a piece of herring. Families raided their life savings, sold their homes and businesses, and squandered fortunes to speculate in the tulip-bulb

---

*The authors recommend to the reader Robert Beckman's excellent book, *Crashes, Why They Happen—What To Do*. Beckman provides fascinating commentary on many of history's more notable financial debacles.

market. Some actually thought the country should switch from the gold standard to the tulip-bulb standard. When the market collapsed, as was inevitable, the nation's world standing was forever changed.

Petal to the Metal

Tulip Madness was at its height from roughly 1634 to the first part of 1637.[2] But it took root much earlier. The hardy tulip came to Europe from the Middle East during the mid-1500s. From Vienna, the tulip's popularity spread to Germany and The Netherlands, to England in the 1570s, and then to France in the early 1600s.[3]

France would see a mini-mania in tulip bulbs, but The Netherlands is where speculation reached its peak. Holland was a world power and a cultural trendsetter. Its fleet accounted for half of all the world's shipping. The Dutch had colonies as far away as the New World. The country was newly affluent; tulips were a way to flaunt that status.

The flowers were pretty, difficult to obtain, and pricey even before Tulip Madness set in. As the flowers became more and more a status symbol, and the De Groots tried to keep up with the Van Helsings, the desire to own tulips blossomed among the masses. At some point, tulip bulbs ceased being an expensive—though harmless—hobby and became the object of the 17th century's most infamous speculative debacle.

■ NOTES FROM A CONTRARIAN PORTFOLIO MANAGER

News of a good investment ripples outward as when a stone is tossed into a still country pond. At first, the ripples are strong and close together, but as they move farther from their source, the distance between them widens and they lose strength. The same is true with investments. The insiders and the early bankrollers see the biggest returns; that's when the investment trend has the most power and is known to the fewest people.

As the investment gathers momentum, it gathers followers. Soon sophisticated, professional investors like managers of pension funds and mutual funds dive in. As the price rises, more people try to ride the wave, among them fledgling individual investors who pull money out of bank CDs in a search for bigger returns. The media trumpets the investment's accelerating rise. Eventually everyone knows the story, the last dollar is in and the ripple fades into nothingness. ▪

As demand for bulbs escalated, it was no longer enough to own just any tulip. Ironically, tulips flawed by a nonlethal virus became the most desirable. The reason: The virus caused the petals to display wild patterns of contrasting colors.[4]

Flowers with dots, ragged petals, or wild stripes that looked like flames became the rage. There were even grading systems to rank and value the flowers: The more striking the pattern, the higher the price.[5]

Cultivators would watch their gardens hoping for mutations that would set their tulip strain apart from others. Discovering a new strain was like striking gold or winning the lottery.

This ruckus would have been but an interesting footnote in botanical history had tulip speculation remained a specialty business. It didn't. Word spread of the fortunes being made and growers sprouted up all over the country. Tulip prices continued to climb. New professions emerged—tulip analysts, for one—as did new industries: packing and shipping, insurance, and even storage vaults.

Tulip speculating became the business of Holland. Nearly 200 years later, author Charles MacKay wrote, "In 1634, the rage among the Dutch to possess them was so great that the ordinary industry of the country was neglected, and the population, even to its lowest dregs, embarked in the tulip trade. As the mania increased, prices augmented, until in the year 1635, many persons were known to invest a fortune of 100,000 florins for the purchase of 40 roots."[6]

For context, in 17th century Holland, the *annual income* of an urban, middle class family was on the order of 200 to 1,000 florins per year. MacKay points out that four fat oxen were worth 480 florins, eight swine 240 florins, two hogsheads of beer 70 florins, and 1,000 pounds of cheese 120.[7] These were items of real value; after a day plowing the field behind the oxen and tending the sheep, a Dutch farmer could eat cheese and wash it down with some beer.

Bulb prices rose still higher. Theft became a problem.

The get-rich-quick crowd moved in; the promoters and profiteers and market manipulators, goosing prices on tulip bulbs just like penny-stock swindlers do with worthless securities today.

Market riggers would sometimes release specially trained animals (dogs, chickens, and pigs were the favorites) into a tulip field to dig up, eat, or otherwise destroy bulbs, creating artificial shortages. Other nefarious traders would buy large lots of a specific bulb and then start a rumor that the field where that bulb hailed from had been obliterated by an invasion of these animals. Naturally, the traders sold their bulbs at a tidy profit when their rumor caused prices to spike.* Greed clouded good judgment.

■ *NOTES FROM A CONTRARIAN BUSINESS REPORTER*

Believe it or not, fraud is a great contrarian indicator that a market is getting overheated. Reporters on the business news desk see it all the time. When a particular sector or investment opportunity gets hot (be it technology stocks, precious metals, silver eagle coins, or wireless communications licenses), the boiler-room crowd will be out there pitching, trying to separate you from your money. Unfortunately, reckless investors too often make it all too easy for these unsavory actors. Investors may be buying, but if they stepped back and considered it carefully for more than a moment, they would see what these glorified penny-stock promoters are selling—nothing. If you start reading about a new wave of particular scams in the newspaper or in your favorite monthly business magazine, chances are good that particular niche, market, or investment has reached an unreasonably bullish extreme. ■

Serious investors employed messengers to deliver news on price changes. But, it was the jump into the market by the middle-class Dutch that finally pushed the speculative frenzy to its ultimate peak. Everyone succumbed to the allure of fast and easy profits. Some people sold their houses, farms, businesses, and livestock to get cash to speculate in tulip bulbs. Others used their property as collateral for deals they'd reached on one of the exchanges. Markets were established in Amsterdam, Rotterdam, and three other cities. Futures markets sprouted. Traders would write contracts guaranteeing delivery of

---

*This reminds us of the hordes of shady stock operators who flourished in the late 19th and early 20th centuries. Their "operations" focused on buying up large blocks of a stock to corner the market, then whipping the rumor mill to squeeze—and knock out—the short sellers.

specific tulip bulbs that they had no intention of fulfilling—they planned to sell the contract to someone else, at a big profit, before it came due.* Initially, tulip-bulb trading had a legitimate purpose and took place only during winter months; that way, growers got their bulbs before the spring planting season. But speculators even perverted that process. Now bulbs were bought not for planting, but for speculation. People clamored for year-round trading.

The futures markets led quite naturally to options markets, where speculators could buy the right to purchase (call options), or to sell (put options) tulip bulbs. Speculators who thought prices would rise bought calls, while those who had a gloomier view purchased puts.

As Tulip Mania played out, already stratospheric prices rose still higher. Eventually, prices were doubling almost *every day*.[8] A trader would pay whatever the seller demanded for the most popular flowers because he believed someone else would pay even more tomorrow. Tulip Madness held no danger so long as prices kept rising.† Dutch economists said that tulip prices would continue to levitate— that unlike other investments they couldn't go down—ensuring an ever-rising standard of living that would make Holland the richest nation in the world.‡ Foreign investors moved into the market, too.

■ *NOTES FROM A CONTRARIAN BUSINESS REPORTER*

If I've learned anything as a chronicler of business, it's to head for cover when someone says, "Things are different this time." In essence, that's what the Dutch believed about tulip bulbs as investments: Unlike other investments, they thought bulb prices could move in only one direction—up. Prices can move in two directions—they can go down, too. The

---

*Readers will no doubt draw parallels to today's commodity exchanges. Remember that commodities futures markets have a legitimate purpose. They exist so those in the trade can lay off risk to speculators who embrace it in pursuit of profits. Even though tulip contracts, in terms of trading and delivery, had much in common with today's commodities contracts, it's one thing to trade in wheat or gasoline (which have real economic use) and quite another to speculate in tulip bulbs.

† All investors, and contrarians especially, should understand that buying stocks using this so-called "Greater Fool" strategy is a very poor idea. This reminds us a lot of today's "momentum" players, also a strategy we abhor.

‡ It is worth mentioning that at the same time this was going on in Holland, the English were plowing their money into ships, armies, and voyages of exploration.

rules of investing that have exerted themselves time and again throughout history will continue to do so again and again. It's just a question of when.

This look at Tulip Mania should remind us that the seeds of speculation are always present. It's easy to succumb when a frenzy spirals, easy to believe the old rules governing value no longer hold sway. But in the end, it's never different. Stocks can be overvalued or undervalued for a short time. Eventually, however, undervalued stocks will rise and overvalued stocks will fall to reflect their true value. Pretending they won't is courting trouble. ∎

Savvy operators did all they could to maintain the momentum. A cobbler in The Hague cultivating tulips in his garden grew a black tulip and bragged of his good fortune. The cobbler was soon visited by tulip traders from another city, who paid him 1,500 florins for the bulb. With the transaction complete, one of them dropped the bulb and stamped it to a pulp. The reason: They, too, had a black tulip. To protect its value, they eradicated the only other known example.[9]

Like stocks in the United States in the late 1920s, tulip trading became part of Holland's social fabric. Parents would name a newborn after the flower of the day, and even common folk would check tulip prices daily.[10] Remember the bulb eaten by the seaman? It was so valuable that it would have paid to feed his shipmates for a whole year.[11]

By 1634, tulip trading was the only business of Holland. The country fell into neglect as more legitimate enterprises were starved of capital.

Paying the Price

The speculation could not continue. Ultimately, there were no more of the "Greater Fools" willing to take those tulips at a higher price. Prices slumped, as they had at times before, but this time did not recover. That sparked panic, and a hefty plunge in prices. Speculators who had purchased tulip-futures contracts at high prices refused to accept delivery at the new lower prices when settlement day arrived.

Stories of default spread, and thousands of Dutch speculators found themselves broke but for collections of largely worthless tulip bulbs. Nobody would buy these bulbs, not even at fire-sale prices.

The poor who had become quickly rich found themselves poor again. Banks failed, accelerating the country's economic slide. Too many years and too much money had been devoted to tulip speculation instead of on the country's other economic interests.

Some speculators in different cities across The Netherlands banded together in hopes the government would step in and restore public confidence in the tulip trade. But government leaders declined, leaving it to the speculators to come to agreement among themselves. The marketeers couldn't agree and, to stop the bickering, the government finally decreed that all contracts made during the mania, or before November 1636, were nullified. Contracts made after that time could be nullified by the purchaser by paying 10 percent to the seller. Neither buyer nor seller was satisfied with that decision: Tulips at one time worth 6,000 florins were now being offered for 500.[12]

Many suits were filed for breach of contract, but the courts refused to enforce the pacts, ruling the agreements were little more than gambling transactions. Finally, the Provincial Council at The Hague was asked to ponder the situation. After several months of review, they did offer an interim solution that the courts again refused to enforce. The mess would take years to clean up and the Dutch economy never again stood at the forefront of the global marketplace.

Lessons from Tulipomania are legion. Have they been heeded? As we have seen, the Dutch drove themselves to financial ruin through tulip bulb speculation. And, in doing so, they lost their empire to the English and the French. Had they not, the language of Wall Street might very well be Dutch. Instead, the English, and not the Dutch, would win the desperate struggle for the New World.

As we will see, however, the Americans would not learn the lesson, either.

THE CRASH OF 1929

The "Great Crash" has assumed a place in both history and legend. How bad was it? Did it cause the deep and tragic depression that followed? Debate continues even today, but there are lessons for contrarians to learn about hype, speculation, and the psychology of the crowd.

The general market reached heights in September 1929 that would not be reached again until late 1954—a quarter of a century later. The Dow Jones Industrial Average shed a sickening 89 percent of its value, falling from its September 1929 peak of 381 to its July 1932 trough of 41.

To equal that today, the Dow would have to fall from its August 1997 peak of 8259 all the way back to 808 in three years—and then not recover until 2022.

The 1929 to 1932 slide followed an incredible run. In the 18-month span from March 1928 to early September 1929, the market doubled, equaling on a percentage basis the gains of the prior five years. Unlike the other mania we've chronicled, the 1928–1929 stock market frenzy started with investors buying shares in solid companies—General Electric, Radio Corporation of America, and Montgomery Ward—and using hard cash. It wasn't until fairly late in the run that investors started using borrowed money to chase stocks.

Of the many factors that contributed to the Great Crash, two are worth noting: the use of borrowed money, or "margin," to buy stocks, and the proliferation of the "investment trusts."

Investment trusts are interesting because they did, for a time, play a role similar to the one mutual funds play today. Originally, trusts gave the individual investor without a lot of cash a direct way to put money in the market and still get diversification.

When trusts first appeared in the United States in the early 1920s, they were run conservatively with strict rules guiding their management.*

As trusts became more commonplace, oversight and account-ability dropped away. The trusts sold shares to the public and used the money however they wished. They had to disclose the value of their holdings when the trust was first listed, and once a year there-after. By 1927, about 160 had been formed. That number doubled in 1927, and 186 more appeared in 1928.[13] By the early months of 1929, new trusts were being promoted at the rate of one each business day.[14]

---

*Originally, investment trusts surfaced in Scotland and Great Britain.

The amount the trusts controlled jumped, too, from about $400 million in 1927 to $3 billion in 1929. This inflow of money created a kind of self-perpetuating chain reaction: The more money that was raised, the more that went into stocks; and the more all that money pushed stocks higher, the more investors felt they had to own them.

One market myth is that everyone was in the market and everyone was buying on margin. That's not quite true. In his book, *The Great Crash: 1929*, author John Kenneth Galbraith says a Senate committee later looked to see just how broad market speculation had been at the time. Member firms of 29 exchanges said that in 1929 they had about 1.55 million customers. This amounted to a bit more than 1 percent of the U.S. population (120 million), or 5 percent of the country's households (29 to 30 million families).[15]

Of the 1.55 million accounts, 950,000 were cash accounts, meaning customers had to pay for the stocks they were buying. The other 600,000 were margin accounts.[16] One other point is worth noting: The trusts themselves made extensive use of margin debt, which meant two major contributors to the Great Crash were concentrated under one roof.

So while it wasn't true that *everyone* was in the market, it was true that nearly everyone was at least *interested in*, and talking about, the market and its movements. The stock-market operators of the time enjoyed the kind of celebrity that figures in sports and Hollywood have today.

In a book called *Once in Golconda*, a British news correspondent working in New York City reported how deep America's love affair with stocks had become: "You could talk about Prohibition, or Hemingway, or air conditioning, or music, or horses, but in the end you had to talk about the stock market, and that was when the conversation became serious."[17]

Golconda, by the way, was a city in India that reportedly made rich every person who passed through it. The city is now in ruins. A fitting analogy, we think.[18]

Setting the Scene

Unlike the market crash of 1987, the 1929 debacle was at least partly tied to a fading economy, though that did not become clear until later. Before World War I, the United States was the world's biggest debtor nation.* But it emerged from that conflict as the world's largest creditor, having been for the first time, the Arsenal of Democracy.

A peacetime boom followed, but was interrupted by a deep slump from 1920 to 1922, with the Dow slipping 25 percent between April 1920 and that December.[19] The economy rebounded into a recovery that lasted into the middle of the decade. Then it stalled again, resuming as a full-fledged boom by the end of the 1920s.

In May 1924, the Dow stood at 90. It would reach 121 by year-end 1924 and 151 by the close of 1925. The next year, 1926, would be difficult: From 151 at the outset, the market was essentially unchanged through the end of February. It fell to 135 at the end of March, before steadying once again.

In 1927, the market began its inexorable and fateful climb, rising 28 percent to finish at 200. The advance that year was steady, and wasn't the product of speculation that would mark 1928.

In 1928, the market rose in big jumps as a quick-buck mentality took hold. Brokers' offices were clogged during trading hours every day.

In March 1928 alone, the market was up 10 percent. Blue chips shed their persona as "widow-and-orphans" stocks, often vaulting 10 to 25 points in a single day. Consider this run of RCA from March 12 to 15: Up $26, up $18, up $7½, up $4. The stock raced from $93.50 to $150 for a cumulative return of 59 percent, according to press reports of the time.

Trading volume, an important indicator, showed that interest in stocks was higher than ever thought possible. Overall daily volume for stocks increased from 3 million to 4 million and finally past the then-inconceivable level of 5 million shares per day in June. On those days, the ticker would sometimes fall hours behind, meaning investors had no idea what was really going on. In November 1928, more than 6 million shares traded hands on several days.

There was a pretty bad break in early December, when Radio actually fell 72 points in one day (it went from $85 to $420 during the year), but the market settled down and resumed its advance.[20]

---

*The common wisdom is that a debtor status is bad for a country's stock market. Ultimately, this can prove true, but it's also fair to say there is no clear direct cause and effect.

For all of 1928, the Dow climbed 97 points, or 48 percent, from its opening level of 203. Following the 28-percent advance of 1927, this stunning performance exerted a mesmerizing pull on investors. RCA quintupled, Montgomery Ward nearly quadrupled from $117 to $440.[21] Trading volume for the year was nearly double that of 1927.

Beneath those figures, however, was a fundamental change in investor behavior. No longer were people buying stocks because they were sound, long-term investments. Investors saw stocks as a way to make money, and make it quickly.

Margin made investing even more alluring: Investors could leverage their capital with borrowed money, putting down as little as 10 percent to buy stocks.[22] Instead of just one or two stocks, margin let investors spread their money between three, four, or even five different stocks. Normally, that would give an investor diversification. But investors then were speculating, buying stocks of questionable quality, and heightening their risk by using leverage.

Here was the attraction: By using borrowed money to buy stocks, if shares doubled in price, investors made 3.5 times their money.

There are two ways to measure the increasing use of margin-buying:

- The jump in volume of so-called "broker loans," and
- And the changes in interest rates charged for those loans.

The interest rates on brokers' loans went to nearly 12 percent at the end of 1928, from 5 percent earlier. Banks could borrow from the Federal Reserve at 5 percent and loan it out for 12 percent, keeping the difference as profit. New York banks made the loans, then became agents linking borrowers and lenders all around the country. It wasn't long before companies outside the financial-services marketplace began making their cash available for loans, instead of using it to finance new plants or purchase equipment. Money flowed in from other parts of the world from institutions looking for the 12-percent return on a loan that was collateralized by the stock investors were buying on margin.[23]

The volume, or level, of these loans would gradually climb skyward, too. From an average of $1.5 billion in the early 1920s, the level of broker loans would rise to $2.5 billion in 1926, and $3.5 billion by the end of 1927. Then borrowing rocketed: $4 billion at the beginning of June 1928, $5 billion in early November, and $6 billion at the end of the year.[24] Broker loans would rise more than $2 billion in 1929; between June 30 and October 4 alone, they rose from $7 billion to $8.5 billion.[25]

All this easy money helped set the stage for the cataclysm to come.

One symptom of a mania is that, as prices rise vertically, the aggressiveness of investors keeps pace. Near a market's top, many people expect the party to go on forever.

Not long before the Crash, margin debt accounted for one-tenth of the total value of shares quoted on the Exchange, and amounted to $5,000 per shareholder.[26] However, the figure underplays the drama, since it was only an average of debt held by both institutional shareholders and typical investors who bought stock only with cash. Margin debt was actually concentrated among active, speculative traders—the investors most likely to sell fast when the market turned ugly.

1929 Arrives

Stocks continued their climb in January 1929 with the Dow rising 17 points. The next month, powerful politicians (mostly members of the outgoing Coolidge administration), and the Federal Reserve Board had serious debates behind closed doors about the level of speculation in the market, and whether it should be checked. News of these deliberations finally leaked out in March, causing another bad break in the market.

Some banks pulled back on their willingness to make broker loans, and with the diminished supply amid all that demand, rates spiked to 14 percent. On March 25, 1929, fear-bitten investors dumped stocks, sending the market down as much as 13 points (4 percent on a Dow index of 300), with the ticker once again running late. Rates on margin loans touched 20 percent, their high-point for the year.[27]

Charles E. Mitchell, chairman of the board of National City Bank, and a director of the Federal Reserve Bank of New York, was the hero of the moment, though he only put off the inevitable. Mitchell said National City would make enough money available so investors wouldn't have to worry that their holdings would be liquidated.[28] The crisis eased. After that near miss, the Fed abandoned its campaign against stock-market speculation.

Leverage even became the preferred method for investment trusts. Goldman, Sachs & Company started its Goldman Sachs Trading Corp. in late 1928, and sold shares to the public at $104 each. It later merged with another trust in 1929, with its share price rocketing from $136.50 before the deal to more than $222 a few days after—*giving it twice the value of the assets in the trust.* It silenced skeptics by repurchasing some of its own stock.[29]

That summer, GSTC would launch two other trusts: Shenandoah and Blue Ridge. Shenandoah shares were issued at $17.50, opened at $30 and reached $36. (By the end of the year, it dropped to nearly $8.00 and would later hit 50 cents.) Blue Ridge was much the same story. And Goldman Sachs Trading took stakes in both. By 1932, Trading Corp.'s shares, which went public at $104, would collapse to $1.75.[30]

It was a hot summer on Wall Street. The Dow rose a sizzling 34 points in June, 16 points in July, and 32 points in August, for a total gain of 28 percent. The 82-point summer advance nearly equaled the gain the Dow saw in all of 1928.

As always, there were a few doomsayers who spoke up about the dangers of margin debt and the speculative fever that gripped the country.

Naysayers were dismissed as curmudgeons. Wasn't everyone making money? It was a new era and American companies were invincible, or so it was believed.

On August 9, 1929, investors got their hint of difficult times ahead. The New York Fed boosted its interest rate from 5 percent to 6 percent, tightening the money supply. For a few days, the market sailed blithely on.

Business was already heading into a downturn, and the conservative Harvard Economic Society was forecasting a recession, though not a depression.[31] However, in a market fed by easy money, even such a small credit-tightening had a big impact.

September 3, 1929 was the market's high-water mark, with the Dow hitting 381—a level it would not eclipse again for 25 years. Since March 3, 1928, Radio had run up 435 percent, Montgomery Ward 251 percent, and General Electric 208 percent.

Two days later, Roger Babson, "a frail, goateed, pixyish-looking man from Wellesley, Mass.," told guests at a financial luncheon that "sooner or later, a crash is coming"—probably one severe enough to throw the country into a deep depression.[32] The Dow fell 9 points on these remarks (about 3 percent), and many big-name stocks were pounded in what came to be known as the "Babson Break." The financial establishment attacked Babson, and *Barron's* derisively dubbed him the "Sage of Wellesley."

Yale professor Irving Fisher, who a month later would make comments securing himself a spot in the Great Crash history, concurred that there might be a drop in stock prices, but "not anything in the nature of a crash."[33] Stock prices recovered, then drifted as the country moved into Fall.

An ominous unease gripped the market.

Every mania has a defining moment, a point when a public figure (or figures) assures the crowd that the good times can go on and on—in essence, that "things are different this time." During the stock-market mania of the late 1920s, it was Fisher. At an October 15, 1929 luncheon for financial executives, Fisher said that "stock prices have reached what looks like a permanently high plateau."[34]

That same day, City National Chairman Charles Mitchell, sailing home from Germany, said "Nothing can arrest the upward movement" of the market.[35]

Unfortunately, like Fisher and Mitchell, the American investing public seemed to think stocks had reached "a permanently high plateau," and believed vested interests could actually make stocks go up at will. The stock market had taken 25 years to double in value; in just two, it had doubled again.

On Monday, October 21, more than 6 million shares traded, putting the ticker more than an hour behind, though a late-day rally avoided a total rout. The losses continued on Wednesday, Oct. 23. The 7 percent decline this day alone was enough to wipe out the 10-percent market speculator.

Thursday, October 24, volume swelled to more than 12 million shares, and during the morning there were often no buyers to take what sellers wanted to give them. Some stocks dropped vertically. It was pure panic, right until noon, when traders learned that banking leaders, including Charles Mitchell, were meeting at the offices of J.P. Morgan. Rumors swirled that organized support would rescue the market and steady nerves. The bankers did decide to pool their resources and support the stock market.

That afternoon, in a dramatic moment in market history, Richard Whitney, vice president of the stock exchange, strode to the post for Steel and bid $205 for 10,000 shares, a price that was several points above the market.[36] The move reassured traders and at day's end the market had shed but 6 points. Though volume was heavy on Friday and Saturday, and prices drifted, it seemed outright disaster had been averted.

It would all come apart.

On Monday, October 28, 1929, the Dow was down 41 points for the day—a drop of 13 percent (equivalent to *1040 points* on a 8,000 level index). General Electric was down $48 (from $290), and Westinghouse $34 (from $175). Bankers again met at the Morgan offices, but this time there was no saving gesture.

Tuesday would clearly be worse.

That morning's *New York Times* carried a front-page banner headline: "Stock Prices Slump $14,000,000,000 in Nation-Wide Stampede To Unload: Bankers to Support Market Today."[37]

It proved to be wishful thinking.

The sun rose that morning, but it was a dark day for most investors. Shares traded at a 33-million-share rate. The ticker was 2½ hours behind.* The Dow fell 30 points (another 13 percent) and only a late-afternoon short-covering rally kept losses from being worse. More than 16 million shares traded, equivalent of 1 billion shares today.[38] The investment trusts were annihilated. Westinghouse, which had closed at $286 on September 3, opened at $131, and fell to $100 before making a comeback to close at $126.

During this horrific week, falling stock prices prompted widespread margin calls. Investors who couldn't cover faced forced liquidation at distressed prices. The level of broker loans, which had grown by $670 million for all of September, contracted by more than $1 billion.[39]

The aftermath was even more agonizing because it was so drawn out. From its September 3, 1929 high of 381, the Dow would fall all the way to 41 on July 8, 1932.

Not for a generation—not until November 1954—would it again close above that 381 barrier.

---

* We can only imagine the terror investors around the country felt because they did not know where their stocks were trading. They knew a financial disaster was unfolding, but had no way to find out how their stocks were faring. Unfortunately, their worst fears fell short of the day's terrible reality.

AVOIDING MANIA MISERY

Horace Annesley Vachell said, "In nature there are no rewards or punishments; there are consequences." A financial mania can be quite tempting. It's easy to understand why even the most seasoned investor succumbs to the pull of easy, fast, and seemingly risk-free profits. It is tough indeed for anyone to keep their money in their pocket as other investors—among them family, friends, and coworkers—seem to be pulling down big profits with very little effort.

Succeeding as a contrarian demands discipline, requiring us to seek opportunities not being trumpeted by the crowd. True, after identifying an out-of-favor opportunity, you want the crowd to join you. That's fine. But contrarians have to avoid manias, when prices for stocks, bonds, real estate, or other investments climb well above true value. Manias are euphoric frenzies that signal a market out-of-whack, whose subsequent blowoff—and blowout—can wipe out all you've worked so hard to amass. It is impossible to read the accounts of man's folly and not be sobered and chastened by the experience.

Contrarians also see the seeds of a mania in speculative fever. So when they observe behavior reminding them of tulip bulbs or blind investment pools, it's a warning to stay on the sideline.

To do that however, we must learn to spot these manias. And after studying Tulipmania, the Crash of 1929, the annihilation of the Nifty Fifty, and the collapse of the Japanese real-estate and stock markets, we offer some clues that will help you differentiate between a mania and a sound bull market.

We've observed that all manias have certain characteristics in common. We would, however, caution that true manias are few and far between. For every true mania, investors will see dozens of speculative frenzies that touch a sector or part of a market, but fall short of being a true mania. And while these frenzies are opportunities to make or lose money, they do not have the devastating fallout that a mania's collapse can cause.

Watch for these signs:

1. Speculative manias almost always come during periods of prosperity. That makes intuitive sense. It's only during periods of prosperity that people have idle money to speculate with. Seventeenth-century Holland had become a financial power. The same was true of the United States in the 1920s, and Japan in the 1980s.* In each case, the country's general standard of living had risen substantially, boosting personal savings, increasing leisure time, and fueling a need for more investment possibilities to recycle the profits from mainstream economic endeavors.

Prosperity alone does not signal the start of speculation; after all, prosperity is an important ingredient for a healthy bull market in stocks, or vibrant markets for real estate, precious metals, or tax-free bonds.

Japan had emerged as a powerful exporter of automobiles and electronics, and its perennially large trade surpluses had made it a wealthy nation. The wealth and savings ethic of the Japanese people—admirable qualities—boosted Japan's appetite for stocks, bonds, real estate, and companies abroad. That appetite drove up the prices of these assets. Eventually the Nikkei would nearly reach 40,000 in a long-term speculative mania that collapsed and drove that market index down in a nasty, multi-year bear market down under 14,000. The collapse also dragged down Japan's real estate market, itself part of the mania, and the banking sector. As we were writing this book, the country's economy still hadn't recovered.

2. Most speculative manias are fueled by easy money and easy credit. An easy-money atmosphere breeds speculation. In Holland, the creation of options on tulip bulbs gave speculators the leverage that made it easy to place big bets on the Semper Augustus bulb. In 18th century Great Britain, later issues of new South Sea Company stock were sold on the "installment plan." In the United States, the use of 10 percent margin grew from $1 billion in 1929 to $9 billion the year of the Great Crash.[40] In Japan, savings accounts paid less than 1 percent, spurring investors to go out and play the market in pursuit of higher returns.

As investments bought using easy credit rise in value, lenders let down their guard, making it progressively easier to borrow more money (the collateral, in this case stocks whose value has been rising, appears sound). Only when the storm hits do the lenders tighten credit, exacerbating the collapse.†

---

* Britain would have its own debacle a century after Holland. England's "South Sea Bubble" would burst, too, leaving many citizens looking at debtor's prison.
† Sometimes, we do learn. When the market crashed in 1987, the Fed immediately and publicly stated it would provide funds needed to maintain liquidity in the markets.

3. All speculative manias are characterized by ever-widening acceptance. In every case we studied, the seeds of a market mania are planted by the wealthy and by professional investors. It was only after the masses jumped in and tried to emulate the market makers that prices really seemed to rocket beyond any semblance of fair value.* Average investors could not buy enough of the Semper Augustus bulb in 1635, or blocks of Montgomery Ward stock in 1929, to really influence the market. But they could buy common tulip bulbs, or highly leveraged 1920s investment trusts. The result: More money chased more investments of increasingly questionable quality.

4. Speculative manias are always supported by authoritative opinion that reassures speculators. Whether it was economists in 17th century Holland, or the unfortunate Dr. Fisher in the 1920s, there will be experts who will justify a mania as merely the proper actions of informed investors. These people usually believe strongly in what they say. They are as blinded by the mania as everyone else.

5. Participants ignore the voices of doom, which really are only the voices of reason.† The Roger Babsons are derided and, worse, may later be blamed for bringing the "good times" to an end.

6. It is impossible to forecast the top in a speculative mania, just as it is impossible to predict a top, or bottom, in normal markets. In a mania, investors lose the ability to think rationally. Any attempt to rationally forecast a price peak can be deadly. All manias are characterized by prices that, in retrospect, are irrational. Prices, having risen wildly, can keep doing so, doubling, tripling, or more. Since the market has lost any semblance of rational value, contrarians must remember that irrationality has no limit.‡

7. It is impossible to invest successfully in a speculative mania. A mania is a lot like a speeding freight train. It accelerates, rockets along, slows at some points, only to speed up again. Getting on and

---

* We aren't saying the wealthy invest without falling prey to a mania. We merely mean that people tend to look at various "experts" to confirm their inclinations, and the wealthy are often assumed to be just that. The truth is, the ever-widening acceptance is partly due to the wealthy and investment professionals going back into the market again and again, and not taking their profits and parking them out of harm's way.

† We discuss this phenomenon in our chapter on contrarian psychology.

‡ This, too, makes sense. After all, for our contrarian buy indicators to work, investors must occasionally send stocks down below their true value. Our indicators tell you when that happens. But if stocks can be oversold, so, too, can they be overbought; that is, they can be driven beyond any rational value.

off at just the right time is near to impossible. More likely, you'll end up standing in front of it, unable to move as it bears down on you.

8. Speculative manias all end with a crash so destructive that its pain is felt for years, even decades, that follow. This may be the easiest way to identify whether or not a mania is playing out. Simply ask yourself if the end of the suspect mania would spell true disaster. Many labeled the 1995 high-technology frenzy as a speculative mania. While many stocks did rise to irrational valuations, the speculation did not draw in enough investors, was not widely accepted enough to be a true mania. When it crashed, it did not spread to other sectors, or cause the market in general to collapse. Indeed, the stocks of good technology companies resumed their rise shortly after. A frenzy, yes. But a true mania, no.

Conversely, look at Japan. The economy there still had not recovered as this book was being put to bed.*

9. As a mania progresses, and the demand for stocks or other investments burgeons, so does the supply. But those newer offerings are always of increasingly questionable quality. At first, only the finest tulips were acceptable. By the end, nearly any tulip was considered appropriate for speculation. In the 1920s, leveraged investment trusts took the place of blue chips and traded at several hundred dollars per share.

10. All manias end abruptly, and with little warning. No matter how much we believe we can avoid a mania, the fact is that manias are most obvious only in retrospect. The happy and successful speculator in August 1929 had no clue the market was about to lose all but 10 percent of its value. What few warnings exist are usually ignored.†

SUMMARY

True speculative manias are rare. We have highlighted two of the more notable. To be sure, there are others. Florida real estate in the

---

*Indeed, during a reporting trip to Japan in 1996, many merchants, restauranteurs, and even taxi drivers in Tokyo and other parts of the country lamented to Bill that things weren't as good as they had been during the boomtime in the late 1980s. The fallout was still being felt.

†Doomsayers have a way of predicting 10 bear markets for every one that actually takes place. Thus, in the heat of mania, their warnings sound like the boy who cried wolf.

1920s, Japanese stocks in the late 1980s, and the precious metals boom of the late 1970s. Since contrarians seek out-of-favor and neglected investments for their portfolios, they should not succumb to one of these stock-market feeding frenzies. If a contrarian successfully identifies a mania, the single best course is to stay on the sidelines: There's no way to predict when it will end.

Endnotes

1. Galbraith, John Kenneth, *The Great Crash: 1929*, Avon Books, New York, N.Y., 1979, p. 69.
2. Malkiel, Burton G., *A Random Walk Down Wall Street*, W.W. Norton & Co., New York, N.Y., 1973, p. 36.
3. Beckman, Robert, *Crashes, Why They Happen—What to Do*, Sidgwick & Jackson, London, 1988, p. 2.
4. Malkiel, p. 35.
5. Beckman, p. 3.
6. MacKay, Charles, *Extraordinary Popular Delusions & The Madness of Crowds*, Crown Trade Paperbacks, New York, N.Y., 1980, p. 94.
7. Ibid, p. 95.
8. Beckman, p. 7.
9. Ibid, p. 10.
10. Beckman, pp. 5–6.
11. Malkiel, p. 37.
12. MacKay, p. 99.
13. Galbraith, pp. 42, 44.
14. Ibid, p. 44.
15. Ibid, p. 69.
16. Ibid.
17. Malkiel, p. 46.
18. Ibid.
19. Beckman, pp. 124–5.
20. Beckman, p. 129.
21. Galbraith, p. 16.
22. Beckman, p. 128.
23. Galbraith, pp. 19–20.
24. Ibid, p. 19.
25. Beckman, pp. 128, 130.
26. Ibid, p. 128.
27. Galbraith, p. 32.

28. Ibid, pp. 134–5.

29. Ibid, pp. 53, 55.

30. Ibid, pp. 55–57.

31. Ibid, p. 62.

32. Ibid, p. 49.

33. Galbraith, p. 69.

34. Galbraith, p. 69.

35. Ibid, p. 83.

36. Ibid, pp. 90–91.

37. *The New York Times*, Oct. 29, 1929, p. 1A.

38. Malkiel, p. 50.

39. Galbraith, pp. 82, 101.

40. Malkiel, Burton G., *A Random Walk Down Wall Street*; W.W. Norton & Co., New York, N.Y., 1973, p. 46.

PART

II

CONTRARIAN BUY SIGNALS

CHAPTER 5

TECHNICAL ANALYSIS: A KEY CONTRARIAN STRATEGY

It is almost always true that the more different anything is from what people are used to, the harder it is to believe.

—*Utopia,* Sir Thomas More

Like all other investors, contrarians have two decisions to make about a stock: when to buy and when to sell. Both can be tough decisions. To make them easier, we rely on two important tools: technical analysis and fundamental analysis. We can use either tool alone, or we can combine the two into an effective system to screen stocks.

We're going to introduce you to technical analysis first, since the two most important "buy" indicators in our contrarian stock-picking strategy are technical tools:

- Our primary indicator, the "down-by-half rule," holds that a stock must be down at least 50 percent from its 52-week high before we can consider it for purchase.

- Our key secondary indicator is that there must be open-market stock purchases of at least $120,000 by company insiders or significant purchases by knowledgeable outside investors.

A stock that's down 50 percent from its high, and has insider buying of at least $120,000, is often an automatic buy.

In this chapter, we'll take a general look at technical analysis. In subsequent chapters we'll study price trends and insider buying. After that, we'll explore fundamental analysis and see how it can be combined with technical analysis to build a winning, contrarian stock-picking system.

TECHNICAL ANALYSIS: THE CONTRARIAN OVERVIEW

Technical analysis is the use of price, volume, and market-sentiment data to forecast the future direction of stock prices. Investors who follow this line of study are known as "technicians," and set themselves apart from the other chief school of investment analysis—the so-called "fundamentalists," who use fundamental analysis.

Fundamentalists look at economic or managerial data that is innate to the performance of the company they are studying. Some examples are such key financial measures as sales, earnings, cash balances, debt loads, and profit margins. They also consider qualitative data such as new products or marketing initiatives. Fundamental analysts use these facts to estimate what a company might earn to project what it might pay out in dividends, and in the end to help decide whether a stock is fairly valued, overvalued, or undervalued.

Technicians, by contrast, believe they can predict future price trends of a stock or other financial asset by using market data such as past price movements. Their logic: Since human nature drives buy-and-sell decisions, and since human nature never changes, technicians believe they can read human action and reaction, again and again, in their charts of stock-price movements. The historic patterns that show up on these charts, technicians reason, are likely to recur, making it possible to forecast future prices based on those of the past.

Other domains of the technician include insider buying, which, like stock-price movements, is not central to the actual day-to-day functioning of a company; and market-sentiment indicators.

Covering every facet of technical analysis would take a whole book by itself, and in the contrarian's library on pages 263–264, we have listed several books worth studying. However, it is difficult to be a contrarian without at least some knowledge of technical analysis, since contrarian investing is largely an attempt to gauge market sentiment, and market sentiment falls within the province of the technician. In these next few chapters, we give you what you need.

Technicians believe that everything known about a share of stock has already been factored into its price. To this analyst, that price is the sum total of all the facts, including opinions and hunches held by investors. Indeed, dyed-in-the-wool technicians aren't particularly interested in the fundamentals of a company. Earnings, dividends, or economic outlook are all of little concern. Technical analysts look to charts showing prices and trading volume.

The very different approaches embraced by technicians and fundamentalists spark a lot of energetic debate between the two schools.

■ NOTES FROM A CONTRARIAN PORTFOLIO MANAGER

I use many fundamental and technical tools. What I use depends on what I'm doing.

When trading commodities, I'm a technician. All I want to see is price movement. I'm not really concerned about volume, crop reports, supply/demand studies, warehouse inventories, or weather reports. I can't react quickly enough to that information.

But, when it comes to stocks, I use both fundamental and technical analyses; one to confirm the other, and vice versa. They're both legitimate tools. Stocks move much more slowly than commodities, and the information is more widely available. The leverage of commodity investing demands very quick reflexes. Stocks don't require such a hair trigger. The endless argument among investors about whether the technical or fundamental approach is the right one is wasted energy. The fact is that they both have their place. ■

PRIMARY BUY SIGNAL: PRICE DOWN 50 PERCENT

The basis of contrarian investing is to gauge market sentiment, and exploit that sentiment for profit when it reaches an unjustified extreme. However, we believe there is no single indicator, poll, ratio, or data-manipulation scheme that will, on its own, provide the contrarian with a reliable signal to buy. Our solution is to combine technical and fundamental indicators into a set of contrarian "buy" and "sell" guidelines that are easy to use.

We must emphasize again that contrarian thinking is a technique for buying and selling a stock ahead of the crowd. That means that, most of the time, we're moving with the crowd, and not against it.

Because contrarians succeed only if they buy and sell ahead of the crowd, we clearly must disregard the technical and fundamental "principles" that already form the basis of the crowd's opinion. Many of those so-called principles are accepted as fact, but are seriously flawed. Even some of what popularly passes for the contrarian philosophy is flawed.

■ NOTES FROM A CONTRARIAN PORTFOLIO MANAGER

One of the technical contrarian indicators that has a long history in folklore is the study of magazine covers. The theory is that when the popular press finally (and belatedly) catches on to a trend as evidenced by magazine cover stories, the contrarian can invest against that oh-so-late opinion. Quite possibly the magazine-cover theory developed a new life when Business Week *published its infamous "The Death of Equities" cover story in August 1979, just before the great bull market began in 1982.**

I remember well the nearly unanimous plastering of Bill Gates' picture on the front of almost every national magazine when Windows 95 was launched. Was this not a classic sell signal on Microsoft? When we were writing this book, Microsoft shares had quadrupled from that point. ■

As this anecdote demonstrates, contrarian investors really need indicators that are quantifiable, and not subjective. That's the beauty of our initial buy signal, the "down-by-half rule." Following research done by Professor John Howe at the University of Kansas, we believe that a stock that has fallen 50 percent or more from its 52-week high is worth a close look. Remember, market sentiment falls into the domain of technicians. The 50-percent price drop is a way to quantify market sentiment, demonstrating that there is a very strong crowd bias against a particular stock. Clearly, any stock that's seen such a

---

** In fairness to *Business Week*, we found and read that article. The article was a chronicle of how high inflation had decimated stock prices. It was not really a predictive piece, but more an explanatory one. The cover title, which is remembered by all, was not an accurate depiction of the story inside.*

dramatic price plunge is unloved and unwanted. Finding anyone who is bullish will be difficult. Our "down-by-half rule" is an objective way of measuring the crowd's opinion.

According to Howe:

- Investors tend to put too much emphasis on the most recent information about a stock. That tends to push the prices of "bad news" stocks too low and "good news" stocks too high.[1]
- "Bad news" stocks experience large price declines, but those drops are followed by a period of above-average returns.[2]
- This initial rebound from the precipitous price decline carries through for about 5 months (20 weeks) after the fall.

Remember, though, that Howe looked solely at one-year holding periods. Other researchers who reviewed longer holding periods found that portfolios of "bad news" stocks tend to see price increases that not only beat the general market, they even outperform portfolios of so-called "good news" stocks that had already seen big price runups. The market-beating performance of the "bad news" stocks tends to last for three years or longer.

On its own, however, a 50-percent price decline would not be a good trading system, since transaction costs could be prohibitive. We need other confirmations, such as insider buying, or a stock price that is low relative to a company's ability to post profits (low P/E stocks).

Nevertheless, the "down-by-half rule" does provide an excellent starting point for contrarian analysis. In all of our research, we found no other technique as effective as this one. Here's why:

1. It adheres to the basic belief that contrarians should only buy a stock when the rest of the crowd views it negatively.
2. It's a means of accurately gauging market sentiment, on a real-time basis, on all stocks.
3. It is an objective, quantifiable guideline that removes emotion from the investment equation. Either a stock is down 50 percent or more, or it isn't.
4. In bear markets, when stocks have been ruthlessly marked down, buying opportunities abound. In a bull market, when most stocks are pricey, fewer stocks are attractive for purchase by contrarians.

> ***The Practical Effect:*** This rule encourages buying when stocks
> are most attractive and discourages buying when shares are
> dear. For a contrarian, that's just as it should be.

Now that we understand the price we're willing to pay, we need
to take a look at how prices move and operate.

Price and the "Random Walk" Theory

When it comes to investing, price is everything. It's an obvious
concept, but is constantly overlooked by most investors. When you
buy stock in a company, you pay a price. Your chief goal is to sell it at
a much higher price. Accurately forecasting the company's earnings,
reasoning soundly, or gauging the market dynamics of its industry
are important, but secondary, activities. Price is supreme.

The best analysis in the world isn't worth a lick if your stock
falls after you buy it, causing a loss. We might have 10 very good
reasons for believing a stock will climb, but if the stock falls, our reasoning is moot. Investors, trying to prove themselves correct, will
often double up on a losing position, as though their buying will turn
the stock around. They take on additional risk, just to prove belief in
their original thesis. In most cases, their money runs out before their
courage does.

If the price of a stock is moving the wrong way, odds are you
will later find your reasoning was flawed, that there were factors you
missed. Buying an additional position is called "averaging down." We
call it making the same mistake twice.

When it comes to the study of stock prices, the investment
world is divided between those who believe that price movement is
not random, and those who believe that it is.

In 1900, mathematician Louis Bachelier published his doctoral
thesis exploring the random nature of price movements. Pioneers
like Bernard Malkiel, author of *A Random Walk Down Wall Street*,
have argued that the movement in stock prices is essentially a "random walk," meaning they can't be predicted in advance.* Disciples of

---

*The "Random Walk Theory" holds that stock prices move in a random fashion, meaning
they can't be predicted using past-price movements. The reason: New information that affects stock-price movements, arrives in a random manner. Since that new information arrives randomly, there's no way to predict changes in stock prices.

this theory argue that all the relevant information about a particular investment is instantly incorporated into its price, meaning there is no way to get an investment edge. These theorists believe it makes the most sense to simply "index" a portfolio to the broader market and not spend time trying to beat indexes such as the S&P 500. There is an impressive amount of academic research backing this notion.

In the opposite camp are those who point out that there are too many instances of people and trading systems that have beaten the market over long periods to give credence to the Random Walk Theory.* They, too, have evidence backing their argument.

If the Random-Walkers are correct, then all technical analysis is destined to fail since a study of previous random events can't be used to predict future random events. That would shatter the contrarian's view that it is possible to beat the market by going against the crowd. If price is a random event, then analysis of price is a worthless endeavor.

Evidence that a particular system or individual can beat the market would seem to bury the Random Walk Theory. However, it's not that simple. Let's assume, for instance, that like many other things, the investment returns of 10,000 individual investors over the past five years will follow the familiar bell-curve. Most investors will fall somewhere around the market averages, a few significantly below, and a few significantly above. Does the fact that only a few investors beat the market mean that price movements are random? Hardly. We could draw the conclusion that prices are not random, and point to the occasional market wizard as proof that it's possible to earn returns higher than the market.[†]

The truth is somewhere between the opposing arguments. It could very well be that prices, in the short run, or day to day, are random events. But the farther out we go, the more confident we can be that stocks will trade at a higher level.

---

*We only have to look at the long-term success rate of the Value Line results to discover an argument that seems to contradict the Random Walk Theory. Stock returns over the past three decades are perfectly correlated with Value Line's ranking system: Higher-ranked stocks consistently outperform lower-ranked stocks. This is too consistent a record to believe that future price movements are merely random.

†However, it is easy enough to puncture that argument. If 10,000 people decided to buy and sell stocks based on daily cloud patterns or the number of station wagons that went by at rush hour, there would be a few with truly spectacular returns. That would be a lot like 10,000 people flipping a coin. Just because a few would get 25 heads in a row, doesn't mean that coin flipping is a non-random event.

> ***The Practical Effect:*** Since contrarians are willing to embrace a long-term view, and since we know that "bad news" stocks tend to rebound and outperform the broad market over longer periods, contrarians can capitalize by going against the grain.

■ *NOTES FROM A CONTRARIAN PORTFOLIO MANAGER*

Woolworth had dropped from the low $30s to the low teens. The stock suddenly had another sinking spell on a bad earnings report. (At the time, people were wondering whether Kmart was going to declare bankruptcy.* For Woolworth, it was a case of guilt by association.) Woolworth shares fell all the way down to $9.50 on heavy volume.

Presumably, at that point, the Random Walk theorists would say that the stock price was accurately reflecting the company's prospects. How, then, do we explain that within a few months the stock more than doubled, with very little change in the fundamental outlook for the company? Does this situation aid the Random Walk argument? We think not.   ■

SUMMARY

Technical analysis is a valid method of study. Often, technical analysis can provide a perspective that's absent in fundamental analysis. Ultimately, contrarian investing begins as a technical study since crowd sentiment falls into the realm of the technician.

Research has shown that stocks that have fallen 50 percent or more from their 52-week high tend to outperform the stock market for up to 3 years. This simple technical indicator is used by the contrarian to measure crowd sentiment in a clear and unambiguous way. A stock cannot be purchased unless this basic criterion is met. There are no exceptions to this rule.

---

* Tony later bought Kmart as a contrarian investment, generating a 53-percent profit for client accounts.

■ ——————————— CONTRARIAN CASE ——————————— ■
MANAGEMENT TURMOIL: TECHNICALLY ATTRACTIVE

Winston Churchill said, "Nothing in life is so exhilarating as to be shot at without result." So, when a big company such as Eastman Kodak, General Motors, or IBM fires its CEO, induces him to resign, or shakes up top management in some other way, take a closer look. Chances are the stock has been a lousy performer and might well be a contrarian play. The reason: These companies almost always face deeply rooted problems that will take years to resolve—and their stock prices reflect it.

The problems are so deep that investors may even fear a bankruptcy filing. When star analysts or market pontificators are making these gloomy predictions in newspapers, magazines, or business-news programs, that's often an indicator that the crowd's opinion has reached an extreme the contrarian can invest against.

Management changes are a technical indicator, since they aren't related to sales, earnings, or any other financial measure (although the board of directors often makes the changes *because* of those financial measures). In a company whose stock is down at least 50 percent, top management changes can serve as another contrarian "buy" indicator.

With GM, it was a bloated, cost-heavy bureaucracy, and competition from higher-quality, less expensive Japanese imports. With Kodak, it was a stultifying culture and leadership that just couldn't decide what businesses the company should focus on. With IBM, investors believed the mainframe computer was dead, and that the company had blundered the shift to desktop personal computers and computer networks.

Let's look at IBM to show how management turmoil can serve as a contrarian indicator.

IBM: THE CHANGE THAT DID COMPUTE

Just before the October 1987 stock market crash, the shares of this computer company reached $175.* They collapsed to a December

---

* These prices are not adjusted for a subsequent split.

1989 low of $94, and recovered to $128 in 1989. At the close of 1991, IBM's stock dropped to $89. By 1993, the company once known as "Big Blue" was being ruefully referred to as "Big Black-and-Blue" because falling fortunes and market share left IBM looking badly bruised.*

IBM had misplayed its shift into desktop PCs and its stock price had fallen into the mid-$40s. It had reported losses in 1991 and 1992 and would do so again in 1993. Change was needed. On January 26, 1993, IBM said it would halve its heretofore untouchable dividend and replace CEO John F. Akers.

That day, the stock traded as high as $53, but closed at $49—up only ⅛ of a point above its day-before closing of $48⅞. Analysts attributed the anemic jump to investor uncertainty that the management change was enough to turn IBM around.

Contrarian indicators were abundant: New stories profiled IBMers who had either retired or been fired, and had seen their retirement cache evaporate because they had parked most of it in "conservative" IBM shares. And one bestseller chronicled—accurately—how IBM fouled up its foray into personal computers, and gave away an operating system called DOS to an upstart startup called Microsoft.

Interesting, from our point of view, was that IBM's stock on this day was down by half from its 52-week high of $100.25, reached the previous July 16. It was also trading at about half of its prior year's sales per share.[†]

The news about IBM didn't get much better in the months after the company said Akers was out. The following February, the company said it would order the first widespread layoffs in its 79-year history. In March, several American chief executives, including Motorola head George Fisher, either said they were not interested or turned the job down outright.

Finally, in March 1993, IBM named RJR-Nabisco CEO Louis V. Gerstner as the new head of the computer company. Judging from the stock's action, investors weren't exactly soothed by the

---

*Tony recalls bidding for a new pension account, when a Trustee deadpanned that IBM stood for "I've Been Mugged." Tony thought, upon later reflection, that if he had been on his toes, the quip might've steered him onto this contrarian buy.

†We'll see in coming chapters on fundamental indicators that this ratio, called the price/sales (P/S) ratio, should pique the contrarian's interest when it falls under 1.0 on a stock that's down by half—as it did in IBM's case here.

announcement. Trading in the $50s when Gerstner was named (the headline on the Associated Press story read: "It's Chips Ahoy for IBM"), the stock would close as low as $41 during the summer. Investors wondered: What does an executive from a "snacks-and-smokes" company know about running a computer firm?

The answer to that question—which should have been: "apparently, quite a bit"—is in the company's stock performance. As our starting point, we'll use the stock's closing price the day IBM said Akers would be replaced, and will exclude dividends and transaction costs for both the stock and the Dow Jones Industrial Average.

Date	IBM Stock Price	DJIA Close	Percent Stock Gain	Percent Market Gain
Jan. 26, 1993	$ 49.00	3298	N/A	N/A
Jan. 26, 1994	56.38	3908	15%	18%
Jan. 26, 1995	74.38	3870	24	17
Jan. 26, 1996	104.76	5271	114	60

Again, it's clear that the strongest performance came in years two and three after Akers was replaced. In fact, even if we use the company's top closing stock price during this stretch ($128) and top market close (5778), IBM still handily outperformed the broader Dow (161 percent for IBM and 75 percent for the market index).

What's more, even after Gerstner took over in March 1993, investors were skeptical that he could run a company in the fast-paced, ultra-competitive computer business. The stock would hit a new low of $41 that August and, after reporting an aggregate $7.83 billion in losses for 1991 and 1992 combined, it would go on to report an $8.1 billion loss in 1993 as it took a panoply of special charges and expenses.

As we know now, however, the company rebounded. The mainframe business stayed strong, in spite of doomsayers' predictions, and the company made some bold moves to play in the emerging arena for networked computers.*

---

*One was the takeover of troubled software maker Lotus Development. IBM used the Lotus Notes software suite to build a base in the networking business.

The Practical Effect: On a stock that's down by half, never underestimate the impact of a change at the top. Though that's a qualitative measure, a distressed company with a new hand at the helm is often fertile ground for contrarian study. Watch what transpires, and see if the company meets some of our other contrarian screening tactics before adding it to your portfolio.

Endnotes

1. Howe, John S., "Evidence on Stock Market Overreaction," *Financial Analysts Journal*, July/August 1986, p. 74.
2. Ibid., p. 76.

CHAPTER 6

RIDING THE PRICE TREND: LOOKING FOR VALUE

Only a fool holds out for top dollar.

—Joseph P. Kennedy

All investing is an attempt to find a trend and ride it for a profit. The bullish investor buys with the hope of selling at a higher price. The bearish investor sells short, looking to buy shares back at a lower price.*

To profit with either of these strategies, a price trend must actually develop. Price trends, then, are the key to successful investing. Contrarians strive to identify what the next trend will be, and position themselves to ride that trend before it begins. We do that by using our contrarian guidelines to spotlight out-of-favor stocks that are compelling values—values we know the rest of the crowd will eventually spot. By then, however, we're already in position to ride that price trend, as those other investors drive up the price of the shares we've already purchased.

---

*In a short sale, the investor borrows an investment (a stock, for example), sells it, and hopes to buy it back at a lower price, returning the investment to the owner. This is usually done at some future date in stocks and futures. *Example:* Sell short Carnegie Steel at $60, buy it back later at $42. Profit is $18 per share.

The study of price trends falls within the purview of the technical analyst. In this chapter, we'll spend some time examining just what price trends are, and show you how to find and follow them.

ATTEND TO TRENDS

A price trend is a *persistent* price movement in one direction. It can be up or down. That persistence defines the trend; without it, there is no trend. Let's consider the graph in Figure 6.1.

As you can see, the price trend is well defined. It is clear, at first glance, that a trend exists. Investors strive to buy at the beginning of the trend, and sell near the end.

The opposite of trend is trendless price movement as shown in Figure 6.2.

This investment offers little opportunity for profit. The price meanders back and forth around the $119 level. Neither buyer nor seller can get an upper hand. Profit potential is limited by the absence of trend.*

Figure 6.1

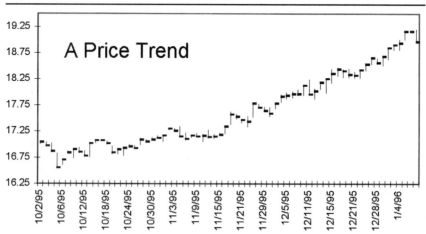

---

* The seller of naked options (one who sells options on a security without owning the underlying stock) can make a profit in this type of situation, but we believe that naked-option selling is a highly risky strategy for an investor with limited capital resources. Naked options offer limited profit potential with virtually unlimited risk.

Figure 6.2

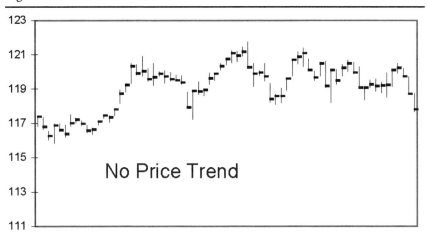

No Price Trend

The earlier a trend is spotted, and the longer the investment held, the greater the profit potential. That's the challenge. Trends are only identifiable *after the fact.* As the price meanders around $119, we wonder if a new trend will assert itself. Soon after, as Figure 6.3 shows, one did:

Once the price broke down from $117, a new trend developed and someone who had sold the shares short would have profited.

What are the characteristics of price trends? Can we learn anything about them that will help identify them before they begin? And do they exhibit behavior near tops or bottoms that signal the

Figure 6.3

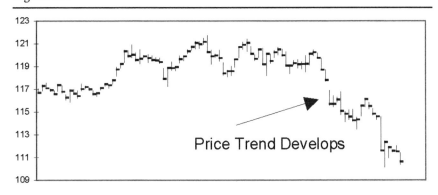

Price Trend Develops

Figure 6.4

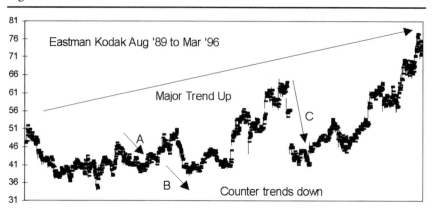

right time to buy or sell the stock? Let's take a look at a stock and see what we can discover about price trends.

Figure 6.4 shows the daily chart of Eastman Kodak from August 1989 to March 1996.

Clearly, the basic trend was up. However, there were three significant counter-trends during that period. If we look at the stock chart for 1992, which comprises counter-trend "A," Figure 6.5 is what we'll see.

This one-year chart depicts a stock in decline. In fact, the stock had made a major "bottom" in the low $30s the year before. This shows why we must analyze a stock—or a market index—in many different time frames to really know where it is in its price cycle.

Figure 6.5

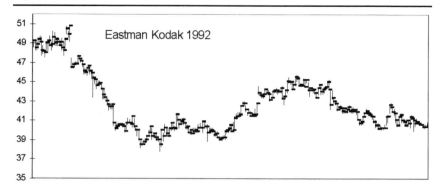

After the major drop marked counter-trend "C," nearly two years would have passed before an investor would realize the stock was in an uptrend. The odds are slim that an investor could have profited from the counter-trend through impeccable timing. Realistically, the only way to have made money on Kodak stock would have been simply to buy it and hold it.

However, close examination offers valuable insights.

PRICE TRENDS AND MARKET SENTIMENT

As contrarians, we strive to gauge market sentiment on a stock. *A trend is the visible expression of current and past opinion.*

A persistent price trend signals the strength of opinion held on a given stock. To illustrate why contrarian investing is so effective over time, consider the life cycle of a bull and bear move.* (See Figure 6.6.)

As a stock bottoms, the last exhausted bulls finally throw in the towel. The stock is friendless. No analysts are pushing it, no mutual fund managers tout it as a great buy. The majority view, if not an

Figure 6.6

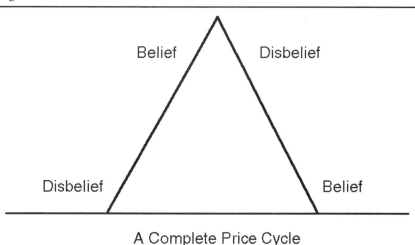

A Complete Price Cycle

---

*We first learned of this concept from Allan Shaw, Chief Market Technician at Smith Barney.

overall consensus, is that the stock is dead money. Indeed, many experts are calling for the stock to hit new lows (that "call for new lows" often piques the contrarian's interest). News about the company is generally bearish, and few investors are drawn to its shares. As the stock begins its first stirrings off the bottom, the rise is met with *disbelief* (shown at the bottom left corner of the pyramid). However, there are few new sellers, since most who would sell already have done so.

Investors, considering the recent drop in the price of the shares, put little credence in this infant bull trend. As the price rise persists (up the left-hand side of the pyramid), investors begin to shift from bearish to bullish. At first, only a few change camps, because disbelief endures. But if the rise continues, and the stock continually starts setting new highs, then buying escalates. Perhaps an analyst puts out the first bullish report; perhaps quarterly earnings beat estimates. Events begin to fuel the price rise, and the trend gathers strength. A general *belief* gradually spreads that this truly is a strong upward price trend that will continue.

As the trend approaches its peak, volume and interest have increased substantially, and most of the crowd believes in the bullish prognosis for the stock. The shares are now popular and on many "buy" lists. Investors treat any price pullbacks as buying opportunities, viewing the shares as a bargain.

Eventually, the stock reaches a peak (at the pyramid's tip), but the absence of bearish news, along with the bullish sentiment, makes the crowd oblivious to the possibility of a major price reversal. While some analysts or market mavens preach caution, or outright gloom, the masses dismiss these warnings. The reversal may be caused by external events, such as a jump in interest rates or inflation, or by problems inside the company, such as delays in an important new product. Whatever the cause, the price reverses course and heads down.

At that point, investor attitude is again one of *disbelief* (upper right side of the pyramid). But this time, the disbelief is that the long, upward price trend is over. Bulls still treat these declines as buying opportunities, believing the bad news to be only temporary. The disbelief persists. But as the price continues to fall, more and more bulls are discouraged as their positions drop into the red. Investors who earlier bought more shares on price pullbacks are now reluctant to do so again. Soon, outright sales begin.

Disbelief has been transformed into *belief* that the price trend is definitely down (lower right side of pyramid). Selling accelerates.

Fresh lows are hit. One by one, bulls turn bearish, and investors continue to sell. Calls for new lows are heard.

Opinion is decidedly bearish, and the stock is once again on few, if any, buy lists. The bottom is finally made. Apathy is the overriding sentiment, and investors look elsewhere for investment opportunities.

As you can see, investors obsess over near-term developments. Most investor sentiment is driven by the current price trend. A rising trend draws investors into a stock, while a declining trend repels them. Few really try to anticipate new trends. The longer the trend persists, the deeper the belief in its persistence. However, at peaks and troughs, the crowd's opinion is usually of an extreme nature. And that extreme is expressed in the actions of investors. Trends peter out with the halt in fresh buying (in an upward trend), or fresh selling (in a downward trend). Once all investors are in, or are all out, there is opportunity for the contrarian. Remember our three-investor example? If all investors are in, or out, an extreme exists. No more money can be brought to bear, so the trend can no longer persist.*

All investors want to buy at the bottom and sell at the top, but as we can see from our pyramid diagram, most do just the opposite. To buy low and sell high demands a contrarian approach.

However, to be contrarians, investors must be able to predict when a trend will reverse, or sense when an extreme opinion has been reached. Few investors make a real effort to do this. Some try haphazardly, many emotionally, but only a small group apply rigorous study. The challenge is that identifying a new trend is really an attempt to forecast the future. That's tough to do with consistency, since short-term price movements are random and can consistently mislead those trying to ferret out trends.

Even so, contrarians have an advantage over other investors because their philosophy prohibits them from buying after long price increases, or selling short after long price declines. Doing either would place them in the majority camp. And while contrarians want the majority to join them *after* they've bought a stock, or sold a stock

---

*Strictly speaking, "everyone" is never in or out. Stock sold by one party is always purchased by another. It is more the nature of ownership that marks the trend. Often, stocks are referred to as being in "weak hands" (uninformed or speculative) or "strong hands" (informed and savvy).

short, they don't want to be in step with the crowd when actually buying or selling the shares.

> ***The Practical Effect:*** The task for contrarians is to figure out when a trend will begin, or where a stock is in the lifecycle of that trend. At its simplest level, this task is an attempt to buy somewhere near the bottom, and sell somewhere near the top.

Trend analysis does not lend itself to neat formulas that can be repeated successfully time and again, so contrarian investors need a set of principles to guide them in each decision. We believe there are some enduring principles in trend analysis, and we will explore them here.

1. Each Trend Is Different

Investors study trends to identify a set of rules that can be used over and over to analyze trends. While many of the rules have some validity, each trend is different. They each develop differently. All rules should carry a warning from the Surgeon General: "Danger! Not to be taken too literally!" The same investment—whether gold, common stocks, or a market index—can have its trend develop differently each time. While some have a tendency to act in a specific way, exceptions are rampant and must be kept in mind. Many times, you will hear that certain investments "trend beautifully." For instance, we're often told that the currencies tend to trend. Sometimes this is true (see Figure 6.7), and sometimes it isn't (see Figure 6.8).

Figure 6.7

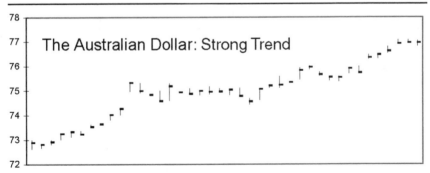

Figure 6.8

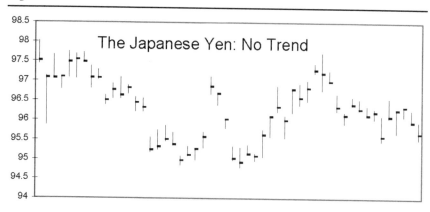

While it is true that currencies tend to have strong price trends, there are enough exceptions to diminish the value of any trading rules based on that idea. You can't be aggressive based on the "tend-to-trend" rule. The danger is that our imaginations "fill in" the future trend. Because some trends begin the same way, doesn't mean they end the same way. The investor can hold on to a mental image, a fictitious hope, as a basis for decision-making. Remember, the mental gymnastics you go through to complete the picture of the trend is a product of your mind—it doesn't really exist.

■ NOTES FROM A CONTRARIAN PORTFOLIO MANAGER

This kind of wishful thinking creates a lot of problems for people. It is very easy to look at a chart, "see" a long-term price breakout, and buy aggressively. Knowing that about 70 percent of all breakouts fail to develop a new trend tempers my enthusiasm for this kind of investing. I find investors are most susceptible to trend imagination after periods of losses. They need a winner to make the year, and this attitude makes them vulnerable to seeing opportunities where none really exist. ■

Let's illustrate how people can read their price charts and see things that aren't really there. Often, their interpretation of the chart is merely a reflection of the biases they bring to the analysis.

As examples, we look at two distinctly different commodity charts from the November–December 1995 period. One is the Live Hog contract, and the other the U.S. Treasury bond contract. Both

Figure 6.9

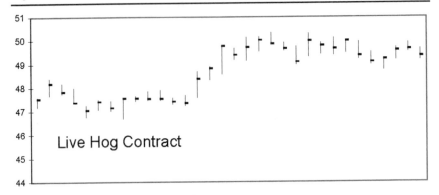

cover the same period, and both trade in the commodity pits in Chicago. The similarities between the two could easily lead an investor to predict they both will follow a similar price trend. After all, the similarities are startling. Investors assume that when price trends show similarities, those similarities will continue ad infinitum.

Let's study the charts shown in Figures 6.9 and 6.10.

While both trends appear nearly identical, it is safe to say that the price of a pig on the hoof is, at best, weakly correlated with the going price of a $100,000 U.S. Treasury bond contract!*

Figure 6.10

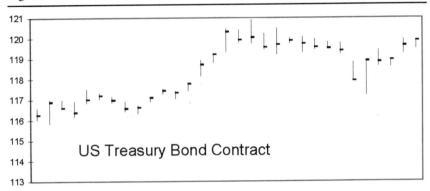

---

*Actually, hogs and bonds are non-correlated. A move in one can't be explained by a move in the other; nor is there any predictive power. There may be some very mild correlation in the case of inflation, but that's hardly definite.

Figure 6.11

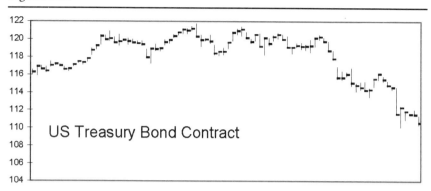

US Treasury Bond Contract

The mind plays a trick, seeking patterns and a similar future resolution. As shown in Figures 6.11 and 6.12, reality proves quite different.

2. Once a Trend Is Obvious, It Is Too Late to Apply Contrarian Investment Principles

Since contrarians philosophically disagree with the majority opinion when buying or selling, their stocks clearly will not have a current price trend in their direction. Trends only exist after there is a shift in opinion and after that opinion gathers strength as more investors climb aboard. Contrarians who look to investments that

Figure 6.12

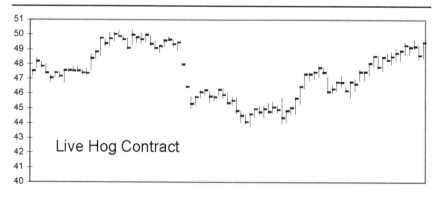

Live Hog Contract

already have strong price trends have deviated from their investment philosophy.

Contrarians wanting to buy or sell short look for one of two things:

- A counter-trend where they buy or sell against (counter to) the established trend.
- Or an investment where there is no trend.

Conversely, an exit (either selling after a long price rise, or buying to replace borrowed shares after profiting by selling short) depends on finding a strong trend against which to work.

In other words, contrarians wishing to purchase a stock look for one of two circumstances:

- The stock has been in a prolonged price decline now exceeding 50 percent.
- The stock has been in a listless, trendless phase after a large price decline.

3. Friendly Trends Work in Your Favor

"The trend is your friend" is an old Wall Street adage, but it's a lesson worth remembering. As investors, we often become so focused on buying and selling that we forget: The profits only come while we're riding a trend.

> **The Practical Effect:** Once you find a trend, ride it as long as you can. That is, there must be a clear reason to force you out. Most of your money is made by sticking with a position, and not through frenetic trading.

That's a key reason we believe contrarian picks should be held for up to three years. Sticking with a stock can be uncomfortable for the contrarian because that means a long period of riding with the crowd. Contrarians, by nature, want to avoid the crowd. But expert investors realize the crowd is only wrong at the entry and exit points. Most of the time, the crowd is correct and uses its money to prove itself correct. Contrarians start with the premise that they will make their move _early,_ and that the masses will eventually see what they saw. That takes time.

4. At the Bottom, Trends Can End Violently, or Softly

Many people believe that a downward price trend ends in a violent selling climax, characterized by heavy volume and a near vertical descent in price. Sometimes that's true. However, long price declines just as often end quietly by simply petering out.

However, it is fair to say that after a long price decline, a rapid drop over a few days on very high trading volume would be one more piece of evidence that a stock has bottomed. This is especially true if there is a sharp price rebound during the week following this climactic price drop. How much volume? We would suggest that double or triple the normal daily average would be a pretty good indicator. By looking at a price-and-volume chart, it should be fairly obvious that a selling climax has occurred. Take care not to see one every place you look! Look at a chart of Eastman Kodak in Figure 6.13, with the stock price on the left vertical axis and volume to the right.

Note how two major bottoms were made in Kodak shares with a fairly unremarkable increase in trading volume. While there was a definite pickup in volume in the weeks and days prior to the bottom, analysis at that time would not likely lead to any definite conclusions. Indeed, the real increase in volume came after the bottom, as the stock, relieved of selling pressure, rebounded.

Figure 6.13

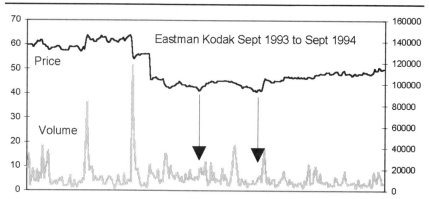

If anything, the huge volume increase that accompanied the first price drop from the mid-$60s to the mid-$50s could have been misconstrued as a "buy" signal. A sharp drop of $10 per share, accompanied by big jumps in trading volume, had all the characteristics of a climactic selloff. But it wasn't the bottom. The stock stabilized for a few weeks, and then embarked on a slow-but-steady drop into the low $40s.

As the chart shows, there were two trends that would have been profitable. The first, a long price decline, would have been profitable for the short-seller. And the second, the long climb back from the low $40s, would have been profitable for the investor willing to buy and hold on. But it's really tough to see any clear selling "climax." In fact, there was a real danger of spotting a signal that wasn't there.

Once you understand that bottoms can be made calmly or sharply, you realize that trading volume, on its own, isn't a great indicator that a stock has bottomed. However, if a stock experiences a long decline of 30 to 60 percent, followed by an almost-vertical drop on a big increase in volume, a bottom may be at hand.

That's a key attraction of our "down-by-half rule"—it gives your analysis a great starting point. A stock that's down 50 percent has probably experienced a selling climax. At the very least, it's a hint that it might be worth pulling out a price-and-volume chart on the stock.

5. At a Major Top, or a Major Bottom, Volatility Tends to Increase

A good price trend is characterized by persistent price movement in one direction. Therefore, an increase in volatility can often signal an increase in a counter-trend movement. If a stock persistently rises, its volatility is quite low. As it approaches a peak, and market players are increasingly uncertain of whether the trend can continue, cycles of buying and selling are more frequent, underscoring the divided opinion. See, for example, Figure 6.14.

The "Five Day Volatility" is simply the five-day standard deviation of the closing price of the stock.* Note how the volatility increased at major turning points.

---

*The standard deviation of return is a statistical tool that measures how likely it is for a stock's return to fall within a specific band. For instance, a standard deviation of 0.50 on a $60 stock means that the stock has a roughly two-in-three chance of being up or down 50 cents, and a one-in-nine chance of being up or down $1.00, which is double the first

Figure 6.14

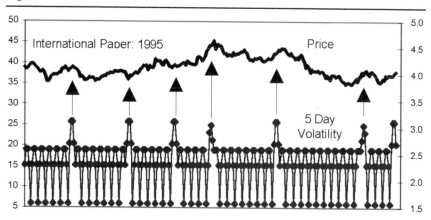

Warning: Volatility sometimes increases at a peak, and sometimes at a bottom. In order to tell where you are, you have to study where the stock has been. If you've been in a good upward trend, and you get a spike in volatility, it may be signaling a peak is at hand. Like other contrarian indicators, volatility is merely one tool, and should be used in concert with other techniques.

Nevertheless, we believe that price tops or bottoms are often accompanied by high volatility, one thing contrarians should look for before buying or selling a stock. We have found some evidence that a spike in the five-day standard deviation of a stock's closing price is a good indicator of a pending price reversal—if it is accompanied by a spike up or down in price.

Measuring standard deviation as an average of the past five trading days has enough sensitivity to be worth study, yet smoothes out the "noise" of day-to-day fluctuations. This is usually most true on a price drop. (See Figure 6.15.) Although this fails often enough to rule it out as a standalone indicator, it is useful as one piece of the puzzle.

---

standard deviation. A discussion of volatility measures is beyond the scope of this book. We select standard deviation because it is accessible to any investor with spreadsheet software. What's more, portfolio risk is very often expressed in terms of standard deviation. Investors with technical software programs have a wide variety of volatility indicators. Of those, we have found "Average True Range" to be the one we use the most. See the Contrarian Math appendix for how to compute standard deviation.

Figure 6.15

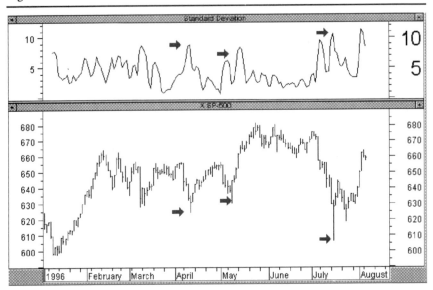

6. No One Can Accurately Predict the Length of a Trend

Some trends explode, either up or down. The best indicator that an investment can continue to trend higher or lower is the completion of an explosive move. More money is left on the table in a bull trend by investors who sell out too early than in any other way. Just when investors believe they've seen the peak, a new and more formidable bullish trend asserts itself.

A glance at the chart of United Technologies in the 1992–1994 period seems to depict a bull trend that's exhausted itself (see Figure 6.16). The move from the mid-$40s to mid-$70s was a profitable run. However, a new move added another 50 points onto the stock, dwarfing the original bull trend.

Investors can't forecast such trends. Contrarians who bought the stock in the mid-$40s, might well sell after the first peak, preferring to seek other, more compelling possibilities. Or they could hold, waiting for an extreme bullish consensus to develop. The risk, of course, is that this extreme bullish consensus never develops.

Figure 6.16

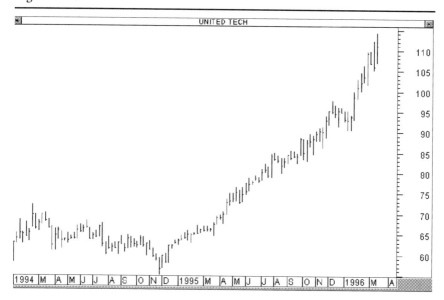

7. *The Best Indicator of a Potential Trend Developing Is the Absence of One*

As night inevitably follows day, a trend will be followed by a period of trendlessness. Put another way, the *absence* of trend is the best indicator that a new trend can develop. It is pointless for contrarians to examine a price chart and try to divine whether last week's increase signals the start of a new trend. There are too many false starts to make this a worthwhile exercise.

However, if the charts reveal a clear pattern of aimlessness—the lack of a trend—contrarians can study the stock more closely, hoping to discern the start of a new trend. The lack of trend can be just another piece of the puzzle, but an important one.* While so-called "V" bottoms happen from time to time, contrarians probably won't

---

* One is reminded of the musings of Sherlock Holmes in *Silver Blaze:*
  "Is there any point to which you would wish to draw my attention?"
  "To the curious incident of the dog in the night-time."
  "The dog did nothing in the night-time."
  "That was the curious incident," remarked Sherlock Holmes.

capture them by buying quickly before the rebound. These are opportunities contrarians must be willing to pass on if they were not monitoring the stock.

Contrarians look for long periods of listlessness for a potential buy signal (this kind of meandering doesn't usually occur at market tops). In general, bear moves tend to take one-half to one-third the time of the prior bullish trend. And, since a lack of a new bull trend is considered to be part of the bear phase, contrarians look for a bear move that has been going on for some time. In other words, the decline should last longer than expected when compared to the length of the rising trend before it. But if the stock has just bottomed, it may be too early to invest. For instance, if the bull trend lasted for 18 months, you might want to wait several weeks or even a few months past the peak before looking at the stock as a potential investment. Naturally, the stock must be down 50 percent from its 52-week high.

As we've said before, research shows it can take between one to three years to correct a bear move on a stock. We can also assume that the bear trend following the bull move lasts from 6 to 18 months, on average.* As is true with all the trend rules we've outlined in this chapter, contrarians should take this one with a grain of salt. But the idea of a bear trend taking from one-third to one-half the time of the bull move offers a *reasonable* time frame when analyzing a stock.

SUMMARY

Perhaps we can graphically summarize a price move and the ideal contrarian response. Figure 6.17 shows price data on our friend Woolworth, the retailer, during the two years from July 1994 to July 1996.

Note that our primary buy trigger, a 50-percent decline in the stock price, would have steered the contrarian clear of this stock during the false upside breakouts in the months prior to the bottom in early 1996. Contrarians must accept that some stocks will drop only

---

* Ben Graham believed that it took 18 to 30 months for the market to overcome the punishment of an individual stock. The length of the typical bull trend, the research on stock-price movement, and the writings of investors like Graham, all point to a two- to three-year holding period for the contrarian.

Figure 6.17

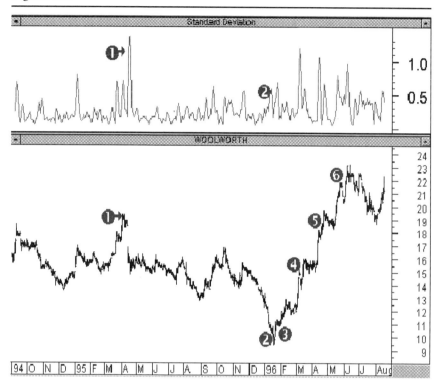

40 percent, and then rally; others 35 percent or even less. However, we need an objective starting point for analysis—as well as one that keeps us from reading too much into a price chart. Our rule that you cannot buy unless there has been a 50-percent price decline can help you avoid false signals.

■ *NOTES FROM A CONTRARIAN PORTFOLIO MANAGER*

We bought the stock because, while the volatility spike was not decisive (and is not needed to signal a top or bottom), the spike in tandem with the 50-percent decline was enough for us to seriously consider the purchase. What put Woolworth shares into the solid "buy" column at the time was:

- *There were no clear developments that could spark a new, bearish trend.*

- *Investors were tossing retailing stocks over the side, believing that consumers were tapped out.*
- *The financial travails of rival Kmart had spawned a case of "guilt-by-association," causing investors to unfairly penalize Woolworth's shares.* ∎

Contrarians who bought Woolworth shares around $10 would also have put in place a stop-loss order to sell the stock if it fell 25 percent from the purchase price. Note that there were no long periods of price meandering. The stock made a classic "V bottom," and turned higher. Contrarians must watch for any quick reversals in a beaten-down stock they might be considering.

Several opportunities to sell at less than maximum profit present a problem. Depending on the investor's anxiety, and other opportunities being considered, the investor could have sold at $15, $19, or $23. All but a sale at $23 would have left some profits on the table, but a sale at even $15 would have meant profits of more than 50 percent.

Contrarians attempt to buy near a bottom and sell near a peak. It is generally easier to buy than to sell.* We want to make our move on an investment before a trend develops. By searching out opportunities where no trend is apparent, contrarians can tip the odds in their favor. Waiting for a clear trend to develop means the investor has broken with the contrarian philosophy. Contrarians must be willing to act before others do. When a trend is established, opinion has already shifted.

Ironically, contrarians who search out opportunities by looking for investments others avoid, make their money by riding the trend—powered along by the money of the crowd. Contrarians don't try to catch every point of the trend, but merely the bulk of it, using their tools to ferret out out-of-favor stocks.

---

* We'll delve much deeper into the selling discipline in Chapter 13 on selling.

CHAPTER 7

INSIGHTS ON INSIDERS: BUYING WITH THE SMART MONEY

Look for a tough wedge for a tough log.
—Pulilius Syrus

Thanks to our "down-by-half rule," you'll never face a shortage of stocks to study. Just because a stock is down 50 percent or more from its 52-week high, however, doesn't make it an automatic buy. We need other signals to help us extract the treasure from the trash. On a stock that's down by half, our "tough wedge" is a rise in purchases by company insiders or by knowledgeable outside investors.

That brings us to our single most important secondary "buy" trigger. We like to call it "buying with the smart money." The rule:

> **A** stock that has fallen 50 percent or more from its 52-week high, and has seen insider buying of at least $120,000 during the past six months (with no selling), is your very best contrarian play.

113

Or:

> **A** stock that's down by half is virtually an automatic buy if purchases by "knowledgeable outsiders" equal 5 percent of the company's total shares outstanding. For an outside investor who already holds 5 percent or more of the stock, an increase in the position of at least 10 percent carries the same weight.

In addition to being a great buy signal, insider purchasing gives contrarians some assurance that the financial and business difficulties of the company are not fatal. Insiders would hardly put their own money into a stock if the situation were hopeless.

There are three concepts at work here:

- First, the stock is trading at a fraction of its former level, fulfilling the basic contrarian precept of buying what the crowd shuns.
- Second, the buying by insiders, presumably the most knowledgeable of all investors, signals the strong potential for a turnaround.
- Finally, the absence of insider selling offers additional assurance that, at worst, the stock may linger at current low levels.

It's much the same with knowledgeable outsiders. In cases where a stock has plunged, and outsiders are buying the stock, the outsiders clearly see value where others do not. That investor has methodically researched the company's prospects and believes its fortunes will change. (We explore investments by outsiders in detail in the two cases at the end of this chapter: Citicorp and Chrysler.)

INSIDER PURCHASING: A CALL TO BUY

One of the greatest risks in contrarian investing is that a stock, beaten down from its high on bad news, looks like a bargain. You buy it, certain a rebound is not far off. But the company's prospects erode still more—and so does its stock price.

Our risk-management rules keep that stock from savaging your portfolio, by forcing you to sell it if its price continues to fall.* And our buy signals help you pick sound stocks in the first place, putting the odds in your favor.

As we said, of all our secondary buy indicators for stocks down 50 percent, insider buying is the single best confirmation that the shares are likely a very good buy.

There is quite a debate over the usefulness of insider selling as a "sell" signal on a stock (we'll take a closer look at insider selling later in this chapter), but research clearly supports the use of insider purchases as a buy indicator. We've expanded that a bit to include buying by *knowledgeable* outsiders. Let's begin by defining just who insiders are, and how we can use them to our advantage.

Insiders are corporate officers and outside directors who have access to "inside"—or privileged—information about a company, its operations, and its prospects. Securities laws demand that insiders, and outside investors who hold 5 percent or more of a company's shares, file timely reports with the Securities and Exchange Commission that detail their buying or selling.

This buying and selling takes many forms, including open market purchases and sales, and the exercise of stock options. These reports must be filed with the SEC by the 10th day of the month following the transaction, so the reports are fairly timely. The filings are a good way to see if insiders are bullish on the company's prospects—particularly, we feel, with a firm whose shares already are down by 50 percent or more.

Are insider purchases a valid "buy" signal for investors? According to the two studies we reviewed, the answer is a strong "yes."

- The first, a study slated for publication shortly after we finished this book, was conducted by professors Carr Bettis, Don Vickrey, and Donn W. Vickrey. The research concluded that outside investors who mimicked the activity of insiders would have earned an annual return that beat other stocks of the same

---

*Recall our rule that if a contrarian stock falls 25 percent from the purchase price, it should be sold. We'll study risk management in greater detail in Chapter 12, Minimizing Risk: Contrarian Strategies.

size and risk by nearly 7 percent per year, after factoring in transaction costs.[1]

In an interview with a national magazine, Bettis said that "high-ranking insiders making large-volume trades systematically outperform the market."[2] The three professors studied trades of 10,000 shares or more by insiders between 1985 and 1990.

- The second study, done by Professor R. Richardson Pettit, Duncan Professor of Finance at the University of Houston, and P.C. Venkatesh, from the Office of the Comptroller of the U.S. currency, analyzed the activity of insiders in all NYSE and AMEX listed companies from January 1980 to August 1987. The two researchers looked at 30,000 purchases and 70,000 sales with an aggregate market value of $7 billion. Their key finding: Insiders tend to increase their *net purchases* (generally by reducing their sales) up to 24 months before a stock generates an above-average return.[3]

  In short, the study concluded, insider activity foreshadows performance: There are more net purchases before a stock rises, and more net sales before it falls.[4]

There was no significant seasonality in either *buying* or *selling*, meaning investors can't expect higher activity during any specific time of the year. However, the two researchers did conclude there was merit in holding stocks for three years—the same holding period both we and others advocate for contrarian stocks.

We need to distinguish between a reduction in selling and an increase in buying. Either can cause "net purchases" of stock to rise. Consider our two hypothetical cases below:

Example 1

    100,000 shares sold
      70,000 shares purchased
      30,000 shares net sold

Example 2

    20,000 shares sold
    30,000 shares purchased
    10,000 shares net purchased

In the second example, even though insider purchasing nearly ceased, there was a "net" increase in insider buying. In other words, the *net* number of shares purchased can increase, even if insider buying holds steady or goes down. We need a stronger endorsement. On a stock that's down by half, we want to see an actual accumulation of shares and an *absence* of insider sales.

Insiders typically buy stock because they think the price is going higher. Patterns of insider buying can sometimes tell us if a stock has reached a true bargain level.

◼ NOTES FROM A CONTRARIAN PORTFOLIO MANAGER

We have two wonderful examples that showcase the merits of insider buying: one example was by design and the other by happenstance. The first, Corporate Express (CEXP), was planned. A seller of office supplies to large companies, CEXP saw its shares plunge from $26.17 to $8.25 (including a one-day drop of as much as 47 percent) because of a warning that problems digesting some acquisitions would produce disappointing earnings in its 1997 fiscal year. Analyst sentiment was decidedly negative. (Said one: "This puts the whole growth-by-acquisition strategy into question.") But one director had purchased 200,000 shares at $10.06 which made me think the insider saw something analysts didn't. We bought the stock on April 23, 1997 for $9.88 per share. In less than four months, the stock was at $17, a 75-percent return. By early September, it touched $20 and several analysts rated it a "buy"— including one who said it was a "strong buy" and that it would climb to $27 within 12 months. Improving prospects, and acquisitions that figured to boost sales and profits, induced us to hang on past our 50-percent return target.

Our favorite example is a Rochester-area company, Canandaigua Wine. After reaching a high of $38.75 on March 29, 1996, the stock cratered to a low of $17 that September 6, as a poor earnings outlook soured investors. From October 17 to October 25, insiders snapped up more than 265,000 shares at prices in the low $20s. The filings were reported in November; nine months later, the stock hit $35.

We had bought the stock for portfolios on October 8, at $21 attracted by the favorable fundamentals, and my belief that the company's wine-

and-beverage businesses would eventually turn. Only later, when the in-sider filings were made with the SEC, did I realize that we had by chance preceded insider buying by a week.

I wish I could say that every purchase was this neat. This one worked particularly well and illustrates how effective our contrarian indi-cators can be (in this case, our fundamental indicators told us the stock was a bargain). However, even had we purchased after the insiders filed, we still would have made a substantial profit.   ■

The more stock that's purchased by insiders—especially stock bought with cash on the open market—the stronger the buy signal. A stock that's down 50 percent that attracts a 100,000-share pur-chase by the president of that company should pique the contrarian's interest.

The More the Merrier

Of course, the larger the purchase, and the more insiders par-ticipating, the more bullish the signal. Six officers and directors, each buying 5,000 to 10,000 shares of stock for cash, is a good signal. Conversely, a single insider purchasing 1,000 shares by exercising stock options, is not compelling (he or she may have political or other reasons for doing so). Each situation is different, and each must be scrutinized within the context of all our other contrarian signals. Purchases of at least $120,000, within a six-month period, is a reasonable threshold.

We established that standard based on research. The average in-sider transaction, according to Pettit and Venkatesh, was $59,000 during the period they studied. To create this secondary buy indica-tor, we essentially doubled that level to $120,000. The reason: We wanted to set a level of buying that could be considered significant. A rate double the average seemed to fill that bill. That level of activity signals a more serious intent than, say, a $20,000 purchase. Prefer-ably, we look for insider buying that goes well into six figures, or higher.

We don't just look at the dollars insiders are bringing to bear. We'd like to see more than one officer doing the buying. Group buy-ing is an even stronger signal because it says to us that this belief in better things to come is held by more than one person. Look at this example to see what we mean:

Good

An officer purchases $120,000 of stock.

Better

Two insiders purchase $300,000 of stock.

Best

Six insiders purchase $400,000 of stock.

Although the average commitment of the six insiders in our "best" scenario (about $67,000 each) was less than both the $120,000 offered by the single officer in the "good" case, and the $150,000 by each of the two insiders in the "better" example, there was broader participation. That, and the higher aggregate dollar amount, makes the final case the most compelling.

Optional Buys

Buying based on stock options mandates extra scrutiny. Corporate officers often exercise granted options, either to hold onto the shares, or (more often) to sell them. If the grants are "non-qualified" options and the stock is held after the options are exercised, it's an even more bullish pronouncement of the company's outlook. Here's why:

With non-qualified options, taxes are due immediately on the value of the stock at option. (Option at $10 on 1,000 shares is valued, for tax purposes, as $10,000.) The value is considered to be ordinary income, and so, is also subject to state, Medicare, and Social Security taxes.

Basically, if insiders acquire stock through non-qualified options, they run the risk of paying taxes on income they might not actually receive. In our example, if the stock drops to $6 after option exercise, the insider paid taxes on $10,000 in income, but if he sells the stock, he will actually only receive $6,000 (plus the tax advantage of the $4,000 capital loss). So, if an insider exercises a non-qualified option and holds the stock, it is generally a bullish pronouncement on the prospects of the company, with a little more intensity thrown in because of the taxes paid when the option is exercised.

Beware of These Buyers

In a few cases, a little extra research can pay real dividends. For instance, in one new trend, corporations have set up loan programs to help insiders buy stock. Sometimes, the acquired shares serve as the collateral for the loan.* Contrarians should treat these cases with caution. Remember, the idea behind insider purchasing as a contrarian buy indicator is that insiders believe enough in a turnaround to actually put their own money at risk. That indicator becomes a lot less persuasive when the corporation provides compensation packages that reduce the amount of risk officers are personally taking.

In addition, the concept of free-will is at issue in our view of insider buying. If insiders are free *not to buy*, and they purchase, that is more significant than situations where insiders are *required* to buy. A little extra digging can quickly establish the facts.†

INSIDER SELLING: A SELL SIGNAL?

We've talked a lot about buying. But what about insider selling? There are many reasons why insiders sell stock, so their stock sales are not necessarily bearish. For instance, even though an officer might be bullish about the company's long-term prospects, college tuition, a new house or estate planning could force an executive to sell some of his stocks. Often, officers have a large percentage of their net worth in their company's stock, and while they remain bullish, it's prudent to diversify from time to time.‡

---

* For ambitious researchers, details of these loans can be found in company proxy statements, and sometimes are detailed in employment agreements tucked inside a company's Form 10-K annual filing.

† There can be other reasons, too. Sometimes insiders (particularly company officers) buy stock because it's the politically correct thing to do in their company. For instance, a new corporate-level executive will buy 500 to 1,000 shares as a symbol of commitment. Sometimes, too, companies *require* key officers to hold an amount of stock equal to some percentage of their annual compensation. These officers, theory holds, will have the best interests of shareholders at heart, since their own money is on the line. Contrarians can often dismiss buying under either of these scenarios as unimportant.

‡ Readers are cautioned that "diversification" is the overwhelming answer of choice when insiders are asked to explain why they are selling. Naturally, this is sometimes the response to

However, insiders may indeed be selling because they are bearish about the firm's prospects.

When it comes to predicting future performance, stock sales by insiders are not as useful an indicator as insider buying.

Although Pettit and Venkatesh found insider selling predictive, it was only mildly so. Insiders have many different reasons to sell. As a general rule, insider activity runs at a rate of two sales for every purchase. This is logical since insiders, as a group, are net owners of stock via options and grants.

However, heavy insider selling after a stock's price has been cut in half is a real red flag. If you buy a stock that's down by half, and see substantial subsequent insider selling, this might be a warning that the stock should be sold.* At times, you may be selling too early. That's okay: Other opportunities abound and capital preservation is an important piece of the contrarian survival strategy.

Putting Insiders to Work

Depending on such factors as your tolerance for risk and the number of stocks you wish to have in your portfolio, you might decide to use insider buying as a mandatory indicator. That is, with a stock that's down by half, you might establish a personal rule that there must be insider buying before you can jump in. Perhaps you would then use our fundamental-analysis indicators to assess the company's financial health. In this way, you buy stocks only when insiders lead the way. This is definitely a more conservative approach, since there will be fewer opportunities.

A cursory study of insider activity for the June–July 1996 period is typical. Although several market sectors had crashed and

---

cover for a stock sale made out of concern for the company's near-term prospects. When a company's shares plunge, perhaps because of a warning that earnings won't meet estimates, it's always worth looking back to see if insiders were selling in the weeks or months before the announcement was made.

*In these cases, selling by multiple insiders would be a potent clue. A sale by a single insider could be for pressing personal financial reasons, and not evidence of a bearish view of the company. (It should be noted that when an insider retires, especially under forced circumstances, sales tend to predominate. A sale by a retiree does not carry the same weight as sales by knowledgeable working insiders, more familiar with the firm's ongoing prospects.)

burned, especially in the high-technology area, only 58 insider purchases were reported, versus 151 insider sales in the Aug. 12, 1996 issue of *CDA Investnet Insiders' Chronicle*, a weekly newsletter devoted to analysis of insider activity.[5] Of those 58 purchases, only two met our primary "down-by-half rule" and also had insider buying amounting to more than $120,000 (we bought both stocks).

While this might initially seem discouraging, it shows that any stocks that do meet our guidelines definitely warrant closer study. After all, insiders are usually owners of stock options which are granted from time to time. Thus, most insiders already have substantial positions in their company's stock. Options are usually granted each year, and when price is down, those options come at a much lower strike price. In essence, that means many insiders already have the ability to buy stock at these depressed prices; if they also go into the public markets to add to their positions, that indicates a pretty strong belief in the company's prospects.

■ *NOTES FROM A CONTRARIAN PORTFOLIO MANAGER*

Insider purchasing is one of my favorite indicators. However, a lot of the time, it is absent in a stock I'm considering for our contrarian strategies. For instance, a change in management is often a catalyst for a turn in the company's prospects, yet management in turmoil is not a good source of insider purchases. The old insiders, unsure of their status, refrain from buying more stock. New managers take some time to get settled, and many are brought aboard with healthy stock options—they don't need to buy stock on the open market.

To me, one of the great attractions in purchasing stocks along with insiders is psychological. If I am investing in depressed stocks, and knowledgeable insiders are staking their own cash along with mine, I have a good basis to proceed and feel more comfortable with my purchase. Therefore, it's much less stressful to stay with the position. I find these types of purchases cause less stress than others. ■

Using insider purchasing as an additional contrarian indicator should appeal to all contrarian investors, especially to those with a more conservative bent.

> *The Practical Effect:* Insider activity can often be used as a tie-breaker. If you have mixed emotions about a particular stock, a look at recent insider activity can usually break the tie convincingly.

On another level, investors can use insider buying as a source of ideas. For instance, you could get a list showing all insider buying during a given week or month, and then check to see if the shares of any company listed are down by 50 percent or more.* In general, anytime you find heavy insider purchasing, check further into that particular stock.

Where to Look

We can get information on insider activity in different ways. Since most filings are still made on paper, and not electronically, quick, electronic access is not available.† Although the SEC maintains the EDGAR database that's accessible via the Internet, insider filings are not part of it.

Therefore, we're left to obtain this information through commercial sources: newsletters, articles from newspapers, magazines or wire services, and other public sources. The *Wall Street Journal*, for instance, offers a weekly column entitled "Insider Trading Spotlight" that highlights several different major events in this area. *Barron's* carries similar information each week.

Newsletters that focus on insider activity are widely available, and some brokerage houses offer this information online. Value Line carries a note on insider buying and selling activity on each stock's fact page. If you cannot purchase any of these reference materials, most public libraries carry some or all of them. Finally, a call to a company's investor relations or public affairs department is often fruitful.

---

* Tony has used this technique occasionally, with great success.
† That is, direct electronic access through the SEC. Information on insider activity is gathered by various vendors who make it available through traditional sources; Bloomberg, ADP, etc.

Summary

On a stock that's down by half, *we consider insider purchasing to be more important than any other indicator of value.*

After a stock meets the initial requirement of being down in price 50 percent or more, contrarians use other indicators to confirm that good value exists. Studies show that insider activity does foreshadow future performance. However, buying is more predictive than selling. Open market purchases by insiders, accompanied by an absence of sales, provides just such a confirmation. Contrarians want to see at least $120,000 in purchases, within the past six months, to indicate serious intent.

Investments by "knowledgeable outsiders" can also be used as a confirming indicator. A stock that's down by half is virtually an automatic buy if purchases by knowledgeable outsiders equal 5 percent of the company's total shares outstanding.

For an outside investor who already holds 5 percent or more of the stock, an increase in the position of at least 10 percent carries the same weight.

■ —————————— **CONTRARIAN CASE** —————————— ■

TOO BIG TO FAIL?
THE VIEW FROM AFAR

Citicorp was America's biggest bank.

And it was in danger of failing.

At least, that was the crowd's opinion. Study the news coverage of Citicorp in the late 1980s and early 1990s and you'll come away shaking your head, convinced the now-healthy, money-center bank could serve as the poster company for contrarian stock-picking.

Looking back, analysts and the news media always seemed to be trumpeting Citi's virtues as its financial condition was quietly eroding, and reading its eulogy as the big bank was on the mend. The result: Investors were buying the stock when they should have been selling it, and selling when they should have been buying.

No wonder so many investors missed out on a terrific turnaround play: a stock that went from a closing low of $8.63 in 1991 to more than $140 in mid-1997—better than a 10-bagger.

The Citicorp case is interesting because it shows why we've built some latitude into our rules for selling a stock. Citicorp is one of those contrarian picks where it paid to hold on beyond a 50-percent profit (see Chapter 13). The bank's shares climbed a wall of worry for the first several years of its turnaround, as market mavens remained obsessed with the problems Citi executives were working to fix. After that, cost-cutting, improved profitability, and a big stock buyback were clear harbingers of rising profits—and a great return on investment.

BORROWING TROUBLE

Under former chairman Walter Wriston, Citicorp was known for its willingness to take risks in pursuit of its stated corporate goal of 15 percent annual earnings growth.[6] True, the aggressive pursuit of growth led to a few problems: Some early forays into the seductive credit-card market were financial disasters, as was an ambitious program to loan money to Third World countries. Even so, Wriston's vision of making Citicorp a global brand name in the financial services arena was successful enough to leave observers wondering if

John Reed would be able to put his own mark on the company when he ascended to the chairman's seat in 1984.

Reed did make his mark, building a hugely profitable consumer-banking business and making Citicorp the nation's second-biggest issuer of credit cards, behind American Express. Said one Wall Streeter of Reed: "He *is* Citicorp."[7]

Unlike Wriston, Reed was noted for accommodation instead of combat, and got high marks from shareholders for his more conservative approach to running the big bank.[8] He was lavished with worshipful praise in 1987 for writing off bad loans the bank had made to Third World countries.*

But Citicorp was setting itself up for trouble: It still had bad loans on its books, and needed extra income to overcome losses from those loans. The solution was to move heavily into commercial and residential real estate lending, and to become a major financier of so-called "highly leveraged transactions"—banking parlance for loaning money to leveraged buyout artists.

Tracking the Shares

Citicorp shares closed as high as $31 in early 1986, drifted back to the mid-twenties, then peaked again just above $34 in the summer of 1987. The October stock market crash that year dropped the shares under $20. They renewed their climb and eclipsed $35 in 1989, before a slow but steady decline took Citi's stock down to $11 in October 1990, as investors finally focused on the bank's problems.

In May 1990, *Business Week* had published a story quoting experts who said investors considering a Citibank certificate of deposit would be better advised to buy Citicorp shares instead. Sure, bad news had driven the shares into the low $20s. But the bank had a great brand name and some very good businesses, experts told the magazine. Besides, as the largest U.S. bank, and the 11th largest in the world, it was probably so big that the federal government could not afford to let it fail.[9]

We can excuse those experts for having second thoughts by Fall. In fact, many feared the bank was going to collapse. Its ratio of

---

* News reports chronicling this move included: "How to Take a $1 Billion Loss and Look Good" (*U.S. News & World Report*), "John Reed's Bold Stroke" (*Fortune*), and "Three Cheers for Citicorp's Initiative" (*U.S. News & World Report*), "Bank Stockholders Should Applaud" (*Forbes*), and "Citicorp Faces Reality—And Finds it Doesn't Hurt" (*Newsweek*).

equity to assets was below minimum federal standards, and most analysts believed the money Citicorp had set aside to cover bad loans was inadequate—short by billions of dollars. Consider some headlines of the day:

- "Citicorp's World of Troubles," chronicling its bad loans.[10]
- "Can John Reed Rock Citicorp Out of Its Rut?" talking about its thin reserves.[11]
- And "John Reed Eats Crow for Christmas," after a dividend cut that Reed had all but promised would not occur.[12]

A contrarian play? At $11.13 on October 29, 1990, the stock was down more than 50 percent from both its June closing high of $25 and from its highest closing price for the previous 52 weeks, $29, recorded in October 1989. Its stock price was about half of its per share book value (a fundamental buy indicator that's one of the most widely watched for a bank or financial-services company).

In fact, Citi shares purchased in October realized a 50 percent return by early June 1991, when they topped out at $17.38.

Had the stock been held, the buyer would have found the stock back in the same $11 neighborhood a year later. In fact, sliding the stop loss up to a 30 percent profit level would have triggered a sale with a 30-percent gain.* The stock dropped again throughout 1991; investors were singing a requiem for Citicorp. Indeed, a bank that had once earned $1.9 billion in 1988, would post a loss of $885 million for the 1991 third quarter. By late December, its shares dropped to $8.63, a price again less than 50 percent of its high for the previous 12 months.

News stories from 1990 and 1991 were a siren's song for contrarians. Some called for a complete collapse; others speculated that Reed, who was now being cast as a failure, was on the way out.

But Citi still had a lot going for it. Most noteworthy was a $590 million investment by Saudi prince Alwaleed bin Talal bin Abdulaziz Alsaud, revealed in February 1991. For our purposes, the prince counts as a knowledgeable outside investor, as Kirk Kerkorian was for Chrysler. (Read more about Chrysler in the following case study.)

---

*Recall that if we hold a stock beyond a 50 percent profit, we use a sliding stop loss to guarantee at least a 30 percent profit if the stock backslides.

The prince's February 1991 investment bulked up Citicorp's balance sheet, and would have reassured an investor who had bought the Citi shares in late 1990. And though Prince Alwaleed's stake was purchased about 10 months before Citicorp stock dropped 50 percent again and bottomed at $8.63 in late December 1991 (leaving it outside the six-month window), it was so large at $590 million that ignoring it would have been a mistake.

The story doesn't end there, however. In February 1992, even though Citicorp shares had nearly doubled from their December low, doubts about its future clearly remained. That month, *Newsweek* published a story contending the big bank still needed a miracle for long-term survival. More than a third of its loans were in arrears, its credit-card business faced an upswing in delinquent payments and its corporate finance group was struggling after losing $1 billion in 1991, the magazine reported.[13]

History shows that Citicorp may have been one of those rare contrarian stocks: A keeper. As the economy rebounded, interest rates fell (usually good for banks) and earnings improved.

Let's consider the three-year and buy-and-hold scenarios for Citicorp, had you bought at the 1990 low, the 1991 low, or after a Saudi prince revealed his big stake.* We track the share price from the two bottoms, not assuming the investor bought there, but merely as a way to track the shares versus the broader market.

First, Table 7.1 shows the three-year returns versus the market, had you bought in October 1990. In Table 7.2, we examine the buy-and-hold record.

Table 7.1

Date	Citicorp Closing Price	Dow Jones Closing Price	Cumulative Stock Return	Cumulative Market Return
Oct. 29, 1990	$11.13	2430.00	N/A	N/A
Oct. 29, 1991	11.00	3061.94	0.00%	26.00%
Oct. 29, 1992	16.75	3246.27	52.00	34.00
Oct. 29, 1993	36.25	3680.59	230.00	51.00

---

*Technically, it was not a contrarian play at that point. But we include it to underscore the significance of big purchases by outside investors.

Table 7.2

Date	Citicorp Closing Price	Dow Jones Closing Price	Cumulative Stock Return	Cumulative Market Return
Oct. 29, 1990	$ 11.13	2430.00	N/A	N/A
Oct. 29, 1991	11.00	3061.94	0.00%	26.00%
Oct. 29, 1992	16.75	3246.27	52.00	34.00
Oct. 29, 1993	36.25	3680.59	230.00	51.00
Oct. 31, 1994	47.75	3908.12	334.00	61.00
Oct. 30, 1995	65.25	4756.57	493.00	96.00
Oct. 30, 1996	98.00	5993.23	781.00	147.00
June 30, 1997	120.56	7672.79	983.20	216.00

Pretty fair compensation for the risk taken.

By following our contrarian rules, depending on what you paid for the shares, it's possible that our 25-percent stop loss would have forced you out of Citi stock for a time. But you could also have repurchased them once they crossed the $11 mark again.*

Table 7.3 (below) takes a look at how the shares performed from their December 1991 low, when the shares were still down 50 percent from their highs, and were again trading at ½ their book value per share.

With a contrarian play, there is usually time to think before you buy and, often, several points at which to purchase. We could have bought these shares for $11, $12, or even $15, and still enjoyed a handsome profit.

Table 7.3

Date	Citicorp Closing Price	Dow Jones Closing Price	Cumulative Stock Return	Cumulative Market Return
Dec. 20, 1991	$ 8.63	2934.48	N/A	N/A
Dec. 21, 1992	20.12	3312.46	133.00%	13.00%
Dec. 21, 1993	37.50	3755.21	335.00	28.00
Dec. 21, 1994	43.13	3767.15	400.00	28.00
Dec. 21, 1995	66.25	5059.32	668.00	72.00

---

*As we'll see, when a stop loss pushes you out of a stock, you can only repurchase it once it passes the price you paid for the shares the first time.

Princely Profits

The prince is an interesting contrarian study. He told *Business Week* he was offered a chance to go in with Kirk Kerkorian on his bid for Chrysler. The prince declined, stating that "buying in at $56 in hopes Chrysler would go to $100 wasn't interesting enough. When it comes to deals outside Saudi Arabia, I don't go against management."[14]

Alwaleed says he has one basic rule when he's contemplating an investment: "Anything that's worth $4 billion and costs $1 billion, buy it."[15]

The $590 million Alwaleed invested in Citicorp bought him convertible preferred stock that paid an 11 percent dividend and was convertible into common stock at $16 per share—only slightly above the $15.38 share price when the deal was inked in February 1991.[16] The stock price dropped after that point.

But his preferred stock purchase was actually his second investment in Citi; Alwaleed already had spent more than $200 million to buy in excess of 4 percent of the bank's outstanding common stock. When asked why he was willing to make such a big bet on a bank most thought was finished, the prince gave an answer that should have any contrarian nodding in agreement: "In the last 18 months I watched the stock go from 35 to 10¾. It was very tempting, almost half its book value. The franchise of Citicorp internationally is unmatched by any other bank in the world."[17]

Alwaleed said the bank's problems were overblown, and could be fixed by management. At the time, he predicted the shares would hit $30 by 1994.

He was right.

The Practical Effect: Anytime a company as big as Citi hits the skids, take a look. As in the case of Xerox or IBM, a company as big as Citi can apply its considerable resources to find solutions to its problems. While, in theory, no organization is too big to fail, in practice, failure is rare. And, when it happens, it is usually a long, drawn-out affair, not a sudden disaster. Therefore, contrarians buying large, out-of-favor companies have the odds on their side. That, combined with compelling financial valuations, make investing in these behemoths of capitalism an excellent risk.

■ ———————————— **Contrarian Case** ———————————— ■
A Giant Stumbles:
The View from Outside

Henry R. Luce said, "Business more than any other occupation is a continual dealing with the future; it is a continual calculation, an instinctive exercise in foresight."

In the early 1980s, thanks to a government-assisted bailout and some fast work by automobile pitchman and CEO Lee Iacocca ("If you can find a better car, buy it!"), Chrysler Corp. became the most celebrated turnaround in the history of Corporate America. The government got paid back seven years early and Iacocca, who agreed to a $1 salary during the turnaround, became an American icon so popular that many suggested he should run for president.

By the end of the 1980s, however, Chrysler was on the ropes again, woozy like a fading prize-fighter who fought one bout too many. Its line of cars was stale, its pension was underfunded by billions, and its losses were so severe that many expected the company to fail. As we will see, it was also a classic contrarian stock play.

Chrysler's New Beginning, Contrarian Style

As any contrarian knows, when things are going too well for a company, there's bound to be a nasty wreck on the highway ahead. Chrysler was no exception.

Iacocca's fame and ego drew him to such projects as refurbishing Ellis Island and the Statue of Liberty, and perhaps diverted his attention from Chrysler. And despite its profitability—or perhaps, contributing to it—Chrysler was still on a very tight budget, which left its pension underfunded and delayed the rollouts of important new models for its car and truck lines.

By 1985, most insiders believed the company could start a modest new-model program. But Iacocca, fearful another recession would bury his car company, did what many companies in Corporate America did at that time: Diverted money away from its main business to buy businesses outside its industry.

By the mid-1980s, Chrysler had started its slide. As so often happens with a good company gone bad, members of the so-called "smart money" crowd kept buying the whole way down. Consider an October 1986 *Business Week* story, "It May Be Time to Hitch a Ride With Chrysler," in which investors rated the company's shares a good buy, because they had dropped from about $23.50 each to $18 (actually half that if you consider a July 1996 two-for-one stock split).*[18]

Two years later, *Business Week* ran a piece speculating that a leveraged buyout might be in the cards for Chrysler because of its "undervalued" stock price. Clearly, the investors who suggested Chrysler was undervalued did not realize how serious the company's situation was becoming.

To be completely fair, other 1988 news reports zeroed right in on the problems facing the carmaker.† Chrysler was losing market share and some analysts began questioning whether the company had the financial muscle to ride out the next recession.[19]

But, many investors still believed Chrysler's problems were temporary and that the carmaker's shares were a good buy. As the stock kept dropping, from a high of $24 in 1987 to a new low of $9.50, the crowd kept buying.

Meanwhile, insiders were starting to wonder how Chrysler was going to survive. As the 1990s opened, Chrysler's stock was trading around $7.50 per share, the debt of subsidiary Chrysler Financial had been downgraded, Japanese cars continued to gain market share and the company's balance sheet was looking ragged.

In March 1990, after Chrysler reported a $664 million loss for the fourth quarter of 1989, cut salaried workers, and closed plants, *Time* magazine ran a piece headlined: "Can Iacocca do it Again?"[20] That Chrysler's travails had trickled beyond business newspapers and magazines and into the pages of general readership news magazines was noteworthy, particularly from a contrarian's vantage point.‡

---

*These prices have been adjusted to reflect a two-for-one stock split in July 1996.

†Among them were a *Business Week* piece by Wendy Zellner, "Why Chrysler's Eagle Isn't Soaring," May 16, 1988, p. 40, and "Iacocca's Time of Trouble," *Fortune*, Feb. 22, 1988, p. 130.

‡When a business story starts getting prominent play in the non-business press, it's often a clear indicator that the crowd's opinion has reached an extreme—in this case, that Chrysler was once again a very troubled company.

In some ways, 1990 was like 1979–1980 all over again. Iacocca looked in vain for a partner with pockets deep enough to improve Chrysler's finances and pay for development of the new vehicles it needed to be competitive.

As Japanese carmakers continued to make inroads that year, Chrysler's sales and profits declined and its stock fell to $5.

At what point did this become a contrarian play? In September 1990, the stock would have met the "down-by-half rule": It bottomed at $4.69, down from its 52-week high of $13 on Oct. 3, 1989. At that point, it was trading at less than book value and at a fraction of its sales per share. On a stock that's down by half, meeting two of our four fundamental analysis indicators makes it a buy.

Something, it seemed, had to give.

Captain Kirk Beams Aboard

That something was billionaire investor Kirk Kerkorian. On Dec. 14, 1990, the 73-year-old Kerkorian disclosed in a securities filing that over the prior several months he had amassed a 9.8 percent stake in Chrysler, worth more than $270 million.[21] Kerkorian said he was a "long-term investor," and planned no takeover, but declined to sign an agreement limiting future stock purchases.[22] By that time, Chrysler shares were still down so far that they had a dividend yield of 8.8 percent, perhaps indicating investors expected a dividend cut. On that count, they would be proven correct.

Trading was frenetic in the three days after Kerkorian's announcement; even so, when the dust settled, the stock had risen just 69 cents per share to close at $6.82. *Business Week* described the stock-price increase as "a nice pop, but not exactly the kind of runup that signals the start of a takeover battle."[23]

Significant insider buying on a stock that's down 50 percent from its high automatically passes our litmus test for a contrarian stock play. But what about big positions taken by outside investors, positions so big that these investors must file statements with the Securities and Exchange Commission? We refer to these non-insiders as "knowledgeable outsiders" and believe their ante should carry the same weight as insider purchases.

If investors like Michael Price or Warren Buffett have the faith to take big positions in troubled companies, as Price did with Chase

Manhattan or Buffett did with Salomon Brothers, these firms rate a second look.

To follow the "down-by-half rule" with Chrysler, you would have had to buy the stock before the Kerkorian announcement. This underscores a key point. We've talked about how, as a contrarian, you must wade in before other investors discover what you already spotted. But once you've made your purchase, you want other investors to pile in, driving the value of your stock higher. Kerkorian's move illustrates what we mean.

When Kerkorian disclosed his stake in Chrysler, Shearson Lehman Brothers Inc. auto analyst Joseph S. Phillippi told *Business Week:* "I'd give anything for a totally honest, eight-words-or-less answer: Why'd you do this?"[24] A lot of other investors were wondering the same thing, spending their time thinking instead of buying. After all, it was possible that Kerkorian would be bought out by Chrysler, leaving others with a hangover. Those who shied away shouldn't feel too bad. There were many reasons in 1990 to hate Chrysler's stock: Its pension was underfunded by $3 billion; it had only a 12.2 percent share of the U.S. car-and-truck market; it had virtually no overseas operations to help it ride out a recession in North America; and it was shackled with a labor contract Sanford C. Bernstein auto analyst Joseph G. Paul described as "the equivalent of cement overshoes."[25]

The stock rose to about $7.50 in March 1991, and dropped to $5 again in December 1991. Had you used our rules, you could have been out after a 50-percent gain, or would have been stopped out with a 30-percent profit after the stock fell back.

But after that, Chrysler shares really accelerated, pushed by the threat of a hostile takeover, big share buybacks, a boost in the dividend, and a turnaround that made Chrysler very much an admired company again.

Along with Kerkorian's investment, something else happened after Chrysler bottomed that would have reassured the investor who bought beforehand: a change in management.

GM executive Robert Eaton was named as Iacocca's successor in March 1992. We've shown how new management can be bullish for a company in trouble. Increasingly, Iacocca had come to be seen as part of the company's problem; the lack of an heir apparent weighted down the shares. Clearly, the Chrysler board understood this and pushed Iacocca to step aside for Eaton.

Table 7.4

| Date | Stock Closing Price | Market Closing Price | Cumulative Returns | |
			Stock	Market
Dec. 17, 1991	$ 5.25	2902	N/A	N/A
Dec. 17, 1992	15.88	3269	202%	13%
Dec. 17, 1993	27.19	3752	418	29
Dec. 19, 1994	23.00	3791	338	31
Dec. 18, 1995	26.88	5075	412	75
June 17, 1996	33.19	5653	532	95

Let's take a look at how contrarians would have done had they picked up Chrysler shares after Kerkorian's big stake became public. Obviously, if bought before his entrance, the returns were even greater. (See Table 7.4.) You also would have done quite well if you had bought the shares based on a change in management (the announcement that Robert Eaton had been recruited from GM to succeed Iacocca). At that point, however, it was a value play, not a contrarian pick, because it was no longer down by half. But we offer Table 7.5 to show how qualitative factors (part of technical analysis) are worth considering—in this case, a change in top management.

We would be remiss if we didn't mention Kerkorian's aborted takeover of Chrysler, if only to make the point that troubled companies are sometimes so cheap that they attract suitors.

Kerkorian was not content to sit and watch Chrysler go through the cyclical upswings and downdrafts all carmakers experience. His stake in the company, purchased for $270 million, would rise in value to nearly $2 billion as Chrysler shares peaked at $31.50 a share. When the shares slid in concert with shares in other cyclical firms as

Table 7.5

| Date | Stock Closing Price | Market Closing Price | Cumulative Returns | |
			Stock	Market
March 16, 1992	$ 8.63	3236	N/A	N/A
March 16, 1993	19.81	3442	130%	6%
March 16, 1994	29.94	3848	247	16
March 16, 1995	20.38	4069	136	26

fears of a slowing economy surfaced, Kerkorian pressed Eaton to do something to recharge his investment.

A boost in the dividend and a share buyback didn't mollify Kerkorian. In April 1995, he launched a hostile, $27.50 per share bid for the company, intending to use Chrysler's cash to finance part of the deal. His bid fell apart because he lacked solid financing, but the bid perked up the stock and spurred Eaton to make other moves to boost the company's stock price.

The Practical Effect: Faced with a large purchase of stock by a knowledgeable outsider in an otherwise hammered-down stock, contrarians should ask the question: "What do they know that I don't?" On a stock that's down by half, when an outside investor takes a big stake in the company, contrarians should take a very close look.

Endnotes

1. Saler, Tom, "How You Can Profit With the Insiders," *Your Money*, July 1997, pp. 22–25.

2. Ibid., p. 24.

3. Pettit, R. Richardson, and Venkatesh, P.C., "Insider Trading and Long-Run Return Performance," *Financial Management*, Vol. 24, No. 2, Summer 1996, pp. 10–20.

4. Ibid., p. 19.

5. CDA Investnet Technologies, 3265 Meridian Parkway, Suite 130, Ft. Lauderdale, Fla., 33331.

6. Loomis, Carol J., "Citicorp's World of Troubles," *Fortune*, Jan. 14, 1991, p. 91.

7. Ibid, p. 92.

8. Boyer, Edward, "Citicorp: What the New Boss Is Up to," *Fortune*, Feb. 14, 1986, pp. 40–44.

9. Laderman, J. M., "Banking on Citi's Consumer Muscle," *Business Week*, May 14, 1990, p. 126.

10. Loomis, p. 90.

11. Weber, Joseph, "Can John Reed Rock Citicorp Out of Its Rut?" *Business Week*, Nov. 12, 1990, p. 116.

12. Meehan, John, and Sprio, Leah Nathan, "John Reed Eats Crow for Christmas," *Business Week*, Dec. 31, 1990, p. 42.

13. "Honey I Shrunk the Bank," *Newsweek*, v.119, Feb. 3, 1992, p. 38.

14. Rossant, John, "The Prince: Inside the $10 Billion Empire of Power Player Alwaleed," *Business Week*, Sept. 25, 1995, p. 90.

15. Ibid, p. 89.

16. Barrett, William P., "A Blank Check It Was Not," *Forbes*, April 29, 1991, p. 40.

17. Ibid.

18. "It May Be Time to Hitch a Ride With Chrysler," *Business Week*, Oct. 13, 1986, p. 158.

19. Levin, Doron P., *Behind the Wheel at Chrysler: The Iacocca Legacy*, Harcourt Brace & Co., New York, N.Y., p. 236.

20. Gwynne, Samuel, "Can Iacocca Do It Again?" *Time*, March 5, 1990, p. 40.

21. Treece, James B., et al., "Kirk Kerkorian Says It Was Just Iacocca Appreciation Day," *Business Week*, Dec. 31, 1990, pp. 47–48.

22. Ibid, p. 47.

23. Ibid, p. 48.

24. Ibid, p. 47.

25. Ibid, p. 48.

CHAPTER 8

FUNDAMENTAL STOCK ANALYSIS

Hit 'em where they ain't.
—William Keeler

Right before the turn of the century, a tiny outfielder for the Baltimore Orioles turned in one of the most amazing performances in the history of baseball. The 5-foot, 4-inch William "Wee Willie" Keeler drilled 1,112 hits for a Herculean .393 batting average. When asked how he did it, Keeler deadpanned: "Hit 'em where they ain't." In other words, hit the ball where the fielders aren't standing. A simple strategy, yes, but one that got Keeler enshrined in Cooperstown with Babe Ruth, Lou Gehrig, and Ty Cobb.

Investors should take note of "Wee Willie's" five-year hot streak, said Ernest C. Kiehne, one time manager of the Value Trust mutual fund operated by Legg Mason Wood Walker Inc. in Baltimore. In a newsletter to clients a few years ago, Kiehne used the Keeler "hit 'em where they ain't" baseball philosophy as an analogy for buying out-of-favor stocks. As analogies go, it's one of our favorites. As contrarians, we'll even take it a step further. With apologies to both Keeler and Kiehne, the secret to success as a contrarian might be phrased as: "What's hot is where you're not."

What do we mean? Contrarians should put their money in asset classes (for instance, stocks, bonds, real estate, precious metals) that are not on investors' hit lists. That's how the contrarian profits; eventually, these assets come back into fashion, propelling higher the value of the contrarian's holdings.

When sorting through stocks, fundamental analysis is a disciplined way to identify out-of-favor companies whose depressed shares represent an investment opportunity for contrarians. Investors use fundamental analysis to gauge whether a stock is overvalued or undervalued by looking at the ratio of share price to other financial measures like profits, sales or book value. For our purposes, we will look at stocks that first meet a technical measure (stock price down 50 percent from its 12-month high), and then meet at least two of four fundamental indicators:

- A price/earnings (P/E) ratio of less than 12
- A price/book value (P/BV) ratio less than 1.0
- A price/free cash flow (P/FCF) ratio of less than 10
- A price/sales (P/S) ratio of less than 1.0

THE FUNDAMENTAL BASICS

When it comes to stock-market analysis, there are basically two schools of thought: the technicians and the fundamentalists. Typically, an investor who subscribes to one school of thought rejects the other. Our goal is not to press the case for one or the other. Indeed, as you're discovering, our guidelines draw from both schools. We need to understand both, so key parts of fundamental and technical analysis can become weapons in our contrarian arsenal.

We're not going to present a start-to-finish lesson on fundamental analysis, since that's beyond the scope of this book. Instead, we'll discuss the basics you'll need to use fundamental analysis for picking contrarian stocks. In this chapter, we'll give a quick overview of fundamental analysis. In the chapters immediately following, we'll delve into proven fundamental-analysis techniques used by investment pros, and demonstrate guidelines for buying out-of-favor stocks.

Our goal is to combine the technical signals (such as our "down-by-half rule" and insider-buying rules), with the fundamental "buy" signals we're detailing here, creating a simple-to-use, but disciplined approach to contrarian investing.

The Practical Effect: You'll know when to buy and when to sell.

The Fundamentalists vs. the Technicians

In most ways, technical and fundamental analysis have little to do with one another. The fundamentalists deride technicians as "tea-leaf readers," while technicians shake their heads and say that fundamentalists seem to spend so much time crunching numbers that they're late pulling the trigger.

Contrarians look for extremes: Stocks, bonds, commodities, or market sectors that are overbought or oversold. Technical analysis can be a good technique for spotting these extreme conditions; when uncovered, these extremes may be investment opportunities. Because technicians often start with a macro point of view—perhaps an overview of the entire economy, or an overview of a particular industry—and then work their way down to ferret out a specific investment, technical analysis is also known as "top-down" investing.

Fundamental analysis is often called "bottom-up" analysis.* Assume you are interested in the stock of a publicly traded company. To decide if that company's stock is overvalued, fairly valued, or undervalued, you make an estimate of the company's future earnings and dividend payouts. That's essentially what the price of a share of stock represents: the market's expectation of the future earnings and/or dividends that will accrue to that share. With fundamental analysis, the starting point of that forecast is the company's income statement and balance sheet. The goal is to calculate some important ratios (P/E, P/CF, P/BV and P/S). These ratios can be compared to the ratios of peer companies, or with a broad market index such as the S&P 500. Only then might the fundamentalist take a look at the overall economy to get an idea of how inflation or interest rates might affect the financial performance of the company being studied.

This truly is a bottom-up approach: from the individual company, to its industry, then to the market, and, finally, a consideration of the overall economy to get a general idea of where the stock market

---

* Note that there are bottom-up technicians and top-down fundamentalists. There is no exclusivity on the direction from which the investment equation is pondered.

might be headed. Put another way, the bottom-up investor goes from the micro to the macro.

The Practical Effect: The investing rules we present in this book combine both technical and fundamental analysis. They work in tandem. Contrarians can use technical analysis as a "screen" to zero-in on a market sector that's been badly beaten down, and then use fundamental analysis to search out the strongest companies in that sector. Or they might employ fundamental analysis to identify stocks worth buying, using technical analysis as a "trigger" to know when to sell.

In this book, our basic rule is first, to search out stocks that are down at least 50 percent from their 52-week highs. If there is no insider buying, we look to see if the stock instead meets two or more of our list of contrarian fundamental indicators (P/BV or P/S ratio of less than 1.0, for instance; more on that in Chapters 10 and 11).

A stock that's down 50 percent from its high is a technical indicator, because it deals with past price movement. Insider buying is also a technical indicator, because it does not relate to the company's innate financial performance. It falls more into the realm of market sentiment—the domain of the technician. But ratios like price/earnings or price/book value are fundamental indicators. They relate to the company's fundamental financial condition and the value the market places on that strength or weakness.

Contrarians don't view fundamental analysis as just a school of thought, but as a tool with which to sift through stocks the quarter-to-quarter investors have relegated to the market-refuse heap. It lets the investor systematically capitalize on short-term inefficiencies emotion creates in the stock market.

THOSE INEFFICIENT EFFICIENT MARKETS

To believe that fundamental analysis (and technical analysis, for that matter) can be used to spot stocks that are either overvalued or undervalued, you have to be willing to believe that the financial markets are not as efficient as proponents of the so-called "Efficient Market Hypothesis" would have you believe.

The Efficient Market Hypothesis holds that securities are always fairly valued, meaning prices reflect all the information that's available about them. There are several versions of this theory:

1. *The "weak-form" hypothesis,* which says all information contained in past price movement is reflected in current market price.[1] If that's true, the trend analysis done by technical analysts, or "chartists," is just time wasted, since all that data is already contained in the price of the stock. Nothing is overvalued or undervalued. If a stock did become undervalued, all the analysts, traders, brokers, fund managers, and individual investors who comprise the "market" would spot the underpriced stock, and immediately bid the shares up to a price level that reflected its true value.

Conversely, if the stock became overvalued, investors would recognize the "sell" signal, dumping the stock and sending its price down to its new—but lower—fair price.

2. *The "semi-strong" hypothesis* holds that the price of a share of stock already reflects all publicly available information about the firm's prospects. That means that, in addition to the historical trading data incorporated in the weak-form hypothesis, the price of a share of stock also reflects all other information publicly available about a company. That includes information on things like anticipated earnings, the company's credit rating, management competence, and the success of products.

According to this theory, while insiders could profit from information known only to them, investors outside the company using a firm's financial statements as a starting point for fundamental analysis are wasting their time trying to find an undervalued stock. In other words, no one can beat the market without "inside information," which is illegal to use and profit from.

3. *The "strong-form" hypothesis* holds that *all* information, even information known only to insiders and not to the market as a whole, is reflected in the company's current stock price at any time.

Ultimately, investors who subscribe to the Efficient Market Hypothesis turn to index funds that track some major market measure (such as the S&P 500), believing it is pointless to try to beat the market.

The Not-So-Nifty Fifty and Other Tragic Tales of Inefficiency

It would appear that, if the prices of all securities in a market at any one time are at fair value, then the market itself must also be fairly valued. Clearly, if we were to believe in the strong form of the Efficient Market Hypothesis, beating the market is an impossibility, meaning the investor would do well enough by diversifying his portfolio between stocks, bonds, cash, and perhaps some commodities. Most of that could be accomplished using market-index funds.

However, professional contrarians know there are points when extremes *do* exist—when the price of a share of stock does not reflect its true value. A stock, or even an entire industry sector, will sometimes be driven to dizzying heights thanks to investor euphoria, fired by a belief that good times can only get better. If that happens, stand clear. Bad news can be a harsh teacher when the big selloff comes.

The so-called "Nifty Fifty" stocks of the late 1960s and early 1970s are just one example of such euphoria. This group of companies, which included Polaroid, were known as "one-decision stocks," because the investor needed to make only one decision: to buy them. The companies were so good their shares would never have to be sold—at least, that was the conventional wisdom at the time. Alas, many proved to be "two-decision stocks" (that should have been sold and profits pocketed after a huge run up in price). At the end of 1972, Polaroid traded as high as 97 times trailing earnings, and McDonald's 81 times earnings, versus 18 times earnings for the Standard & Poor's 500.[2] When the big bear market came in 1973, eradicating 40 percent of the S&P's value, these "one-decision" stocks were clobbered. Polaroid dropped from $126 on December 31, 1972 to $19; McDonald's from $76 to $30.

Many times, a perfectly good company or reasonably healthy industry sector will become "oversold." Usually, it's because investors overreact to bad news by dumping shares and driving prices down below a company's—or industry's—true value. These are possible buying opportunities for contrarians. Of course, not every hammered-down stock is a buy; often the low stock price reflects a deep and fundamental change in the company's prospects that has altered its long-term value as an investment.

Consider these two scenarios, potential opportunities for contrarians that stand as partial evidence the markets are not as efficient as some would have us believe:

First, a high-flying technology stock, trading at a very big multiple to its earnings (a very high P/E), whose price plunges after it warns that earnings will fall short of Wall Street's consensus estimates. We've seen this all too often: A company's stock nose-dives after its CEO warns that the soon-to-be-released quarterly earnings report is likely to disappoint investors. Was the stock efficiently priced days and weeks before the earnings announcement? Clearly, insiders knew of the problems even before the announcement, which would seem to contradict the Efficient Market Hypothesis.

Our second example is when an entire market, whether it's the Dow Jones Industrial Average, the Bolsa in Mexico, or the Tulip exchange in 17th century Holland, is at a high level one day and plunges the next. Scholars point to the 508-point debacle in the Dow on October 19, 1987 as a poignant example that seems to contradict the Efficient Market Hypothesis. Was the Dow efficiently priced in the weeks leading up to the Crash? If so, how could that valuation change overnight, and then reassert itself in the months that followed? Did anything really change?

Stock prices are a reflection of expected future earnings and dividends. The same is true of a market index. The index is determined by the prices of the stocks contained in it. And those stock prices are reflections of expected future earnings and dividends. In the strong form of the Efficient Market Hypothesis, even information known only to insiders is said to be factored into the stock price. If that's true, even before insiders disclose earnings problems, or warn that a highly touted new product has flopped, that share of stock should already have been fairly valued. Even after the earnings warning, there should be no price plunge. Clearly, as experience demonstrates, markets are not completely efficient, at least not in the short-term. Investors overreact, pushing shares either too high on good news, or too low on bad news.

With the benefit of hindsight, we can all look back and see the warning signals that were missed. But in October 1987, did the fundamental or technical underpinnings of the stock market undergo such a fast and dramatic change that a one-day, 23-percent market crash was warranted? According to one study, the answer is no. Yale University's Robert Shiller polled 1,000 investors—those with big money and those with modest individual accounts—and concluded the selling did not reflect a change in market prospects, but was touched off by the fall in the market itself. In short, people sold stocks because stocks were falling.[3]

If you think by now that we hold absolutely no stock in the efficiency of the markets, don't. Markets are fairly efficient. But not completely. The markets' overall efficiencies are marred by some short-term aberrations when they become overbought or oversold. To become a successful contrarian, you must understand and believe these short-term mispricings can be exploited for profit. That's the essence of contrarian investing. Fundamental analysis is an effective way to uncover these opportunities.

Contrarians need context when picking stocks. Merely because a stock has fallen a long way does not make it an automatic buy. We need some objective reason to believe that a company's stock promises market-beating returns. This promise comes from valuable company assets that can be used or sold, new products that can boost profits, or cash from operations that can be used to buy back shares. Fundamental analysis is a good way to assess a stock's potential.

In the next several chapters, we discuss four fundamental ratios that can aid stock selection: price/earnings (P/E), price/book value (P/BV), price/free cash flow (P/FCF), and price/sales (P/S). Each can help you "hit 'em where they ain't."

SUMMARY

In fundamental stock analysis, we use quantitative and qualitative data about a company's operations to assess whether the firm's stock is undervalued, fairly valued, or overvalued. We do this to try and profitably exploit short-term inefficiencies in the stock market, buying when other investors won't. These fundamental tools are useful for picking stocks. The four we focus on are low price/earnings, low price/book value, low price/free cash flow, and low price/sales.

Endnotes

1. Brigham, Eugene F., *Financial Management: Theory and Practice*, Sixth Edition, p. 249.
2. Jubak, Jim, "Sometimes Growth Isn't Enough," *Worth*, February 1996, p. 108.
3. "The 'Efficient Market' Was a Good Idea—And Then Came The Crash," *Business Week*, Feb. 22, 1988, pp. 140, 142.

CHAPTER 9

THE POWER OF
LOW P/E RATIOS

*D*on't fight forces; use them.

—R. Buckminster Fuller

We all take risks in our lives. We trade the familiarity of a job in our hometown for another in a city far away. We give up the freedom to relax with families and friends on evenings and weekends and take on debt to go to graduate school. We eschew the virtually guaranteed income from a Treasury bond to buy shares in a computer-software company. All these decisions involve risk. The new job may bomb, and the new city may have long winters. The graduate degree may put us in a deep hole financially, yet not advance our career. The software company may go bankrupt.

Why do we take these risks? In essence, each decision is an investment. We give up something now in hopes of getting something even better in the future. In making those decisions, however, we factor in risk. We make an economic decision that weighs the shot at a bigger payoff against the chance that our current situation will worsen.

Investing in stocks is the same kind of risk/reward game. To tip the odds in their favor, contrarians can look for stocks with low

147

price/earnings ratios. A stock's P/E, its price/earnings ratio, is a key fundamental analysis tool for contrarians. Used correctly, P/E ratios can help contrarians zero in on good investment opportunities and reduce risk. Many studies bear this out.

CALCULATING P/ES

The "trailing" P/E ratio is calculated by dividing a stock's price by its earnings per share in the most recently completed fiscal year. In other words, if a company's stock is trading at $20 per share, and the firm had earnings per share (EPS) of $1 last year, its P/E is 20 ($20 stock price/$1 EPS = P/E of 20). The company is said to be trading at 20 times trailing earnings.

Some analysts use a variation of trailing P/Es by using the aggregate earnings from the four most recently reported quarters, even if those four quarters are not all in one fiscal year. Assume it's August, and you are pondering Morgan Buggy Whip as a contrarian play. Morgan's fiscal year ends December 31. To calculate a P/E this way, you would look up the earnings per share from the first two quarters of the current year (the first quarter ending in March, and the second that ended in June) and the earnings from the final two quarters of last year (the third ending in September and the fourth ending in December). You would add the four quarters of earnings together and divide that total by the current stock price to arrive at this variation of trailing P/E.

There is logic behind this method. By using the most recent numbers available, some experts believe we get a more current picture of a company's financial performance. This is particularly true if a company's earnings are accelerating, or, as is usually the case with a stock down by half or more, are falling.

For contrarians using a 52-week range to calculate the percentage decline in a share of stock, using the P/E from the most recent four quarters is reasonable and logical. The *Wall Street Journal*, in its daily stock tables, reports P/Es using this method. So do many brokerage houses.

The company's P/E for its projected, or "leading," earnings also can be calculated. If the same stock is trading at $20 per share, and it's expected to earn $3.00 per share for the current year, then the company is trading at 6.67 times leading earnings ($20 stock price/$3.00 projected EPS = 6.67 P/E).

When studying the P/E for a particular prospect, a couple of things are worth noting:

- If a stock is trading at 20 times trailing earnings, and 6.67 times leading earnings, it's clear that the company's earnings per share are expected to improve. Business might be accelerating to boost profits, or the company could be buying back stock (reducing the number of shares the profits must be apportioned across).

  Sometimes a one-time charge reduces past earnings, or a one-time gain is expected to boost them in the current year. The one-time charge could be for costs associated with layoffs, and the gain could come from the sale of a factory.

- If the reverse were true; that is, if the shares were trading at 6.67 times trailing earnings, and 20 times projected earnings—then the company's earnings are expected to decline.

As an example, let's look at two California companies that Tony bought for client accounts in 1996: Read-Rite (RDRT), which makes key pieces for computer hard drives, and Applied Materials (AMAT), which makes semiconductor-manufacturing equipment.

RDRT

    Price $13.75, Trailing P/E 5.41, Leading P/E 9.17, 52-week range $12.625–$49.50

AMAT

    Price $25.75, Trailing P/E 7.22, Leading P/E 6.50, 52-week range $25–$59.875

High-technology companies are often difficult to analyze. New technologies can leapfrog their products. And their shares are often whipsawed by investors; that is, bid up beyond fair value when times are good, and unfairly punished at even the slightest hint of bad news. Some contrarians avoid tech stocks in favor of shares in established, well-capitalized companies, especially those in basic industries with well-recognized names. However, in 1996, technology stocks that just months before were trading in the stratosphere, had fallen into deep disfavor. Let's walk through an example using these two companies to see how a contrarian might ferret out low P/E stocks. Our example also demonstrates how combining technical analysis (top-down) and fundamental analysis (bottom up) can create a winning investing discipline.

A 1995 frenzy for semiconductor, Internet-software and computer companies burst badly in 1996 and had many investors despairing over the futures of these firms. Computer sales had slowed and prices for computer chips (especially for memory chips) were in freefall. Investors who gorged themselves on these stocks the year before decided the party was over and dumped the shares like leftover punch on New Year's Day. News stories chronicled the tough times ahead for tech companies and analysts crafted eulogies for the stocks they had been touting only months before.

For contrarians, these graveside pronouncements marked investment opportunity. Newspapers, financial magazines, brokerage-house research, and television reports tell contrarians what industries are being hit hard in the stock market, giving those investors a place to start their search. This represents the kind of "top-down" approach many technical analysts use with success. From there, however, contrarians can employ some fundamental-analysis screens (such as P/Es of less than 12) to pick out the most promising stocks. This shows how technical and fundamental analysis can complement each other. We can also see how contrarians are set apart from more conventional "value" investors. The difference, again, is that contrarians look for extremes. In 1996, companies in other industries sported low P/E ratios. The auto industry was one. But these other industries were not universally feared or hated as were some subsets of the technology sector.

Both stocks in our example, therefore, fit some of the initial criteria demanded by a contrarian investor:*

1. Both were in out-of-favor sectors (semiconductor equipment for AMAT and PC components for RDRT.)

2. Both stocks had dropped more than 50 percent from their 52-week highs, showing that investor sentiment was very negative on each.

3. Both were trading at low P/Es.

---

*However, as we said, many times contrarians and value investors are buying the same stocks. The difference is the approach that the two different types of investors take to picking stocks, and the fact that contrarians look for extreme opinions to exploit.

4. And with Read-Rite, five insiders had combined to purchase 58,000 shares of the stock.

The two companies fell out of favor with the rest of the high tech crowd, but had the financial muscle to weather a downturn. Both were leaders with solid financials. Read-Rite in 1995 had more than $1 billion in sales and earned more than $100 million. Debt was a mere 15 percent of assets. A fall in demand for disk drives, and difficulty making the switch from old-technology products to new, drove the company's share price into the cellar. Long term, however, many analysts projected the company's earnings would grow at a double-digit clip, particularly because foreign markets (Europe, Japan, and developing Asia) had a very low level of PCs per household compared with the United States. Even in the United States, big corporations were only beginning to embrace the fastest new computers and complex, memory-consuming PC operating systems. New software and Internet applications were creating the need to store much more data—meaning bigger disk drives.

Applied Materials was the biggest U.S. maker of the equipment used by the companies that churn out computer chips. It had more than $3 billion in sales in 1995 and had net earnings of more than $450 million. Semiconductor sales had been growing at a 40-percent annual clip, prompting companies such as Motorola, NEC, Cirrus Logic and others to plan new factories, bolstering orders for equipment. When it became clear that computer sales were slowing down, that inventories of chips were too high and that prices were crashing, plans for many new plants were postponed or shelved. Predictably, investors clobbered the stock prices of chipmakers, as well as the shares of companies that sold equipment to them.

Even so, chip sales were projected to grow from $180 billion in 1995 to $330 billion by the turn of the century, creating a need for the new factories. And even if prices stayed low, chipmakers would have to become more efficient, demanding the latest in equipment.

One final point: During the upsweep of hype in the chip business, analysts recommended the stocks of equipment companies such as Applied Materials, pointing to plans in the industry for *$40 billion* worth of new plants. Even if construction was slowed down or shelved for some of the plants, clearly there was still a lot of business for AMAT to grab. The company's stock, in a word, was unduly punished.

As our example shows, P/E ratios are a useful indicator when trolling for stock plays. Contrarians like to find these beaten-down stocks. The reason for these beatings vary: Maybe it was a bad earnings report, litigation, poor cost controls, an accident at one of the company's factories, or negative news about one of its products. Sometimes, as Read-Rite and Applied Materials illustrate, entire industries fall out of favor. Cyclical stocks, such as General Motors or Ford, reach their low points during the depths of a recession, get bid up before the economic rebound, and languish late in an economic cycle. By that time, investors have moved into supposedly "safer" consumer stocks such as Coca-Cola or McDonald's.

When a company or a sector falls out of favor, their shares tend to sport minuscule P/Es. Of course, if the company is losing money, there would be no P/E. When investors are smitten with a company's prospects for fast-growing profits, they bid up its stock, elevating it to 30, 40, or 50 times earnings, or more.

Investors will pay more on a price/earnings basis for a computer-networking company whose earnings are expected to grow at a 30 percent clip, than for a cleaning-chemicals company whose earnings are only increasing 10 percent a year. If we assume both are expected to earn $1 next year, and the market is trading true-to-form, shares of the computer-networking company might trade at $30 (a P/E of 30 on $1 per share of expected earnings), while the cleaning-chemicals company would be at $10 (a P/E of 10 on $1 per share of anticipated earnings). Stocks with higher projected growth rates typically carry higher P/Es. The common wisdom is that such "growth" stocks offer better returns and also pose less risk than a solid company with short-term problems and a stock price in the compost heap.

However, the opposite is often true.

Many studies show that diversified portfolios of low P/E stocks actually give investors better returns than high P/E stocks, while also posing much lower risk.

To understand why, we must first show how big a role P/E ratios play in investor psychology.

P/E RATIOS: GROWTH VS. VALUE

P/E ratios help define the two major investment schools: growth and value. Growth investors tend to go after companies that are increasing sales and earnings at a quick clip, say, 20 percent or more a year. These stocks sport high P/Es, a ratio in line with (or even greater than) the rate at which the company's profits are growing. Peter Lynch, the long-time manager of Fidelity's Magellan fund, is perhaps the best-known, growth-stock guru. Yet, even he said that it's dangerous to pay too much for growth.

Some experts think high P/E ratios and high projections of growth play off each other and create a trap for investors drawn in by gaudy forecasts. It's like an infinite loop in a computer program: A company's high rate of earnings growth causes its shares to trade at a high P/E; those high P/Es induce analysts to forecast higher growth rates for the company's earnings.[1]

There is a relatively new subset of growth practiced by "momentum players," many of them running some of the industry's bigger growth funds. Momentum players concern themselves less with a stock's valuation than they do its prospects to boost earnings and, hence, its share price. In an accelerating bull market (be it the stock market as a whole or just its hottest sectors), momentum players may for a time outpace the pack. They will pay up for a stock, as long as they think someone else will take that stock off their hands for a higher price. This is sometimes called, appropriately, "The Greater Fool Theory."

Momentum investing as a buying-and-selling discipline is the antithesis of the contrarian style. Contrarians might well ride along as the market moves a stock they already bought. But you can bet those contrarians bought the stock long before it became popular with the crowd.

Aside from growth, the other major investment school is value. Value investors search for bargains—shares they feel don't reflect the true value of the company's assets, franchise, management, product lines, technology, and growth prospects. Growth investors also claim to look for bargains (though their idea of a bargain might be a stock that's trading at 30 times earnings, with projected profit increases of 50 percent a year). The difference is that value stocks are usually out of favor with investors.

Remember "Wee Willie" Keeler? If he had been reincarnated as a portfolio manager, he would say value stocks were the ones where investors "ain't." And while growth stocks do well in a raging bull market, value stocks tend to do a lot better when the stock market is languishing and largely directionless. The late Benjamin Graham was probably the father of this discipline, and Warren Buffett, his star pupil, the best practitioner.

Contrarians and value investors do have some qualities in common. Contrarians, too, look for bargains, particularly among companies that are out of favor with Wall Street. The difference is that contrarians want extremes. Contrarians often buy into a stock, or a market, that's so far out of favor even value investors won't touch it.

David Dreman is the best-known proponent using P/E ratios as a way of gauging investor sentiment about a stock or market sector. He also has the courage of conviction: In August 1987, after watching as the market moved into what he thought was overvalued territory, Dreman did something he had never done before—he went to 30 percent cash in client accounts. At the time, Dreman Value Management managed $3 billion for clients.[2] His move was vindicated that October.

LOW P/E STOCKS: PUTTING PUNCH IN A PORTFOLIO

What constitutes a "low P/E" stock? That depends. Dreman believes that if the S&P 500 is trading at 15 times last year's earnings, and a stock is trading at 12 times earnings or less, the low P/E criteria is met.[3]

In an article published shortly after his death, Benjamin Graham suggested investors look for companies with P/E ratios less than 40 percent of the highest P/E the company had sported during the past five years.[4] For instance, if the highest P/E on a stock during the previous five years had been 25, that stock would have to be trading at less than 10 times trailing earnings to qualify as a low P/E stock (high P/E of 25 × 40 percent = P/E of 10).

The lower the P/E, the more the stock is being shunned by the market, and the more inclined contrarians should be to do the research and see if it is a buy. Sometimes you'll even be interested in "No P/E" stocks—shares of companies notching losses. Usually, however, the trailing 12-month P/E will just be a very low number.

Many academic studies show the power of low P/E ratios. Let's consider a few:

1. Sanjoy Basu, finance professor at McMaster University, studied P/E ratios and investment returns of about 500 NYSE stocks during the 14 years from 1957–1971. Basu took the stocks at the end of the year, ranked them from highest to lowest according to price/earnings ratios, and divided them into five equal parts (quintiles). Equal amounts of money were invested in each stock and the stocks were sold after one year and replaced by a new set that met the same parameters (see Table 9.1).

The median P/E for the stocks in the top fifth was 35.8, though that figure also includes companies with losses. The median P/E for the bottom fifth was 9.8. Over the 14 years of the study, the highest P/E stocks had an average annual rate of return of 9.3 percent, while the lowest P/E stocks returned an average of 16.3 percent.[5] Using Basu's research, a $100,000 investment in low P/E shares would have grown to $828,163 after 14 years, while the same amount invested in the high P/E stocks would have grown to only $347,282. A big difference! In fact, over that period, low P/E stocks would have returned more than twice their high P/E counterparts.[6]

There's more, Basu found. Low P/E stocks were actually less risky.[7] Beta is the measure of a stock's volatility and correlation with the broader market. A positive beta means the stock moves up when the market rises, and falls when the market drops. A negative beta means the stock moves opposite the broader market. The S&P 500 has a beta of 1.0. A stock with a beta greater than 1.0 is riskier than the market, while any stock with a beta less than 1.0 is considered less risky because it moves less than the market.

Table 9.1   Investment Results of New York Stock Exchange Industrial Companies According to Price/Earnings Ratios, April 1957 through March 1971

Portfolio	1 (Highest P/E)	2 (Highest P/E without loss companies)	3	4	5	6 (Lowest P/E)
Median price/ earnings ratio	35.8x	30.5x	19.1x	15.0x	12.8x	9.8x
Average annual rate of return	9.3%	9.5%	9.3%	11.7%	13.6%	16.3%
Market risk (beta)	1.11	1.06	1.04	.97	.94	.99

Source: Tweedy, Browne

Basu found that high P/E stocks had a beta of 1.11, meaning for every 1 percent move in the broad market, the high P/E stocks moved 1.11 percent in the same direction. Put another way, the stock would move in the same direction as the market (up or down), but 11 percent more. Low P/E stocks, by comparison, had a beta of only 0.99, meaning they were slightly less risky as the market. In other words, low P/E stocks gave more bang for the buck, with less risk than their high P/E cousins.

Indeed, other studies have found that whatever volatility these stocks have is focused more to the upside than the downside. In other words, if volatility is measured by how much a stock moves in excess of the market, then when low price/earnings stocks move more than the market, it's usually up and not down.

A naysayer to contrarian investing (and there are many) might counter that this data is old and that things are different now. But there are other, more recent studies that have reached the same conclusion that low P/E investing is valid.

2. Roger Ibbotson, founder of Ibbotson Associates, looked at all NYSE stocks from December 31, 1966 to December 31, 1983. On each December 31, he ranked them according to their P/E ratios and sorted them into deciles, or 10 equal parts. (See Table 9.2.) He looked at the returns generated during the 18 years from the end of 1966 to

Table 9.2   Investment Results of New York Stock Exchange Companies According to Price/Earnings Ratios, Dec. 31, 1966 through Dec. 31, 1984

Decile	Compound Annual Return	Ending (12/31/84) Value of $1.00 Invested on 12/31/66
1 (Lowest P/E ratio)	14.08%	$12.22
2	13.81	11.67
3	10.95	7.21
4	10.29	6.43
5	9.20	5.32
6	6.43	3.27
7	7.00	3.62
8	5.57	2.80
9	5.50	2.77
10 (Highest P/E ratio)	5.58	2.81

Source: Tweedy, Browne

the end of 1984. His findings: If an investor purchased a portfolio of stocks that made up the lowest tenth of the NYSE on each December 31, and traded them for the lowest tenth on each subsequent December 31, that investor would have earned an annual compounded rate of 14.08 percent for the 18 years. An investor who each year bought the tenth of the market with the highest P/E ratios, should have seen the portfolio compound at an annual rate of 5.58 percent. For reference, the NYSE as a whole would have returned 8.6 percent while U.S. Treasury bills compounded at 7.4 percent.[8]

Because of the long horizon, the return of the low P/E portfolio was dramatically higher than the high P/E portfolio. Every $1 invested in the low P/E portfolio became $12.22 after 18 years, while every $1 invested in the high P/E portfolio became $2.81.[9]

The low P/E effect seems to be even greater with small-capitalization companies.* Investors will often hear others talk about small-cap, medium-cap and big-capitalization companies. The definition for each class varies. We set $150 million as the smallest market-cap stock a contrarian should purchase.

3. Dreman, in a study done with Michael Berry of James Madison University, looked at the relationship between market caps, P/Es, and annual returns over a 20.5-year stretch ending October 31, 1989. This study, much larger than previous ones, involved 6,000 companies. They were ranked according to their market caps and rank-ordered into five equal groups. Companies in each of the five groups were again sorted into five groups, this time ranked according to P/E ratios. The portfolios were adjusted every year and the investment returns were calculated. (See Table 9.3.)

An investment in the quintile of companies with the lowest P/E ratios, among the 20 percent with the smallest market caps (an average of $46 million), and rebalanced each October 31, generated average annual returns of 18 percent. Compare that to only 13 percent earned for the biggest-cap companies with low P/Es. If the small-cap companies with the highest P/Es were purchased, the average annual

---

*Capitalization is the market value of a publicly traded company. It is computed by multiplying the number of outstanding shares by the current market price. A company with 10 million shares and a stock price of $15 has a market capitalization of $150 million. Although the definition varies, a small-cap company might be one described as having a market cap of less than $1 billion.

Table 9.3   Annual Investment Returns for Low versus High
Price/Earnings Ratio Stocks within Market Capitalization Categories
for the 20½ Year Period Ended Oct. 31, 1989

Market Cap Category	Average Market Cap October 31, 1989 (Millions)	Price/Earnings Ratio Category				
		Lowest P/E 1	2	3	4	Highest P/E 5
1 (Smallest)	$ 46	18.0%	15.3%	10.2%	7.0%	4.1%
2	127	15.7	13.7	10.0	6.5	7.4
3	360	17.0	15.1	10.6	7.4	8.2
4	1,031	13.8	12.9	10.3	8.5	7.1
5 (Largest)	5,974	13.0	12.4	9.1	10.5	8.7

Source: Tweedy, Browne

return was only 4.1 percent, while the large-cap companies with the
highest P/Es returned 8.7 percent.

An investment of $1 million in the small-cap, low-P/E port-
folio that was refreshed each year grew to $29.7 million over that
20.5 years, while the same investment in the big-cap, low-P/E stocks
grew to $12.2 million. A $1 million investment in the small-cap,
high-P/E portfolio grew to only $2.2 million, the study found.[10]

4. Another study done by Basu for a 17-year period ended in
1980 came to a similar conclusion: 19.1 percent average annual return for the small-cap, low-P/E stocks, and 13.1 percent for the big-
cap, low-P/E stocks. However, Basu said the lowest-cap, big-P/E
stocks returned 14.4 percent on average.[11] Basu looked only at NYSE
stocks for this study.

5. Dreman retested his theory again more recently, this time
looking only at companies with market caps of less than $1 billion.[12]
He looked at 3,500 companies over 25 years, sorting the companies
into three groups: The 20 percent with the lowest P/E ratios, the
middle 60 percent, and the highest 20 percent. He rebalanced the
portfolios quarterly. His finding: an average return of 18.1 percent
for the low P/E group, 13.3 percent for the middle group and 9.3
percent for the highest group. Dreman also found that the performance difference between the low- and high-P/E stocks was greatest
for small companies.

Other research concludes that the low-P/E method works equally well, if not a little better, for stocks in such developed economies as the United Kingdom, Germany, France, and Japan.[13]

Understanding why the low-P/E strategy works so well goes right to the core of contrarian investing. It's the same reason that an estimated 75–80 percent of all professional money managers fail to beat the market. Earnings are much harder to predict than investors believe.

A study reported by *Forbes* magazine in 1987 found that analysts were overly optimistic in the earnings forecasts rendered for companies trading at very high multiples of trailing earnings. Earnings reported for 1986 fell 73 percent shy of the estimates the analysts had posted in mid-1985. Although analysts' estimates are generally not this far off the mark, it shows how difficult it is to predict the future, even for an experienced professional.

In his Ph.D. dissertation, Harvard Business School researcher Sudhir Krishnamurthi found the same results. Looking at 1,250 closely followed companies for a five-year period ending in 1981, the researcher concluded that consensus forecasts for earnings reports due out in less than a year were off by an average of 30 percent. Other studies have found that the average miss was 17 percent, 24 percent, and an incredible 60 percent in the recession year of 1974.[14]

Don't be too hard on the analysts; estimates by company executives (off an average of 15 percent) and the office-equipment and computer group (off by 89 percent) were in many cases, much worse.[15] And while it is true that analysts can be wide of the mark, they can also be right on the money. The upshot in those cases: When earnings come out as expected, the stock stays put.*

■ *NOTES FROM A CONTRARIAN BUSINESS REPORTER*

I've been covering public companies since the mid-1980s, and still find earnings day—and the weeks leading up to it—a fascinating example of what these academic researchers found. Wall Street has some very fine financial minds, able to reflect quickly on the meaning of a new product,

---

*Contrarians can err in believing that analyst recommendations can be bet against consistently for profit. In a 1996 snapshot study of 40 stocks that met our contrarian criteria and were covered by Smith Barney, analysts had "buy" recommendations on 12, and no outright "sell" recommendations.

executive change, acquisition, or divestiture. Even so, it's been my experi-
ence that the analyst's estimates either overshoot or fall short of the ac-
tual earnings per share reported by the company. That's not a criticism.
Bigger companies are an amalgamation of many different businesses,
each facing unique financial, competitive, and managerial challenges.
Smaller companies, though less bulky, often experience much quicker
changes of fortunes. One example: a semiconductor company that under-
estimates the speed with which the market will embrace faster chips—
and gets left sitting on a huge inventory of slower chips.

For analysts, the forecasting game gets even harder when the com-
pany's management refuses to give guidance. In that case, being right to
the precise penny per share is a superhuman accomplishment. It may be
more surprising that they get it right so often, given the cards stacked
against them. It is no wonder that a good analyst can literally be worth his
*weight in gold.** ∎

Earnings forecasts are based on a company's past performance.
Studies have shown that the fast-growers, the companies whose earnings have been rising at clips of 20 percent or more for the previous
four or five years, are the ones that sport high P/E ratios. They are
also the likeliest to disappoint. Research shows that earnings often follow a "random walk," meaning there is no relationship between what a
company has earned in the past and how it will do going forward.[16]

> ***The Practical Effect:*** Low-P/E stocks, by contrast, already
> have bad news built into their prices, meaning more bad news
> exerts little extra downward pressure on them. Investors want-
> ing to play the low P/E game need to have patience. Those who
> do will be rewarded.

This was demonstrated in another study done by researchers
Josef Lakonishok, Robert Vishny, and Andrei Shleifer. The three
professors ranked all companies listed on the NYSE and AMEX

---

*Assuming a gold price of $400 per ounce, and an average analysts' body weight of 155
pounds (an admittedly off-hand estimate), an outstanding analyst could be paid in excess
of $1 million per year. A fair number are!

Table 9.4 Investment Returns in Relation to Price/Earnings Ratios for all New York Stock Exchange and American Stock Exchange Listed Companies, April 1968 through April 1990

Holding Period Following Portfolio Formation	P/E Ratio Decile									
	Highest P/E Ratio . . . . Lowest P/E Ratio									
1st year	12.3%	12.5%	14.0%	13.0%	13.5%	15.6%	17.0%	18.0%	19.3%	16.2%
2nd year	10.1	11.3	12.4	14.3	16.7	16.4	18.0	18.5	18.3	17.4
3rd year	11.8	13.8	15.7	17.1	17.1	19.1	19.8	18.8	18.8	19.5
4th year	11.1	12.4	14.5	15.1	15.7	15.9	19.8	19.9	20.5	21.4
5th year	11.9	12.9	15.1	16.7	17.1	16.8	19.6	20.1	21.1	20.7
Average annual return over the 5-year period	11.4	12.6	14.3	15.2	16.0	16.7	18.8	19.1	19.6	19.0
Cumulative 5-year total return	71	80	95	103	110	116	137	139	144	138

Source: Tweedy, Browne

according to P/E ratios, and divided them into 10 equal parts. The first portfolios were formed April 30, 1968, and new portfolios were formed each subsequent April 30. Each portfolio was held for five years and the study ended April 30, 1990.[17] The results are shown in Table 9.4.

Low P/E portfolios beat high P/E portfolios, and quite handily. Almost uniformly, as the P/E fell, average annual returns grew, until the final decile, when returns dropped off slightly. The study also showed some of the best returns came in the third, fourth, and fifth years the portfolio was held. That fits in with our finding that contrarians will see some of the biggest returns in the third year after buying a stock.

SUMMARY

Low P/E stocks are fertile ground for the contrarians. Once stocks have fallen 50 percent or more from their 52-week highs, P/E analysis can determine which stocks are priced cheaply in relation to their power to earn money. Ample academic research underscores the benefits of low P/E investing. A P/E ratio of less than 12, based on either trailing 12-months earnings, or last fiscal year earnings can be a confirming indicator. Alternatively, stocks trading at less than 40 percent of their highest P/E ratio over the last 5 years, or stocks trading at a P/E less than the P/E of the S&P 500 can be similarly considered. Whichever formula is used, the application of a low P/E screen before purchase has been shown to have great benefit in a contrarian portfolio.

Endnotes

1. Bauman, W. Scott, and Dowen, Richard, "Growth Projections and Common Stock Returns," *Financial Analysts Journal*, July/August 1988, p. 79.
2. Rohrer, Julie, "Portfolio Strategy: Value Vindicated?" *Institutional Investor*, v.22n1, January 1988, pp. 53–55.
3. Dreman, David, "The Glories of Low P/E Investing, *Forbes*, June 27, 1988, p. 172.
4. Oppenheimer, Henry R., "A Test of Ben Graham's Stock Selection Criteria," *Financial Analysts Journal*, September/October 1984, p. 69.
5. Basu, Sanjoy, "Investment Performance of Common Stocks in Relation to Their Price-Earnings Ratios: A Test of the Efficient Market Hypothesis," *Journal of Finance*, June 1977, p. 666.
6. Tweedy, Browne Co. L.P., *What Has Worked in Investing: Studies of Investment Approaches and Characteristics Associated With Exceptional Returns*, Tweedy, Browne Co. L.P., New York, N.Y., 1992, pp. 14–15.
7. Basu, p. 666.
8. As cited by Tweedy, Browne, *What Has Worked in Investing*, pp. 15–16.
9. Ibid.
10. Browne, pp. 18–19.
11. Ibid, pp. 17–18.
12. Dreman, David, "Boring is Best," *Forbes*, Nov. 6, 1995, p. 372.
13. Chisholm, John R., "Quantitative Applications for Research Analysts," *Investing Worldwide II*, Association for Investment Management and Research, 1991, as cited by Tweedy, Browne, p. 20; also, Levis, Mario, "Stock Market Anomalies: A Reassessment Based on the U.K. Evidence," *Journal of Banking and Finance*, 13, (1989), pp. 675–696.
14. Dremen, David, "Why High P/Es Are Dangerous," *Forbes*, Aug. 3, 1981, pp. 104–105.
15. Ibid, p. 104.
16. Ibid.
17. Lakonishok, Josef, et al., "Contrarian Investment, Extrapolation, and Risk," *The Journal of Finance*, December 1994, pp. 1541–1578. Tweedy, Browne, *What Has Worked*, pp. 19–20.

CHAPTER 10

BOOKING ON LOW PRICE/BOOK

Not one tenth of us who are in business are doing as well as we could if we merely followed the principles that were known to our grandfathers.

—William Feather

Just as a low P/E strategy is an attempt to buy a company's future earnings at a discount to true value, the low price/book value (low P/BV) filter is aimed at buying a company's assets "on the cheap."

The Practical Effect: A contrarian opportunity exists when a company's stock price is less than its book value per share; in other words, when the stock has a P/BV ratio of less than 1.0.

THE BOOK ON BOOK VALUE

A company's "book value," or net asset value, is an accounting measure used to compute what the business would be worth if the company were liquidated. We calculate book value by subtracting all liabilities from all assets.

In the strictest sense, book value is equal to total assets, minus intangible assets (such as goodwill and patents), minus current liabilities (debts coming due in less than a year), minus long-term liabilities and preferred stock (which take precedence over common stock), less any other obligations (such as money owed to an underfunded pension). So the formula for book value per share (BV/S) is:

$$\frac{\begin{array}{c}\text{Total Assets}-\text{Intangible Assets}-\text{Current Liabilities}-\\\text{Long-Term Liabilities}-\text{Preferred Stock}\end{array}}{\text{Number of Shares Outstanding}}$$

For shares outstanding, use the number of common shares on the company's balance sheet at the time you are making the calculation. The BV/S figure itself is often carried in a company's financial statements. It is also readily available as part of the analysis of companies supplied by advisory services such as the Value Line Investment Survey.*

There are some caveats. Book value is an accounting measure, meaning it is not necessarily a perfect reflection of a company's true value. For instance, accounting rules require a company to carry most assets on its books at "historical" values—that is, the price paid for the asset, less any applicable depreciation. Some assets, such as buildings, were depreciated as they aged, so they might fetch more in a sale than they were worth on the books. Others—land, for example—may have seen their values rise over time. In our land and building examples, the assets are on the books at a value that's much, much lower than what they might fetch if purchased by an informed buyer.

Benjamin Graham used a simpler approach to calculating book value, which he called the "net current asset value." His definition: current assets (cash, receivables, and inventory) minus all liabilities that take precedence over the company's common stock. These would include current liabilities (such as accounts payable), long-term debt, preferred stock, and pension liabilities. Notice that by using "current assets," he was not including any value for a company's real estate (land and buildings), or equipment. And while accounting rules would also have us subtract "intangibles" such as goodwill or

---

*Indeed, Value Line publishes a weekly list of companies with the lowest P/BV ratios, just as it does with low P/E stocks. It's not a bad place to look for investment ideas.

patents, Graham recommended that investors include them, particularly where such assets have an estimable market value.[1]

Graham used to look for companies trading at a price that was two-thirds or less of their stated book value. For instance, if a company's book value was $16 per share, Graham would consider it a buy only if it were trading at $10.67 per share or less ($16 × 66 percent = $10.67).

Graham found that, over a 30-year period, his annual return on well-diversified portfolios of such stocks was about 20 percent, much better than the historical market average of 11.9 percent for the S&P 500. Over time, those extra returns would mean huge dividends for someone saving for a college education or for retirement. For instance, a $20,000 portfolio invested in stocks generating an average return of 10 percent per year would grow to $348,000 in 30 years. But that same portfolio, growing at 13 percent, would total $782,000 during that same period. A difference of three percentage points makes a major difference over time.

Before we consider some of the research backing the low P/BV strategy, let's take a look at some low price/book value companies that illustrate the point.

The first, shown in Table 10.1, is RJR-Nabisco (RN), the big tobacco and snack-foods company. To give it context, we compare it with one of its peer companies, Philip Morris (MO), which has interests in tobacco, beer brewing, and foods. Consider these numbers from November 1996 (see Table 10.1).

RJR's stock price had already been under pressure because of fears about the massive legal liabilities it might face from lawsuits filed by smokers, and from states seeking to recoup money for health problems caused by smoking. A jury had found in favor of a smoker

Table 10.1   RJR Nabisco and Philip Morris, November, 1996

	RJR-Nabisco	*Philip Morris*
Stock Price	$29.00	$93.00
Trailing P/E	23	13
Book Value	$36.00	$17.00
Price/Book Value	0.8	5.4
52-Week Range	$26–$35	$85–$107

Table 10.2   Three Steel Companies, August 1996

	British Steel	*USX*	*Bethlehem*
Stock Price	$26	$28	$11
Trailing P/E	—	8	14
Dividend Yield	10.2%	3.5%	—
Price/Book Value	0.7	1.7	1.0
52-Week Range	$23–$31	$27–$38	$11–$14

Note. The ratios for British Steel were computed from the underlying stock trading in London, BST's primary exchange. The ratios hold true for the ADR.

who survived lung cancer. Then, after a sweet start, sales of RJR's low-fat "Snackwells" cookie line were going flat. In fact, RJR said it would lay off 4,200 workers to cut costs. An investor could buy $1 worth of RJR assets for 80 cents. With Philip Morris, the investor was paying $5.40.*

Another company, in a different industry, was British Steel (American Depository Receipts: BST). A comparison with two peer companies, USX Corp. (X) and Bethlehem Steel (BS) in August 1996, is enlightening, as illustrated in Table 10.2.

All steel stocks were depressed because of short-term economic fears, and concerns that steelmakers weren't able to make price hikes stick. However, development in emerging markets such as China and Eastern Europe promised robust growth, long-term. British Steel plays in a lot of these markets, meaning its prospects were perhaps better than peer companies. And its stock was selling at a discount to its book value, while its peer companies were selling at a premium.

Now let's take a look at a low P/BV stock that was a contrarian play. Illustrated in Table 10.3 is our friend, Read-Rite, the disk-drive parts maker, in Aug. 1, 1996.

As you can see, Read-Rite at this point represented a classic contrarian play. At $10.50, it was down 78.8 percent from its 52-week high of $49.50, and therefore met the down-by-half rule. It

---

*Neither company was a contrarian stock under our guidelines, since neither was down by half. From their highs, RJR would have had to fall to $17.50, and Philip Morris to $53.50. This illustrates that, while a tobacco stock may *appear* to be a contrarian play because there's an element of fear associated with it, that does not necessarily make it a "buy" under our guidelines. Truth be known, most investors at the time were holding on to their tobacco stocks and many analysts and portfolio managers viewed Philip Morris quite favorably.

Table 10.3   Read-Rite, August 1, 1996

	RDRT
Stock Price	$10.50
Dividend Yield	—
Book Value/Share	$11.68
Price/Book Value	0.899
52-Week Range	$9.63–$49.50
Trailing P/E	7.66

was trading at 7.66 times trailing earnings and its price/book value was 0.899—meaning it met two of our four fundamental contrarian indicators.

The stock would later jump into the mid-$30s, powered partly by improving prospects and then by a hostile takeover bid.

MAKING IT PAY

Henry Oppenheimer, an associate professor of finance at the State University of New York at Binghamton, tested Graham's premise. He studied the investment returns of stocks trading at 66 percent of their net current asset value or less during a 13-year stretch from Dec. 31, 1970 to Dec. 31, 1983. He rebalanced the portfolio each year. His findings: The mean average annual return of those stocks was 29.4 percent, versus 11.5 percent annually for the NYSE and AMEX indexes. A $10,000 investment in the low price/net current asset value (P/NCAV) portfolio at the beginning of the study would have grown to $254,973. Comparable figures were $37,296 for the NYSE-AMEX index and $101,992 for over-the-counter stocks.[2]

In a neat bit of understatement, Oppenheimer concluded that "on the whole, performance, when measured from any perspective, would have been quite satisfactory."[3]

The returns were not consistent, year over year. During one three-year stretch, the low price/net current asset portfolio returned only 0.6 percent per year, compared with 4.6 percent for the broad market portfolio. That supports the earlier point that contrarians must stick with their picks for at least three years.

Oppenheimer made two other interesting discoveries. First, the degree to which a company was undervalued by the market was key. In fact, on average, Oppenheimer found that the companies with the lowest ratio of stock-purchase price to net current assets offered the best returns. Those returns were well-ordered: The closer the stock price was the company's net current asset value (and hence the bigger the ratio), the smaller the return an investor would realize.

Finally, although Graham always counseled investors to buy shares in companies that had positive earnings and paid dividends, Oppenheimer found that "if anything, firms operating at a loss seem to have slightly higher returns and risk than firms with positive earnings."[4]

Tweedy, Browne Co. L.P., a value-oriented investment firm, took a look at both Graham's low price/net current asset value strategy, and one that used the more conventional low price/book value (low P/BV) approach, to show that investors can use both methods to earn market-whipping returns. Tweedy, Browne looked at 7,000 companies in the Compustat database, screening for those whose:

1. Shares were trading at 66 percent of their net current asset value, or less;

2. Were trading at no more than 140 percent of their book value (1.4 times book value).

Only companies with market capitalizations of $1 million or more were considered, although those that were acquired, merged, or went bankrupt were included in the results. Twelve years were considered, with portfolios being formed each April 30 from 1970 to 1981. The price/book value stocks were broken into nine groups. The lowest group consisted of stocks trading at less than 30 percent of book value, while the highest group was composed of stocks trading at 120 to 140 percent of book value. For each of the 12 portfolio formation dates, Tweedy, Browne calculated the returns for holding periods of six months, one year, two years, and three years after the stocks were picked.

The returns generated by both the portfolio of stocks trading at 66 percent of their net current asset value, and at a low ratio of price/book value, trounced the high price/book value portfolio and the S&P 500 in every holding period observed.

As we see in Table 10.4, the stocks trading at 0 to 30 percent of book value had an average return of 88 percent over the three-year

Table 10.4   Price in Relation to Book Value, Stocks Selling at 66% or Less
of Net Current Asset Value, April 30, 1970 through April 30, 1981

Stock Selection Criteria	3-Year Holding Period Avg. Return	3-Year Holding Period S&P 500
140%–120% of book value	48.9%	27.7%
120–100% of book value	45.3	27.7
100–80% of book value	51.5	27.7
80–70% of book value	57.9	27.7
70–60% of book value	62.1	27.7
60–50% of book value	72.6	27.7
50–40% of book value	77.9	27.7
40–30% of book value	73.5	27.7
30–0% of book value	88.0	27.7
66% of current NAV	87.6	31.5

Source: Tweedy, Browne

holding period, compared with 48.9 percent for the 120 to 140 percent of book value stocks, and 27.7 percent for the S&P 500. The
Graham-style portfolio (shares at 66 percent of net current asset
value) returned 87.6 percent.

An investor who, on April 30, 1970, invested $1 million in
stocks selling at less than 30 percent of their book value, and who
rolled that investment into a similar group of stocks each April 30
thereafter, would have ended up with more than $23.3 million as of
April 30, 1982. That compared with only $2.6 million for the S&P
500, the Tweedy, Browne study concluded.[5]

The return was even better for companies trading at 30 percent
of book value in which debt as a percentage of equity was 20 percent
or less. These "unleveraged," low price/book value stocks returned a
total of 113.7 percent on average over a three-year holding period,
compared to 98.8 percent for the Graham-style picks, 53.8 percent
for the high price/book value stocks and 27.7 percent for the S&P
500.

Other studies demonstrate the validity of the low price/book
value approach to investing:

1. Roger Ibbotson looked at the relationship between stock
price as a percentage of book value and the returns those NYSE-
listed stocks earned shareholders over an 18-year period ending Dec.
31, 1984. Sorting the stocks into deciles (10 equal parts) starting on

Dec. 31, 1966, and re-ranking them each Dec. 31, Ibbotson found that the 10 percent of stocks with the lowest price as a percentage of book value generated compound annual returns of 14.36 percent, compared with 6.06 percent for stocks in the highest decile. The compound annual return for the market-capitalization-weighted NYSE Index was 8.6 percent during the period of the study.[6]

2. Eugene Fama and Kenneth R. French looked at stock returns from July 1963 to December 1990 and found that low price/book value stocks provided the best returns within each capitalization category of stocks: small, medium, and large. But the very best returns were achieved by low P/BV small-cap companies. Fama and French looked at all non-financial companies listed on the NYSE, AMEX, and NASDAQ. They ranked them according to price as a percentage of book value and sorted them into deciles. Each price/book value decile was ranked according to the company's market capitalization and sorted into 10 equal parts again.

In the decile with the highest price/book value stocks, large-cap stocks returned an average of 11.2 percent per year, while their small-cap counterparts returned an average of 8.4 percent per year.

However, in the decile with the lowest price/book value stocks, big caps returned an average of 14.2 percent per year, while the low P/BV small-cap stocks returned a staggering 23 percent per year. Interestingly, when all companies in the lowest price/book value decile were thrown together, the average annual return was 19.6 percent, according to the researchers.[7]

3. Josef Lakonishok, Robert W. Vishny, and Andrei Shleifer looked at the returns from five-year holding periods for low price/book value stocks, finding that the final three years of that period accounted for the best returns. They looked at all NYSE and AMEX companies, ranking them into deciles from the highest to lowest ratios of price/book value. The study began on April 30, 1968 and new portfolios were created each April 30 thereafter. It concluded with data as of April 30, 1990. Each portfolio was held for five years.

On average, the highest price/book portfolios—which the researchers called "glamour stocks"—returned 9.3 percent annually during their five-year holding periods, compared to 19.8 percent for the lowest price/book value stocks.[8] The low price/book value shares, which they called "value stocks," returned an average of 17.3 percent the first year, 18.8 percent the second, 20.4 percent the third, 20.7 percent the fourth, and 21.5 percent in the fifth and final year of each holding period.[9]

This study also looked at risk, and whether low price/book value shares were riskier than high price/book value stocks. You might think low price/book stocks, being clearly out of favor with investors, might pose more risk. They didn't, the study found. Low price/book value stocks outperformed high price/book stocks in the worst 25 months of the stock market during the research period, as well as in 88 other months when the market dropped.[10]

How could that be? As we've said, contrarian investing doesn't just offer solid investment returns. It also reduces risk. Shares trading at a low price in relation to book value are usually out of favor for some reason. They have been mauled after a bad earnings report, are cyclical stocks suffering because investors fear a recession, or belong to companies facing major litigation. Much of the bad news is already reflected in the stock price. Many times, more bad news or even a break in the market has little effect on these beaten-down shares. Research shows that the downside for a well-diversified portfolio of stocks exhibiting contrarian value characteristics is less than the potential downside of the market as a whole. Its upside is much greater.

One last note on the price/book value study done by Lakonishok, Vishny, and Shleifer. True, they found that low price/book value stocks lose less than their high price/book value counterparts in down markets. But, these cheap stocks also beat their high-priced brethren during the best 25 months the market had during the study. They returned an average of 14.8 percent in each of those months, compared with only 11.4 percent for the high price/book value shares.[11]

Other research shows that the low price/book value effect doesn't just hold true for U.S. stocks. Among the studies are two worth considering:

1. Morgan Stanley looked at the stocks of all the companies in its international database during the 10 years from 1981 to 1990. About 80 percent of those companies were non-U.S. firms. The stocks were ranked according to their prices as a percentage of book value and sorted into 10 equal parts. Stocks in the lowest price/book value decile enjoyed a compound annual return of 23 percent, compared with 17.9 percent for the Morgan Stanley Capital International

Global Equity Index and 13.8 percent for the decile of stocks with the highest prices as a percentage of book value.

2. Three investment experts, including William F. Sharpe, a Nobel Prize winner in economics, looked at stocks in France, Germany, Switzerland, the United Kingdom, Japan, and the United States. In order to see if low price/book value stocks offered investors bigger returns than high price/book value stocks, they studied an 11½-year span from January 1981 to June 1992. They used the S&P 500 Index for the United States and the Morgan Stanley Capital international indexes for the other countries. The researchers divided the indexes in half according to market capitalization for each country: The top half, composed of the high price/book stocks for each country, were labeled the "growth" portfolio; the low price/book stocks, the "value" portfolio.

The monthly return for each of the two portfolios for each country was the return of the underlying stocks in the portfolios, weighted according to their market capitalization. The researchers then computed the cumulative difference between the investment returns generated by the value stocks over the growth stocks. In other words, they calculated how much more an investor would have

Table 10.5 The Extra Investment Returns from Value Stocks as Compared to Growth Stocks in France, Germany, Switzerland, the United Kingdom, Japan, and the United States, January 1981 through June 1992

Country	Cumulative Extra Investment Return from Value Stocks vs. Growth Stocks over 11½-Year-Period January 1981 through June 1992
France	73.7%
Germany	17.7
Switzerland	42.7
United Kingdom	31.5
Japan	69.5
United States	15.6
Global (i.e., all of the above)	39.5
Europe	31.9

Source: Tweedy, Browne, *Financial Analysts Journal*

reaped by investing in the value portfolios than they would have in the growth portfolios for each country.

Table 10.5 shows performance differences for the countries studied. In each market, the value portfolio beat the growth portfolio: The performance difference ranged from 15.6 percent more in the United States to 73.7 percent more in France.[12]

When searching out low P/BV stocks, here are some tip-offs to watch for:

1. Graham liked to find stocks trading at two-thirds or less of the company's net current asset value.

2. David Dreman, who specializes in low P/E stocks, buttresses that technique by looking for low P/BV stocks of companies with balance sheets in which debt is less than 40 percent of capital.[13]

3. Tweedy, Browne says investors trying to ferret out low price/book value shares should be on the lookout for these indicators. All will strike a chord with contrarians:

   • Low P/E ratios
   • Low price/sales ratios
   • Low prices in relation to "normalized earnings," that is, what the company would earn if it had the average return on equity for its industry, or if it had the average profit margin on sales for its industry*
   • Current earnings that are substantially depressed from prior levels of earnings
   • And a stock price that has dropped substantially from previous levels, meaning the company's market capitalization has dropped significantly (we recommend at least 50 percent)

When evaluating companies that meet these criteria, also look to see if any:

1. Show heavy insider buying (at least $120,000 is our guideline);

---

* Profit Margin = Net Income/Sales

2. Are seeing their shares being accumulated by other companies, or big-name investors;

3. Are buying back their own stock;

4. Or have replaced top management—particularly with executives from outside the company.

Any of these four technical analysis indicators hint that others see value where the general market does not, warranting a closer look at that stock.

Summary

After finding stocks down 50 percent from their 52-week highs, contrarians can apply four different fundamental screens as confirming indicators, looking for stocks that meet two of the criteria. Using two provides a cross-check and additional confirmation lacking in a single indicator. For instance, companies in the grocery business often sport minuscule prices to sales per share; however, this is the norm and not a contrarian indication. Among the four indicators to use are stocks trading at less than book value. A great deal of research shows that stocks trading at a low ratio of price/book value outperform the broad market while reducing portfolio risk. A P/BV of less than 1.0 helps a stock qualify as a contrarian play.

Endnotes

1. Graham, Benjamin, and Dodd, David, *Security Analysis*, McGraw-Hill, New York, 1988, pp. 318–319.

2. Oppenheimer, Henry, "Ben Graham's Net Current Asset Values: A Performance Update," *Financial Analysts Journal*, November/December 1986, pp. 42–43.

3. Ibid, p. 43.

4. Ibid, p. 46.

5. Tweedy, Browne Co. L.P., *What Has Worked in Investing: Studies of Investment Approaches and Characteristics Associated With Exceptional Returns*, Tweedy, Browne Co. L.P., New York, 1996, p. 6.

6. Ibid, p. 3.

7. Ibid, p. 8.

8. Lakonishok, Josef, et al., "Contrarian Investment, Extrapolation, and Risk, *The Journal of Finance*, December 1994, p. 1547.

9. Ibid, p. 1548.

10. Ibid.

11. Ibid, p. 1570.

12. Sharpe, William F., et al., "International Value and Growth Stock Returns," *Financial Analysts Journal*, January/February 1993, pp. 27–31.

13. Maturi, Richard J., *Stock Picking: The 11 Best Tactics for Beating the Market*, McGraw-Hill, New York, 1993, p. 8.

CHAPTER 11

PANNING FOR VALUE: CASH FLOW AND PRICE/SALES

There are more fools among buyers than among sellers.

—French proverb

Financier Donald "The Donald" Trump once told *The Wall Street Journal* that "Cash is King." He was only partly right. In truth, cash flow is king. That's especially true for contrarians sifting the muck for out-of-favor stocks. They look for companies with low price/earnings ratios (P/E), and they want companies selling at a fraction of book value; but contrarians also like to have companies with a good cash flow.

BUYING CASH FLOW ON THE CHEAP

With a stock that's down by half, we can use fundamental ratio analysis as a confirming indicator. And one of the most valid fundamental ratios is cash flow.

Cash flow allows a troubled company to keep paying that fat 5-percent dividend, or to buy back shares to placate disgruntled shareholders and support the stock price. Cash flow gives that company maneuvering room to pull clear of its problems. And cash flow lets it rebuild existing businesses, acquire other promising companies, or even start new ones. Cash flow is raw power. Cash flow *is* king.

As we do with earnings and assets, contrarians want to buy cash flow on sale. Can that be done? In a word, yes. In this chapter, we're going to show how a low price/free cash flow (low P/FCF) ratio can serve as a confirming buy indicator on a contrarian stock.

> *The Practical Effect:* On a stock that's down 50 percent from its 52-week high, a P/FCF ratio of less than 10 (in concert with one other of our contrarian fundamental indicators) is enough to make a stock a "buy."

The Skinny on Cash Flow

Cash flow is one of the more difficult accounting concepts to master. Entire books are devoted to calculating cash flow, and its close cousin, "free-cash flow."* We need a quick introduction to the concept before we demonstrate how a low P/FCF ratio can be used as a contrarian indicator. We should say here that contrarians probably won't have to actually calculate cash flow. Nearly any brokerage report on a company will include cash-flow figures, computed by a professional analyst. Even so, contrarians must understand the importance of cash flow, and how it is computed, in order to have confidence in using it as a confirming buy indicator.

Cash flow is the flow of funds both in and out of a business. It can be negative as well as positive. A firm that has more cash coming in than going out has a "positive" cash flow. A company with less cash coming in than is going out has a "negative" cash flow. A company with persistent negative cash flow is headed for serious financial problems. Often the solution is to sell more stock, which "dilutes" the value of each shareholder's stake.

We calculate cash flow by starting with a company's net income and adding back such "non-cash" accounting items as depreciation and amortization. Because depreciation reduces a company's

---

* Various research focuses on different types of cash flow: Some look at cash flow and others at free cash flow. We based our rule on free cash flow because it's a tougher hurdle for a company to clear and puts the odds even more in your favor.

book profits, but does not actually take cash out of the till, many investment analysts consider cash flow a better measure of a company's health than reported profits.

Example

1. Company earns net income of $10,000,000.
2. This net income includes, as an expense, $500,000 in equipment depreciation. (This is an accounting entry only. No cash is actually spent.)

    Result: Cash flow equals $10,500,000.

Still other investment experts contend another cash-flow measure—"free-cash flow"—is an even better indicator. Several accounting definitions for free cash flow (FCF) exist. Cash-flow gurus Kenneth S. Hackel and Joshua Livnat say free cash flow is the amount of cash generated by a business that exceeds the amount needed to buy inventories, replace equipment, or build new factories.[1]

Good business managers recognize the need to invest for future growth and they make those investments when needed. But some companies generate more cash than their businesses need to grow. That surplus is free cash flow, cash that can be used to buy back stock, boost dividends, buy complementary businesses, or create hot new products.

One good definition of free cash flow is:

$$FCF = Pre\text{-}tax\ Income - Capital\ Spending$$

While others look at "Surplus Cash Flow":

$$SCF = Pre\text{-}tax\ income + Depreciation - Capital\ Spending$$

As you can see, analyzing and defining cash flow and free cash flow requires a thorough grounding in accounting. Since this knowledge is highly specialized, it is okay to rely on professional analysis to save time.

One easy way to find companies that generate more cash than they need is through Value Line, the investment-information service. Value Line's weekly listing of "Biggest Free Cash Flow Generators" ranks companies by the ratio of cash taken in to cash needed

to pay dividends and update factories and equipment. Wall Street
analysts and their stock reports offer cash flow and its cousins as a
standard piece of analysis. Other information services that offer individual company reports, like Standard and Poor's, also calculate
price/free cash flow figures.

Let's take a look at a comparison between RJR Nabisco and
Philip Morris in 1996. As we said in Chapter 10, neither of these
stocks qualified as true contrarian plays because their shares were not
down 50 percent. Neither were the shares trading at P/FCF ratios of
less than 10. But tobacco companies are huge cash-flow generators and
provide good examples of what a low P/FCF stock looks like.

Company	CF/Share	Free Cash Flow/Share	Price/FCF
RN	$5.10	$6.02	11.04
MO	7.95	2.82	16.78

As we can see, RJR traded at a lower multiple to free cash flow
than Philip Morris. This becomes more significant when we recall
that it also is a low price/book value stock. When using our four
fundamental indicators (low price/earnings, low price/book value,
low price/sales, and low price/free cash flow), we often find companies that meet two of these four ratio requirements.

The Practical Effect: A stock that's down by half and meets
two of our four fundamental indicators qualifies as a buy.

A company meeting all four of our fundamental-ratio indicators
would have to be scrutinized very carefully. It might well be too sick
to survive. Today's ratios can change dramatically tomorrow, so
contrarians must be skeptical of any stock that appears to have too
much going for it—from a contrarian standpoint, that is. A market
pricing a stock very cheaply on every level might be signaling more
trouble to come.

Cashing in on Cash Flow

Several studies demonstrate that buying low price/free cash
flow stocks is another way to pick superior stocks and reduce risk.

David Dreman looked at the 750 largest public companies from 1963 to 1985, ranked their stocks based on cash flow to market price, and measured their subsequent returns. The stocks with the lowest price/cash flow ratios generated a 20.1 percent total annual return, versus 10.7 percent for companies with the highest price/cash flow ratios.[2]

As part of their in-depth look at contrarian investing, professors Lakonishok, Vishny, and Shleifer studied the returns investors could reap by picking low price/cash flow shares. The professors ranked all companies on the NYSE and AMEX according to their P/CF ratios, for a 22-year period ending in 1990, and arranged them in 10 equal groups (deciles). As we can see in Table 11.1, the low price/cash flow stocks consistently outperformed the shares of companies with high price/cash flow ratios.[3]

Note, for example, that lowest price/cash flow stocks returned an average of 20 percent per year, compared to 9.1 percent for the highest price/cash flow stocks. The lowest price/cash flow shares provided an average cumulative return for the five-year stretch of 149 percent, compared to only 54 percent for their highest price/cash flow counterparts.

The professors' research underscores that contrarians can score by giving their strategy time to work. The low price/cash flow stocks, which made up 20 percent of the companies in the study, *did not* beat the high price/cash flow stocks, which comprised 20 percent

Table 11.1   **Investment Returns in Relation to Price/Cash Flow Ratios for all New York Stock Exchange and American Stock Exchange Listed Companies, April 1968 through April 1990**

Holding Period Following Portfolio Formation	Price/Cash Flow Ratio Decile									
	High P/CF Ratio . . . . *Low P/CF Ratio*									
	Percent Returns									
1st year	8.4%	12.4%	14.0%	14.0%	15.3%	14.8%	15.7%	17.8%	18.3%	18.3%
2nd year	6.7	10.8	12.6	15.3	15.6	17.0	17.7	18.0	18.3	19.0
3rd year	9.6	13.3	15.3	17.2	17.0	19.1	19.1	20.2	19.3	20.4
4th year	9.8	11.1	14.6	15.9	16.6	17.2	18.2	19.2	22.3	21.8
5th year	10.8	13.4	16.1	16.2	18.7	17.7	19.1	20.9	21.2	20.8
Average annual return over the 5-year period	9.1	12.2	14.5	15.7	16.6	17.1	18.0	19.2	19.9	20.1
Cumulative 5-year return	54	77	96	107	115	120	128	140	147	149

Source: Tweedy, Browne

of the companies, in every one of the 22 years looked at in the study. For holding periods of one year, for example, the average return of the low price/cash flow stocks were better than the average returns of their more-expensive counterparts in 17 of the 22 years. For three-year holding periods, the low-priced free cash flow stocks beat the higher-priced stocks in 20 of the 22 years. And for five-year holding periods, the average returns of the low P/CF stocks were better than the higher-priced counterparts *in each one* of the 22 years studied.[4]

> ***The Practical Effect:*** Time and again, our research has shown that returns using a contrarian strategy improve tremendously when we hold stocks for two to three years. Lower transaction costs, and long-term capital gains advantages are additional benefits.

In addition, the three professors found that low P/CF stocks— like low P/E stocks and low P/BV stocks—appear to reduce risk if placed in a well-diversified portfolio. Low P/CF stocks declined substantially less than high price/cash flow stocks during the worst 25 months of the market looked at in the study. This was also true, although to a lesser extent, in the next worst 88 months. The returns of both stock groups were about even in the 25 best months of the market, and in the next-best 122 months of the market.[5]

If you had wanted to buy high P/CF stocks, and keep pace with their low P/CF counterparts, you could have done so only with exquisite market timing. Contrarians do not rely on market timing. They rely on purchasing stocks at compelling valuations.

Hackel and Livnat conducted a similar study covering the period 1980 to 1994. The researchers' approach was much more involved than looking at low price/free cash flow stocks, but their conclusions were about the same.

Hackel and Livnat included in their portfolio only the companies whose ratio of market value/free cash flow was in the bottom 20 percent of all companies selected, after applying other valuation filters. (They looked for companies with debt/equity ratios below 0.40, etc.) In other words, they ranked the companies in descending order based on free cash flow ratios. Only firms in the bottom fifth were considered low market value/free cash flow stocks.

The new portfolios were chosen each December 31 (for the 1980 portfolio, the stocks were chosen December 31, 1979), held for one year, and traded in for the new portfolio. In their book, *Cash Flow and Security Analysis*, Hackel and Livnat state that their "free-cash-flow portfolio" generated an average annual return of 19.2 percent, 4.1 percent above the S&P 500 for the same period.[6]

POCKETING PROFITS ON LOW PRICE/SALES STOCKS

The final fundamental analysis tool in the contrarian's kit is the price/sales (P/S) ratio. When analyzing a stock, investors focus a lot of attention on a company's earnings. Are they growing? At what rate? Is that rate sustainable? Earnings are important. But so are sales.

> ***The Practical Effect:*** Under our guidelines, any stock that's down by half, has a P/S ratio of less than 1.0, and meets one other of our fundamental indicators qualifies as a contrarian "buy."

Centering on Sales

After George M.C. Fisher was hired away from Motorola to engineer a turnaround at Eastman Kodak in 1993, some analysts began pushing for deep layoffs, a strategy that dramatically slashes costs—and can just as dramatically boost profits.* But Fisher would not be pressured. Indeed, by way of reply, Fisher would often tell reporters: "You can't cost-cut your way to greatness, you've got to have growth." Fisher wasn't talking just about growth in profits, but growth in sales.

If a company's sales aren't growing, its chance for sustained profits go out the window. And sometimes, even when a company's sales are rising, profits aren't. Startup costs for a new product, one-time charges to settle a lawsuit or pay for layoffs, or an outlay for an acquisition can squelch profits in a given quarter. Stagnant, or falling, profits often

---

*Bill began covering Kodak just before its CEO was ousted by the company's board of directors and Fisher brought aboard.

translate into a meandering, or falling, stock price. We need to think of sales as the "raw material" for all the other good things we want: rising earnings, a boost in dividends, and, a higher stock price.

A cursory look at a company's income statement reveals why a growth in sales is referred to as "top-line growth." The first line on an income statement is always net sales, or total revenues, or whatever that company calls the money it takes in from its businesses. From that, the company subtracts its expenses: wages for its workers, costs for raw materials, advertising and new equipment, write-offs, interest payments on its debt, and the taxes it owes on its sales. Whatever is left is the company's profit—its bottom line.

It sounds pretty basic—until we look more closely. Every year, the cost of doing business increases. Workers get raises, materials get more expensive, healthcare costs continue their advance, and taxes rise. Fisher told Bill that, at Kodak, costs rose by about $300 million each year. That's why Fisher put so much emphasis on sales growth. Without that "raw material," sustained profit growth wasn't possible.[*]

Indeed, a company that does not increase sales has to cut costs just to stay even. And a firm can only do that so long before a long-term decline begins.

■ *NOTES FROM A CONTRARIAN PORTFOLIO MANAGER*

I was once on a conference call for portfolio managers and the speaker was trying to explain how a major layoff at a Fortune 100 company was good for the company and its stock price. This "downsizing," or purging, of 5 percent of the company's work force had prompted a 10-percent jump in its stock price.

Quipped one wag: "I guess if they laid everybody off, the stock would triple." ■

Companies often fall into trouble, but only some of them become contrarian opportunities. One way to evaluate that opportunity is by using the stock's price/sales (P/S) ratio. Like other ratios, it is expressed in terms of stock price as a percentage of sales per share.[†] With a stock that's down 50 percent from its 12-month high,

---

[*] And when sales growth did finally stall, Kodak's stock price plunged and the company had to announce yet another layoff.
[†] Sales/Share = Total Sales/Total Shares Outstanding.

the low P/S ratio can be used as one of two fundamental-analysis "buy" indicators.

We define a low price/sales ratio as one that's less than 1.0. Computing it is easy.

Example

- A company has sales of $700 million.
- It has 100 million shares outstanding.
- The stock is trading at $6.00.

1. Compute sales per share ($700 million in sales/100 million shares outstanding = $7.00 sales/share)
2. Divide this number into the stock price

   $6.00 stock price/$7.00 sales per share = P/S ratio of 0.85

This ratio simply means that the market is valuing each dollar of sales per share at 85 cents. Or, put another way, each dollar value of stock is backed by $1.16 in sales ($7 sales per share/$6 stock price).

Is a low P/S ratio a valid contrarian "buy" indicator? Experts say yes. In his book, *What Works on Wall Street*, author James P. O'Shaughnessy looked at the returns generated by low P/S stocks over a 43-year period ending in 1994.[*7] His question was simple: How would investors have fared had they dedicated $10,000 to the 50 stocks with the lowest P/S ratio each December 31? He studied the period 1951 through year-end 1993. The holding period for each stock was one year (which is why the last purchase was made in 1993, but the study ended in 1994).

The result: A compound annual return of 16.01 percent, compared with 12.81 percent earned in a broad basket of stocks with market capitalizations greater than $150 million. The difference between the returns: $10,000 invested in the low price/sales portfolio grew to $5.9 million, while the same amount placed in the basket of stocks yielded only $1.7 million.

Conversely, if an investor bought the 50 stocks with the highest P/S ratios, the annual compound growth rate was only 4.72 percent.[8] This underperformance by high P/S stocks confirms the wisdom of buying low P/S stocks.

---

[*] O'Shaughnessy's book is an excellent study of many different portfolio-management systems. Indeed, it's a must-have for any serious investor.

In fact, low P/S stocks beat stocks in general in 28 of the 43 years studied and was the most rewarding of all quantitative investment strategies O'Shaughnessy examined; he looked at several dozen.

■ NOTES FROM A CONTRARIAN BUSINESS REPORTER

During our research, both Tony and I were struck by how consistently this low-valuation theme repeated itself. Time and time again, a low-valuation ratio (such as a low P/E or low P/S ratio) led to portfolio performance that was better than the broad market. Even more interesting was how high-valuation ratios would result in a portfolio that performed significantly worse than the market.

- *A high P/E approach underperformed the market.*
- *A high P/S approach underperformed the market.*
- *A high P/FCF approach underperformed the market.*
- *A high P/BV approach underperformed the market.*

If you really think about it, though, this makes real sense. When you buy a stock sporting a low valuation, you are essentially buying it on sale—getting a bargain. We look for bargains when we shop for groceries or cars, and should think the same way when shopping for stocks.   ■

One thing we should note, however, is that all the strategies O'Shaughnessy studied required investors to rotate their portfolios each year. That runs up transaction costs, eating into returns—particularly for individual investors buying relatively small blocks of stock each time. What's more, as our research and some of our case studies show, "bad news" stocks often don't generate their biggest returns until the second or third year after they are purchased.

Let's look at a stock that met the low P/S criteria in August 1996 as we were researching this book. We'll pair up competing chipmakers, Intel (INTC) and Advanced Micro Devices (AMD).

August 15, 1996

Symbol	Price	52-Week Range	P/S Ratio
INTC	$81.625	$49.81–$83.25	4.45
AMD	13.125	10.25–36.00	0.57

Intel is the world's leading maker of microprocessors, the "brains" of any personal computer. Advanced Micro Devices had for many years been a successful cloner of Intel chips, but was finally forced to design, make, and market its own microprocessors. It slipped behind and, to catch up, acquired a smaller chipmaker called NexGen that had better technology. Production problems, a slowdown in PC sales, and concerns about the amount of money AMD would need to build its own chip factories zapped the company's shares. However, in its favor was a big side business with computer networkers, a huge growth area in the computer industry.

These factors alone did not necessarily make AMD shares a contrarian buy.* While AMD met two important criteria—a price decline of 50 percent and a low P/S ratio, contrarians often avoid high-tech stocks. Many are flash-in-the-pan "story" stocks that are tough to analyze without expert knowledge. Comparing it with a peer company gives some perspective and, for those smitten with tech shares, a starting point for further analysis.

The Price is Right

If O'Shaughnessy is right, and low P/S stocks offer the best returns, why is that so?

First, while earnings are subject to a whole series of accounting maneuvers, sales are straightforward. That's why the P/S ratio is more dependable; unlike earnings, it's tougher to massage sales figures. Second, companies with low P/S ratios tend to be established enterprises that have a solid core of sales.[9] Interestingly, companies with low P/S ratios often sport some of the other contrarian fundamental indicators discussed: low P/E ratios and low P/BV ratios, among them.

Xerox had all the elements of a classic contrarian purchase. It was a large, well-established company with excellent products, a brand-name franchise, and depth in both financial and management talent. And as part of a planned transition, Kearns would give way to a protégé, Paul A. Allaire. Allaire would build on some of his mentor's policies, but would make some of his own changes, too,

---

*Tony did eventually purchase AMD shares for a contrarian portfolio he manages, because it did meet our fundamental indicators. He bought the stock at $12.63 Sept. 4, 1996 and sold it at $47 on March 12, 1997.

such as selling the financial-services businesses and moving very aggressively into digital copiers that could be tied into computer networks.

The Practical Effect: Generally, when a company falls on tough times, investors tend to downplay the ability of management to bring about change. In fact, investors often magnify the problems, pushing the stock down well below fair value.

Large companies such as Xerox have deep pockets, a brand name, good technology, and a big base of customers. Sure it takes a lot to turn a big ship around, but remember that it's also hard to sink one.

SUMMARY

Research is compelling in showing that stocks with low price/free cash flow ratios are attractive investments. The contrarian uses a P/FCF ratio of less than 10 as a confirming indicator that the stock has been sold down to an extremely low valuation. This, combined with other contrarian indicators, helps screen potential picks. Since cash flow analysis is often technical in nature, requiring a thorough grounding in financial accounting, contrarians rely on professional analysts for these numbers. Time is better spent on other tasks.

Once a stock exhibits a 50 percent or greater price decline, the hammer is cocked and the contrarian seeks the confirmation needed to pull the trigger and buy the battered stock. Substantial research has shown that a low P/S ratio can provide that corroboration. While we don't believe that a low P/S ratio, in combination with a 50 percent price decline, is enough to warrant purchase, this ratio in concert with one of our three other fundamental screens is enough to warrant purchase. A P/S ratio of less than 1.0 is a validating indicator.

Contrarians want to avoid buying stock in a company that's headed out of business. Getting shares in a name-brand firm like

Xerox dramatically reduces that risk. On a stock that's down by half, look for those that meet two of our four fundamental financial ratios:

- A P/E of less than 12.
- A P/BV ratio of less than 1.0.
- A P/FCF ratio of less than 10.
- And a P/S ratio of less than 1.0.

■ ——————— **CONTRARIAN CASE** ——————— ■

RESTRUCTURING PLAYS:
FUNDAMENTALLY ATTRACTIVE

A big company doesn't have to fire its CEO to be a contrarian stock. Restructuring plays can generate nice returns, too. They demand patience because the payday is very often two or even three years away. But that payday can be well worth the wait.

Bad news—especially bad news that seems to linger—can really sink a stock. Sometimes a company is afflicted with several different problems that combine to keep investors away. Let's look at one of those companies: Xerox Corp.

XEROX: A DOCUMENTED TURNAROUND

If you had the chance to buy shares in a troubled brand-name company, and you could earn 10 percent on your money while you waited for management to fix the problems, would you do it? Of course. So would we. Apparently, however, most others would not. Xerox presents an interesting contrarian study because it was a blue-chip stock exhibiting several of the key indicators we've outlined.

Everything we're going to discuss was in plain view, and yet, most people missed it.

In late 1990, Xerox shares closed as low as $9.70, while sporting a $1 per share dividend. This means the stock was yielding a bit more than 10 percent.* The firm was facing tough times, to be sure. Key markets such as Europe and Latin America were experiencing wrenching economic problems. And, though investors weren't sure of it at the time, the United States was in for a full-fledged recession.

Xerox faced other difficulties, too. But these were of its own making. As we all know, Xerox invented the photocopier, marketing its first machine, the 914, in 1959. The 914 was an immense success, creating an entire new industry. But no company as profitable as Xerox enjoys its monopoly forever. Those big profits were an open invitation for rivals to move in on the market. Move in

---

* Stock prices have not been adjusted to reflect a three-for-one stock split the company finalized in 1996. The low, adjusted for the split, was $9.70 per share.

they did. By the late 1970s and early 1980s, Xerox was in big trouble; its Japanese rivals were selling copiers for less than it cost Xerox to make them.

Shortly after taking over as chairman in 1982, David T. Kearns realized that Xerox could be heading out of business. It would take a long time, maybe even the rest of the decade. Nevertheless, the company was destined for ruin, and Kearns knew he had to act fast.

He forced the company to embrace Total Quality Management, a self-improvement philosophy that focused on total customer satisfaction. TQM worked, and by the late 1980s, Xerox's profitable copiers were wowing customers again. But as part of Kearns' fix-it strategy, Xerox diversified into businesses that weren't a Xerox strength: financial services, property-and-casualty insurance, and real estate. When those businesses stumbled, so did Xerox.

In 1990, for instance, Xerox, which only the year before had won the Malcolm Baldrige National Quality Award, took a $375 million write-off to shut down a real-estate venture. Partly because of that boondoggle, Xerox would report year-end earnings of only $1.66 per share, down from $6.56 the year before. Management recognized the problem and decided the company would get rid of any business that could not provide a 15-percent return on equity.

The contrarian buy signals were all there: At $9.70 a share, the stock was down slightly more than 50 percent from its Dec. 5, 1989 high, meaning it met our initial "down-by-half rule." It also met two of our four key fundamental indicators: It had a P/E of about 7.0 and sported a P/BV ratio of 0.6. The subjective signals were also there: troubled businesses and investor concern that those troubles could not be easily fixed.

One last point: The immense dividend yield meant a nice income stream even if the dividend were cut, as the market obviously expected it would be.

Xerox would weather the recession, buttress its office-equipment business and, eventually, sell off its insurance and financial-services businesses. In Table 11.2, you can see the results. Although we generally advocate selling a turnaround play within three years after purchase (or after a 50-percent rise in stock price), the fact that you would still be getting a 10-percent return on your original money would have been a pretty strong inducement to hold on.

Table 11.2 shows how you would have done versus the broader market had you stayed in the stock.

Table 11.2   Xerox, October 1990 to August 1997

Date	Stock Closing Price	Dow Close	Pct. Stock Gain (Cumulative)	Pct. Market Gain
Oct. 26, 1990	$ 9.70	2436.14	N/A	N/A
Oct. 28, 1991	20.55	3045.62	112%	25%
Oct. 26, 1992	26.08	3244.11	169	33
Oct. 26, 1993	24.08	3672.49	148	51
Oct. 26, 1994	36.13	3848.23	272	58
Oct. 26, 1995	42.67	4703.82	340	93
Oct. 28, 1996	46.38	5972.73	378	145
Aug. 5, 1997	83.88	8187.54	765	236

Endnotes

1. Hackel, Kenneth S., Livnat, Joshua, *Cash Flows and Securities Analysis*, 2nd edition, Irwin, Chicago, IL, 1996. This work is generally regarded as the best text available on the topic of cash flow analysis.

2. Maturi, Richard J., *Stock Picking: The 11 Best Tactics for Beating the Market*, McGraw Hill, New York, 1993, p. 22.

3. Lakonishok, Josef, et al., "Contrarian Investment, Extrapolation, and Risk," *The Journal of Finance*, December 1974, pp. 1541–1578. Also see O'Shaughnessy, James P., *What Works on Wall Street*, McGraw Hill, New York, pp. 25–26.

4. Lakonishok, et al.

5. Ibid.

6. Hackel, Kenneth S., and Livnat, Joshua, *Cash Flows and Security Analysis*, 2nd edition, Irwin, Chicago, IL, pp. 433–444, 1996.

7. O'Shaughnessy, James P., *What Works on Wall Street*, McGraw-Hill, New York, 1996.

8. Ibid, pp. 105–106.

9. Sturm, Paul, "A Value Picker's Best Friend," *Smart Money*, May 1996, p. 63.

CONTRARIAN SELL SIGNALS

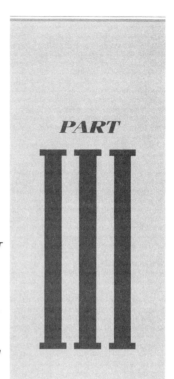

PART

III

CHAPTER 12

MINIMIZING RISK: CONTRARIAN STRATEGIES

The dinosaur's eloquent lesson is that if some bigness is good, an overabundance of bigness is not necessarily better.

—Eric A. Johnson

When investors look at a stock for purchase, they typically focus on return, asking: "How much can I earn on this investment?" What they don't often ask is "How much risk must I take to get that return?" Contrarian investing is a way to deal with both of those questions. We can buy beaten-down stocks, but we have to address the risks that come with buying the shares of companies in distress.

In this chapter, we're going to look at what works, and what doesn't, when it comes to managing stock-market risk. Just as we have with analyzing, buying, and selling contrarian stocks, we've composed a simple set of rules to help you manage risk. They are:

- No single stock should constitute more than 5 percent of a contrarian portfolio. Three percent is an even better cutoff.

- Make sure each investment "theme" (rising interest rates, for example), makes up no more than 20 percent of your portfolio.

Fifteen percent or even 10 percent is a better limit to avoid concentrating your risk.

- If a stock falls 25 percent from the price you paid for it, sell it. Indeed, with each stock you buy, put in place a stop-loss order that does this for you automatically. Sell your losers and look for better opportunities.

THE TRADER'S VIEW

We can learn a lot by studying the risk-management strategies of a commodities trader. Contrarians aren't traders because they're not trying to pick off quick profits through a series of lightning-fast transactions. Even so, contrarians face the same challenge as the frenetic trader in the soybean pit—controlling losses to avoid total collapse.

In futures trading, risk control and money management is everything. (Since this isn't a book about commodities trading, we'll ask you to accept some of this without a long explanation. We have included a list of good sources, however, in Appendix B, The Contrarian Library.) Indeed, risk control is even more important than deciding when to buy or sell a commodity. Since futures trading depends so much on leverage—using a little bit of equity to control large dollar amounts of futures contracts—the trader is taking on a lot more risk than someone simply buying stocks with cash.

For instance, when investors buy a gold contract, they are buying the right to take delivery of 100 ounces of gold. If gold is trading at $400 when the contract is purchased, the investor controls $40,000 worth of gold. The broker will ask only that $2,000 in "margin," or good-faith money, be deposited to hold that position. That means that a $12 dip in gold will result in a $1,200 loss.

That loss will wipe out more than half the investment, and can come in just a few moments' time. In trading a $200,000 account, it is not unusual to have a movement of $10,000, or 5 percent, in a single day. Compare that with the conservative bond market, where an entire year could pass without a 5 percent loss.

With such a high level of risk, the commodity trader has to be quick to cut his losses short. If he doesn't, those losses can sap all his capital. The commodity trader's obsession with risk should be taken to heart by *all* investors—even contrarians buying stocks. Yet, as we noted earlier, most investors focus on the *return* they hope to earn and give only passing thought to managing *risk*. That's a mistake: As an investor, you can't notch long-term profits if you lose all your money in a series of short-term unprofitable stock picks.

THE ESSENCE OF RISK

Risk is defined in many ways. To some, risk is the portfolio's volatility (how violently it goes up and down relative to the market). To others, risk is defined as the potential for total loss.

We define risk more specifically. Risk is the event, or events, that so discourage investors that they abandon the long-term investment strategies that generate higher returns. Therefore, we need to invest in a manner that keeps us from becoming discouraged, from abandoning our strategy, or from quitting altogether. If we stick with a good investment plan, we can profit in the long run by enjoying the positive returns of common stocks over time.

■ *NOTES FROM A CONTRARIAN PORTFOLIO MANAGER*

During the two decades I have been managing money, I've seen a lot of investment strategies that can work if followed consistently over time. Buying and holding a diversified portfolio of blue chip stocks can work. Buying stocks with strong Value Line rankings can work. Following good analysts can work. Hiring a good money manager or buying a good fund can work.

In short, there are plenty of ways to approach the stock market and make money. But I've found that the greatest risk facing stock-market investors is the loss of more money than they can tolerate, usually in a bear market. Fear of still more losses puts them on the sidelines for years afterward, meaning they miss a good portion of the next bull market. Little wonder that investors tend to increase their risk near the end of bull markets, and slash their risk toward the end of bear markets.

Much better to temper enthusiasm when things are good and develop enthusiasm when things look bleak. This is what contrarians do and it helps them stay the course. ■

The Long-Term View

Investing is a marathon, not a footrace. Every investor should develop a well-reasoned strategy that leads to long-term profits. Surviving over a long period gives the strategy time to work. This focus on the long run—coupled with a sound strategy—assures success.

Let's consider a simple example of two fictitious investors, Randall and Allison, both using the same investment strategy. One succeeds, the other doesn't.

Randall decides he will buy a stock index fund that tracks the S&P 500. He will hold that fund for 20 years, and sell it at retirement. Simple. His co-worker, Allison, intrigued by the idea, decides to do the same.

Randall, excited about the potential return, goes to his bank and takes out a personal loan for $25,000 to use as his retirement grubstake. The 8 percent initial interest rate on the loan, he reasons, is less than the long-run annual return of 10 to 12 percent he expects to earn from his index fund. The monthly payment is well within his means. The interest rate is adjustable, meaning it can rise or fall with general interest rates. But since the Federal Reserve seems to have inflation in check, Randall doesn't expect his payment to rise anytime soon.

Allison invests $25,000 from her savings account. One year later, inflation surfaces. Interest rates have risen two percentage points and, in response, the stock market has dropped 15 percent. Randall and Allison have each lost $3,750 ($25,000 × 15 percent = $3,750). Both regret the loss, but figure they will make it up—and then some—over the long haul. Randall admits to a bit of nervousness, but can easily handle the slightly higher payment on his floating-rate loan.

Two years into the strategy, the stock market has dropped another 10 percent, but shows signs of bottoming. Interest rates have started to retreat, as a mild recession takes hold. Both Randall and Allison have less than $20,000 in their retirement accounts. The recession has been tough on their employer but, fortunately, both still have jobs. Their local bank hasn't been so lucky, however. Burdened by a portfolio of bad loans (they lent too freely when times seemed good), the bank is forced into a merger with a larger, cross-town rival. As part of the merger terms, the new bank owner calls in all demand loans of less than $100,000.

Randall pleads with the bank, to no avail. The new managers are sympathetic, but are reining in the kind of lending that got Randall's bank into trouble in the first place. He has no choice but to sell his mutual fund, and makes good on the losses by draining savings that were earmarked for the down payment on a new car.

Randall is out of the market.

Meanwhile, Allison is profiting because of her patience and discipline—and a risk level much lower than Randall's. As a bull market takes hold, Allison sees her mutual fund jump 40 percent over the next three years.

Randall totals up his costs:

Two years' interest	$ 4,800
Loss on investment	$ 5,875
Total Loss	$10,675 (42 percent of his investment)

Both investors had the same strategy. Both intended to see it through. Both made precisely the same investment. The difference between them: their level of risk.

Randall ignored the risk of leverage and was unable to remain invested into the long run. We believe most investors fail because they pay too little attention to risk. They take a stock tip from a friend and bet heavily without doing any of their own research. They borrow money to take bigger stock positions, without considering what will happen if the market turns against them.* Or they embrace a "get-rich-quick" strategy, hoping to strike it big right now in gold-rush fashion, with no thought of making it into the long run.

With proper risk control, we can consistently make the wrong investment decision and still show a profit. To see what we mean, let's look at another example.

Al takes $100,000 and buys four $25,000 U.S. Treasury bills maturing every three months. Believing he can forecast the direction of the stock market, Al decides to take half of the interest as each T-bill rolls over and use the money to buy index options on the S&P 500. Five years later, Al has made 20 losing option trades in a row. He's never been right. But his $100,000 account has risen to $111,000—all from the half of the interest he didn't use to buy

---

* As the bull market raged while we were writing this book, Tony heard of several investors (not his clients) who borrowed against their 401(K) retirement accounts and used the loan proceeds to buy stocks on margin in their regular trading accounts. Talk about taking risks!

options. In other words, his account grew in value because of the money he didn't place at risk in the market.

Al has correctly controlled his risk and survived his own lack of investment skill. In fairness, it's unlikely he would make 20 losing trades in a row. While Al certainly hasn't meaningfully increased his investment capital, and has lost ground to inflation, his original investment remains intact.

Seeing that an investor can be wrong 20 times in a row, and still make money, we begin to understand the importance of risk management. We see we can improve our investment performance by spending more time evaluating our risk, and less time worrying about return. That's a lesson that goes against our gut instinct. We concentrate on picking good stocks, and often think very little about the risk that's posed by those stocks, or by our investment strategy.

■ *NOTES FROM A CONTRARIAN PORTFOLIO MANAGER*

I've been approaching the investment problem from the risk perspective for so long that I sometimes find it difficult to warm up to investment ideas that seem to promise huge returns.

If a client calls me to get my opinion on a stock that looks like it has the potential to be a big winner, my first reaction is to assess the downside risk: What can go wrong, when can it go wrong and how much will it cost us if it does go wrong? Invariably, I conclude that the hoped-for return faces very long odds and carries too much risk.

This, among other factors, reinforces my belief that investors tend to underestimate the risk of a long-shot stock, while overestimating the risk of a conservative investment such as a stock that has been unfairly beaten down by investors.

Knowing how difficult risk assessment is for me, an investor who practices it daily, I can understand why so many investors have bad investment experiences—they have no risk-assessment strategy. ■

Sidestepping Risk Traps

If you have a sound investment strategy—such as contrarian investing—you can make money if you can survive into the long run, which gives your strategy time to work. The best way to survive is to avoid placing more in any single investment than you can afford to lose. Investors find it difficult to calculate the loss they can afford, or feel comfortable with. We'll show you how to do that later. But first let's consider some of the typical pitfalls that trap investors.

Failing to control risk by investing too much in a single idea stems from one of several mindsets that only mean trouble for the investor. Learn to recognize these in yourself:

1. *Get Rich Quick!* You want big returns, and want them now, either because you are impatient, or still worse because you are trying to make up for past losses. Maybe you're jealous of others who brag of their success. Or perhaps you have financial problems you want to resolve with one swing with the proverbial "10-bagger." The upshot: You load up on two or three stocks and look for the big score. In pursuit of those big returns, you take on too much risk. That risk is your eventual undoing.

2. *Confusing Brains with a Bull Market.* You've made several good calls in a row during a healthy bull market and start believing you are invincible. That the whole stock market has risen—accounting for most of your success—doesn't enter your mind. You don't bother diversifying, convinced that each pick will be a success. You think about writing down your strategy so your family will have it in case something happens to you. Maybe you'll even consider writing a book. Worse still, you're so full of yourself that you're openly disdainful of others' ideas.

Eventually, you take a huge position in one of your "can't-miss" stocks and are wiped out when that stock tanks and you ride it into the ground (probably even doubling or tripling up all the way down). Amazingly, you probably still believe that you had it right and that everyone else was wrong.

3. *The Tip Victim.* You make a big bet on a "whisper stock," one that's recommended by a coworker, a friend, or Marvin the taxi driver. Once you buy on that tip, you become paralyzed, afraid to sell because you might miss the big gains that seem just around the corner.

Market tips from others should be ignored. First, possessing true inside information and acting on it for profit can land you in jail. Second, even if the tip is quite above-board, if you depend on someone else's tip to buy a stock, how can you be sure they'll be around to tell you when to sell?

4. *Hooked On the Idea.* You become so taken with an idea that you lose your objectivity. This is a fairly common mistake. Investors often repeat investment themes, no matter how dubious, until they become utterly convinced of their validity.*

In fact, research shows investors may cling to a pet theme even when they have little success to show for it. Profits seem irrelevant. Gold bugs will accumulate the metal for years, convinced gold is such a compelling investment that they will eventually be rewarded for their unwavering belief. The investor who buys the same stock, year after year, without factoring in the changing market the company faces, or the new risks those changes pose, is guilty of the same error.

How do you know when the hook is out? Try making the opposite argument. If you're in love with a stock, try making the bear case for it. If the market is heading higher, try arguing why it will go down. If you can't, you've become so taken with your logic that you can't see how it might be flawed. You're so convinced that you're willing to take any kind of pain to be proved right in the end. As a result, you keep buying, and you don't spread the risk by diversifying.

Maybe you'll eventually be proved right. But the heightened risk, and the cost of lost opportunity elsewhere, makes this a very poor investment strategy.

5. *Lack of Knowledge.* You don't do your risk research and don't understand the risk. A mutual fund advertises its return. Whenever a stock is recommended, the price target is usually mentioned, but rarely is the downside risk. When people buy on a tip, or pick a fund, or invest in a stock, they usually have little knowledge of the risk they run. Even when risk is clearly stated, investors will often gloss over it, or fail to take the time to understand the nature of that risk. Investors should be able to recognize the risk of an investment as easily as the potential return. If they can't, they should not make the investment.

---

*Basically, if a hot market keeps rising, it enters a self-perpetuating stage: The market goes up because investors believe it will go up; so investors keep buying more stocks, which pushes the market up, thus confirming the wisdom of buying more. Eventually, of course, the wheel stops turning.

■ *NOTES FROM A CONTRARIAN PORTFOLIO MANAGER*

Even a casual study of stock market history shows that in any single year, the market can decline by 20 to 25 percent. It has done so many times and will no doubt do so again.

Do investors, fully invested in common stocks in IRA rollover accounts, or perhaps using borrowed money, understand this? Are they ready to take a $40,000 hit on a $200,000 investment?　■

RISK MANAGEMENT RULES

Now that we've explored the destabilizing potential of risk, let's look at how to properly manage it, using more of our simple guidelines.

Since contrarians buy out-of-favor investments, they do not generally pay a high price. Nevertheless, a stock that has dropped from $50 to $25—a 50 percent plunge—can just as easily drop another 50 percent to $12.50. Like any other investor, contrarians must not stake big portions of their portfolios on single ideas under the mistaken idea that risk has been greatly reduced or eliminated just because the portfolios are filled with beaten-down stocks. Contrarians must always assume that even their down-by-half investments carry their own elements of risk.

Let's take a closer look at our risk-management rules:

1. *No single stock should constitute more than 5 percent of a contrarian portfolio,* and preferably less. In fact, we believe 3 percent is ideal. This implies a portfolio of 20 to 35 different stocks. Such a diverse portfolio diffuses the risk, meaning a drastic decline in one stock won't drag down the value of our portfolio.

Our second rule broadens this risk-management concept.

2. *Limit your exposure to a specific industry or investment theme to 20 percent or less of a portfolio's value. A preferable level is 10 percent.* Even at only 10 percent of a portfolio, this rule allows you to hold stock in as many as three companies per industry. (If one theme comprises 10 percent of a portfolio, and you observe our other rule of limiting your investment in any one company to 3 to 5 percent of your portfolio, you could still buy shares in three different companies in that one industry. Three companies at 3 percent of the portfolio is less than the 10-percent cap on any one industry.)

We want to avoid concentrating our stock picks around a single thesis or theme that might have a big group of stocks rising or falling in concert with one another. Contrarian opportunities are often concentrated in specific industries. For instance, if you find a utility stock that is down 50 percent in price, chances are others will be, too. The reason for the drop may be related to the fundamentals of the industry (for instance, a jump in the price of coal that's used to fire powerplants). The factors driving down the price of one stock will drive down the others, making it easy to build your portfolio around just a few industries. But that's dangerous, because it dramatically boosts the chances of taking big losses all at one time.

Keep in mind that all stocks within a specific industry tend to be highly correlated, meaning their prices will go up or down in lockstep with one another, and usually because of the same catalyst. (We'll explain more about correlation shortly.) For example, if you buy shares in six different steel companies, you may consider yourself well-diversified. But owning six steel stocks simply means your risk is concentrated in the steel industry.

If the shares of gold-mining companies are attractive because they've been beaten down, try to diversify by company, but keep the overall gold exposure to 10 to 20 percent of the portfolio's value. In other words, limit yourself to three gold stocks (at 3 percent each) or four (at 5 percent each).

All gold mining stocks, absent an event that affects one specific company, will tend to move together because they all operate on the same relationship between the cost of mining the gold and the price it receives in the marketplace. If the idea is a good one, all four mining companies should show a profit. If poor, all four will show a loss. Therefore, no one company should comprise more than 5 percent of the entire portfolio.

Twenty percent invested in a single idea using stocks that all move together is the same as having 5 percent in each of four stocks.

Since four stocks in the same industry will tend to be highly "correlated," meaning their prices will move largely in unison, limiting each to 5 percent of the portfolio's total value is much less risky than having 5 percent in each of 10 companies related by theme or industry.

We've spoken a lot here about not filling your portfolio with too many stocks from similar industries. But neither do you want too few. Sometimes, the risk you face is with a single company that falls on tough times, independent of the market conditions in its industry. By purchasing more than one gold stock or steel stock that is down at least 50 percent from its 52-week high, so-called "event risk" is minimized. "Event risk" is the chance an event specific to one company—that is, independent of your thesis (for instance, a mine peters out)—strikes like lightning, causing a big loss.

Investing too much in a single industry isn't the only way to concentrate—and heighten—risk. Investment "themes" can have the same effect. Perhaps a contrarian theme is the resurgence of inflation. Everyone is sanguine about inflation and you believe low energy prices have encouraged inflation-igniting consumption. If so, purchasing two gold stocks and one energy stock is preferable to three gold stocks.* But even with the diversification between two industries, both holdings ride the same inflation thesis. Both industries, therefore, face the same risk: *that inflation doesn't rise.*

Of course, you might not have enough money to allow for the broad diversification we advocate here. If you invest in a particular theme, but can afford to buy shares in only one company, try to pick the company with the strongest finances. Some easy ways to gauge a company's financial strength:

- The bond ratings of either Standard & Poor's or Moody's Investors Service, or;
- The Value Line stock safety rankings, or some other recognized rating system.

Again, since many contrarian stocks are companies in distress, it's important to pick firms that have the financial muscle to ride out their problems. Companies with too much debt, or consistently falling sales, need to be studied carefully before their shares are added to a portfolio.

This brings us to our final risk-management rule.

---

* Gold, and gold stocks, are often viewed as a good way to hedge against inflation.

3. *Limit your losses on any one investment to 25 percent of the purchase price.** A $5,000 position on a particular stock in a $100,000 portfolio calls for a stop loss of $1,250 ($5,000 × 25 percent stop loss = $1,250 downside limit). This limits your loss on any one stock to only 1.25 percent of your portfolio.

Here's why:

- Since we contend that no one stock should constitute more than 5 percent of your portfolio, in a $100,000 portfolio the amount of money invested in any one stock should not exceed $5,000 ($100,000 × 5 percent = $5,000).

- By using a 25-percent stop-loss order on each stock you buy, you cannot lose more than one-quarter of your investment on any one stock ($5,000 outlay for one stock × 25-percent maximum loss = $1,250).

- That 25-percent stop loss limits your potential loss on any one investment to 1.25 percent of the portfolio's total value (the $1,250 downside limit = 1.25 percent of a $100,000 portfolio).

You can begin to see how our guidelines are designed to work together. In short, we won't invest more than 5 percent in any single stock, and we want to be out of that stock if its price falls 25 percent from what we paid for it. This may seem like a large loss tolerance, but the stop-loss level must be set to allow for normal market fluctuations, mistiming (getting in before the actual bottom), and the primary goal of cutting losses before they become debilitating.

As we've seen, even a 25-percent loss on one stock has a very small impact on the value of the overall portfolio. This stop-loss rule, coupled with the other two rules prohibiting us from concentrating too much money in similar stocks or investment themes, work together to limit our downside risk. If contrarians adhere strictly to these three simple rules, it is nearly impossible to lose all their capital. Indeed, the mathematical probability of losing the entire portfolio is so low that it's not even worth considering. And that means the odds of getting into the long run are very good.

---

* We advocate the use of a 25-percent stop-loss order to meet this rule, and cover its use in Chapter 13, Contrarian Selling.

Heed the following three "don'ts":

- Don't invest more than 5 percent of your portfolio in any one stock and, better yet, keep that investment to 3 percent.
- Don't concentrate more than 20 percent of your portfolio in any one industry or common theme. Better still, keep that industry or theme risk to 10 percent of the portfolio's value.
- Don't take more than a 25-percent loss on any single stock.

■ NOTES FROM A CONTRARIAN PORTFOLIO MANAGER

These are very simple rules to use, but they are invaluable. Often, an investor's enthusiasm will crowd out good judgment.

No matter how excited I may become over an investment, my rules prevent me from loading up on it. And when the idea doesn't work out, they also force me to admit the mistake and bail out. This, for me, is usually the toughest thing to do.

Sometimes, I buy something as a hedge against another investment, meaning a stop loss isn't as important as when I'm buying a stock for profit. It all depends on my reasons for making the investment.

I do find, though, that these rules keep me grounded in reality, and often, will save me from myself. ■

Don't "Average Down"

If you're the type of investor who finds it difficult to sell after the stock you've bought drops into the red, don't feel bad. It's human nature to want to leave as a winner. But resist the urge to buy more, called "averaging down," a move many investors make to bring down their average cost on a stock. If a contrarian pick falls 25 percent, sell it and move on. Remind yourself that the stop loss is designed to get you into the long run, where the real profits are. Ignoring the stop loss, while occasionally the correct thing to do (because the stock rebounds), is usually the path to disaster. As a contrarian, you have to cut your losses short, and a mechanical dollar-stop is the best way to do that consistently.

In certain cases, when the stock that you've sold continues to meet our guidelines, you can buy it back, *but only at a price slightly higher than you paid the first time.* You pay the higher price to confirm that a rising price trend has begun and, after failing once with the idea, to prove that your reasoning remains valid.

Example: You have a $200,000 account and decide to buy 1,000 shares of Absolom Brothers Crackers at $10 per share (1,000 shares × $10 each = $10,000, or 5 percent of your $200,000 account). The stock is down more than 50 percent from its $25 high and investors are avoiding it, but you believe a turnaround in the cracker market is imminent. The stock falls to $7.50 and you sell, taking your $2,500 loss. Your stop loss of 25 percent of the $10 purchase price is triggered with a loss of $2.50 per share: A $10 purchase price – a $2.50 drop in share price = a $7.50 stop-loss trigger.

You still believe cracker stocks are poised to pop (the Food and Drug Administration is studying the health risk of cookies), but you have to wait until the Absolom shares show some life. You place a good-until-canceled order to buy 1,000 shares at $10⅛.

Most investors would double up on Absolom once it fell enough to irritate, believing they could lower their average cost and boost their returns on the way back up. That is a flawed strategy. If more bad news strikes (cookies are found to prevent cancer), and Absolom drops from $7.50 to $5.00, the loss widens to $7,500. The doubled-up hit of $7,500 is nearly 4 percent of the account value of $200,000. At that level of loss, the risk of losing all of your money to a string of bad trades is no longer theoretical. It could happen.

From an emotional standpoint, Absolom has become a stock that's now nearly impossible to sell. Many people who fail in the stock market do so because they can't let go of their mistake stocks. Eventually, they get locked in to too many losers and are unable to get out of those positions. Their capital is tied up and isn't generating profits—or worse, it gets vaporized. The contrarian rules we're outlining have an interesting effect: Over time, you'll find that you winnow out your losers and end up with a portfolio filled with winners.

By waiting for Absolom to hit $10⅛, the contrarian is allowing the stock to prove itself a worthy investment. If it rebounds, that means your timing was off the first time around. At $10⅛, up from the low of $7.50 per share, the stock is now clearly in a new upward trend. True, you've given up a $5,240 move (a $2.62 rise × 2,000 shares = $5,240). However, the contrarian is making a statement. If the stock was a buy at $10, it should be just as good a buy at $10⅛.

It is a fallacy to believe that if $10 is a good price, then $7.50 is better. In that case, the stock's action is not confirming the contrarian's premise for buying it in the first place. Perhaps the thesis is flawed, or perhaps you were just too early. But, by waiting for it to reverse course before buying it again, you give yourself a better chance of avoiding the losses that often are incurred by averaging down.

Remember, when you average down on a loser, precious capital is kept from other, better opportunities. You spend too much time, energy, and money—your most important investment assets—trying to shepherd along this type of position.

■ *NOTES FROM A CONTRARIAN PORTFOLIO MANAGER*

Averaging down gets people into a lot of trouble. I always feel that if I pick a stock, and it doesn't work out, I don't want to compound the error by averaging down. If I do, it creates all kinds of problems. If the stock goes lower after the second purchase, it's pretty clear I've bought into a downtrend that is continuing to run. Averaging down is like reaching out to catch a falling knife; you never know which end you are going to grab.

Owning a loser consumes a lot of energy. But owning a loser twice is far worse. Not only is the dollar loss larger, but the situation tends to sap my confidence and affect my ability to think through other opportunities. I get defensive, and make decisions to avoid the mistake of my last investment instead of focusing on the merits of the current opportunities.

I've learned. Now, when I buy a stock and its promise doesn't pan out, I cut it loose. There are simply too many other ideas and other stocks out there to shackle myself to one mistake. ■

Manage risk by understanding the risk in your portfolio. To control overall portfolio risk, you must understand the risk of each stock and its relationship to all the others in the portfolio. Investors may think they are well-diversified because they own a 50-stock portfolio. The reality is that the 50 stocks they've chosen tend to move as a group, up and down, in lockstep with the broader stock market. Such poorly chosen portfolios only substitute the risk of individual stocks with the risk of the stock market. One stock won't kill you. But you could be mortally wounded when the whole market goes down.

Managing risk is a key attraction of contrarian investing. Contrarian stocks have for the most part already had their bear market when we buy them. So when the overall market goes through its bearish throes and drops 25 percent, contrarian portfolios tend to suffer a lot less.

However, even the most astute contrarian will not entirely escape that carnage.

MAXIMIZING RETURNS

To maximize investment returns over long periods, money has to be put at risk. To boost investment returns, there is simply no substitute for increasing risk in a calculated manner. The financial markets are a way for investors both to lay off risk, and to take on risk. Those who take on calculated risk must, in the long run, be compensated for that risk by getting a higher return. Speculators and investors are providing a service and, if they come to believe that assuming risk is not a profitable enterprise, they will stop doing so.

■ *NOTES FROM A CONTRARIAN PORTFOLIO MANAGER*

This is a concept that took me a long time to understand. When I heard others say that you had to be fully invested in common stocks at all times, I knew they were saying this because stocks, over time, offered returns that were higher than competing investments. That was an oversimplification. What I finally realized was that the real message was not to stay invested in stocks, but to keep money at risk. Most people find the stock market to be the easiest way to put their money at risk. ■

The need to put money at risk does not mean staying invested in U.S. common stocks. To do so through a bear market exposes the investor to inordinate risk.

The Practical Effect: If an investor can keep money at risk, and can diversify by choosing markets and investments that rise and fall at different times and in different degrees from one another, the overall risk of that investor's portfolio will be reduced without forfeiting the opportunity for profits.

Investing will always carry risk. But if we can build a portfolio of investments diversified by types of risk, and if most those investments will have positive returns over time, we have bullet-proofed our portfolio as much as possible.

The Correlation Conundrum

To identify investments that are not highly related to each other in terms of their price movements, we must consider the *correlation* of the price movements between the individual investments in our portfolios.

We've talked about our rule limiting holdings of stocks in similar industries or of common themes to 10 to 20 percent of the portfolio. That means you must keep stocks whose price movements are highly correlated to 10 percent or less of your total stock holdings. To make sure you observe that diversification rule, you need to know just what *correlation* actually is.

True diversification is a concept some investors have a tough time understanding. While you certainly want to have all your investments show a profit over the long run, you would prefer they not do so all at the same time. If they are all generating the same returns simultaneously, they must all be correlated with one another. That's dangerous since stocks that all rise together, will likely all fall together. In a bear market, that can be fatal.

By assembling a portfolio of non-correlated stocks, you still will make your profit, but the big swings in your account value (up or down) will be muted, and you will more likely survive into the long run.

If two investments are perfectly correlated, it means that they always move in the same direction, at the same time and to the same degree. If this happens, we say the two stocks have a correlation of positive 1.00 (+1.00). When you drive your car down the highway, your rear tires are perfectly correlated. They both move in the same direction, at the same speed, at the same time.

When two things are *negatively* correlated, it means that they always move in an opposite direction, at the same time, and at the same speed. Two children on a teeter-totter are perfectly negatively correlated. When one moves up, the other moves down at the same time and at the same speed. We call this a correlation of negative 1.00 (−1.00).

When two things are noncorrelated, there is no telling how one will move in relation to the other because there is no relationship in their movement. When a leaf falls from a tree in your backyard, it has no relation to the temperature of your morning coffee. We call this a 0.00 correlation.

Finally, when two things are *weakly* correlated, it means there is some relationship, but that relationship is poor and is a weak predictor of price movement. That would be a correlation of −0.50 to +0.50. For instance, if it's raining outside, we can assume that some people will be using an umbrella. So, umbrella use is highly correlated to rain. But, if we had to predict whether the next person coming out of a building would have one, we'd have to say that the correlation, while there, is weak. The next pedestrian may or may not use one.

The good news is that we can compare the past price movements of different assets to each other and, using correlation analysis, can determine whether the prices of the two assets move in concert with, or independent of, each other. (If you have Microsoft Excel, or another popular spreadsheet program, correlation analysis is easy. See Appendix A, Contrarian Math, for some formulas.) For instance, if you buy a typical blue-chip American stock, it will have a very high (+0.90 or better) correlation to the 30-stock Dow Jones Industrial Average index. Your stock may not always move exactly like the Dow, but during a bull market, it will likely share in the wealth.*

Conversely, few stocks escape a down market intact, so the blue chip stock also is likely to fall when the bull market gives way to the bears.

Of course, if you own equal shares in all 30 stocks in the Dow, in the right proportion to the index, you are perfectly correlated to that index. All you've done is traded your risk exposure to one stock for the risk of the Dow index. And that risk can be greater than holding a single stock!

Indeed, investors take on much more risk than they realize. Consider the following examples of some of the surprising—but hidden—risks we are taking through some high-profile mutual funds.

---

*This is not the same as beta. A stock could be highly correlated to the stock market, but have a very low beta. A stock could have a correlation of 1.00 but a beta of 0.70.

- Correlation of the S&P 500 to a popular growth mutual fund: 0.92

- Correlation of the S&P 500 to a popular value mutual fund: 0.95

- Correlation of the S&P 500 to a popular small cap mutual fund: 0.89

Until now, you might have believed that if you own equal dollar amounts of each of these three funds that you've diversified away some of this risk. Here is the truth:

1. You have reduced your risk to an event related to a specific fund (a scandal over trading practices, the departure of a successful manager, or a run on the fund by investors after a big loss).

2. You have reduced your risk against an investment style falling out of favor (growth works well in a strong bull market, while value seems to succeed more in trendless markets).

3. You have reduced the risk that devastating losses in one stock will hammer the fund.

However, you have substantially *increased* stock market risk, since these broad portfolios of stocks now mimic the movement of the broad market. In other words, you have reduced the risk that a plunge in one stock will cause a big portfolio loss. But you've substituted that risk for the risk of a big loss if the overall market experiences a major drop. Yet, most investors in this situation would think they've diversified away that risk.

From an overall portfolio standpoint, all investors accept a lot of risk. While we want to limit our risk on a specific investment to 1 to 2 percent of our portfolio (using a stop loss), the very nature of investing means accepting risk. We can't really eliminate that risk from our portfolio if we still want a shot at fairly big returns over time, since the market rewards those who take on additional risk.

It is important to understand that the risk is there. If the result of that understanding is to prompt a more conservative approach or more knowledgeable technique in selecting investments, then that awareness is certainly a positive thing.

Table 12.1   50-Percent Gains Over Six Years

Year	Portfolio A		Portfolio B	
1	$100,000		$100,000	
2	$110,000	+10%	$120,000	+20%
3	$120,000	+9%	$135,000	+12%
4	$130,000	+8%	$122,000	−10%
5	$140,000	+7%	$119,000	−2%
6	$150,000	+7%	$150,000	+26%

Let's put it another way. If we had two investments that, over time, each returned an average of 12 percent per year, and the price movements of the two investments were weakly correlated, we would have less risk than if we had two investments that were perfectly correlated. The reason: The two weakly correlated investments won't always move up and down together; that is, their combined performance would tend to smooth out the portfolio's gyrations.

The bigger swings in the portfolio's value caused by the two perfectly correlated investments are unsettling to most investors. Large swings tend to spark a fear of losses—a fear that can sometimes take an investor off a game plan that is well-conceived, but needs time to work. Consider the two ways of making 50 percent gains shown in Table 12.1.

Which portfolio would you rather have? Which would you be more likely to stick with? Which would let you continue a consistent, disciplined strategy, and which one would cause you to panic and perhaps change your game plan? Both A and B get you to the same destination, but how many investors would have the fortitude to stick with Plan B? After all, you'd have to sit through two consecutive years of losses. If we can reduce the volatility, if we can "quiet" our portfolios, we can more assuredly get into the long run, which is where the big profits are made.

■ NOTES FROM A CONTRARIAN PORTFOLIO MANAGER

When people experience major stock-market losses, they engage in a crude form of volatility analysis and retreat to cash. Since the stock-market volatility was much greater than they anticipated (resulting in losses), these investors reduce volatility by selling stocks and putting the proceeds into cash.

Unfortunately, these investors compound their mistake by overestimating future volatility (and losses) by staying in cash. Only until stocks have clearly resumed their upward advance do these investors believe downward volatility has been eliminated, and move back into the market. Actually, in buying stocks, they've added volatility.

This jerking and lurching is very expensive. The cumulative effect of poor timing, taxes, transaction costs (and emotional pain) results in poor returns over time. Most people are much better off taking a middle course that they can accept in all markets. Smaller, but consistent, returns are preferable to making a lot in one year only to lose a lot the next. ■

Asset Class Myopia

Reducing risk includes controlling how much is invested in each individual investment, as well as how the individual investments correlate to each other. If you buy two paper companies, you may believe you've diversified away your risk. But barring some company-specific event, the two stocks will move in tandem. Of course, if you believe that the paper industry is a good contrarian play, you're better off buying five companies (at 3 percent of the portfolio each) instead of one, but transaction costs or a small portfolio size may not allow that luxury.

Nevertheless, with five paper companies or one, you still have the risk of both the paper industry and the stock market.

We believe that since investors gravitate to areas where they have access to the greatest amount of information, American investors are generally overweighted in U.S. stocks. Contrarians should view all investments as the same, and broaden their focus to consider investments from all around the world. Two decades ago, the United States accounted for about two-thirds of the world's stock market value. Today, that ratio has reversed: the U.S. represents around 40 percent.

Many of the very best investment opportunities are now in overseas markets, where the higher efficiencies of the American market do not yet exist. Inefficiency breeds opportunity.

Growth rates are also worth noting. While the U.S. economy chugs along at 2 to 3 percent a year, many overseas markets are growing at double or triple that pace. The governments in some of those countries fight to hold down their growth rates to keep inflation at bay.

> **The Practical Effect:** To diversify, investors must look across many different types and classes of investments.

We believe that contrarian investors should be just as comfortable investing in foreign markets, commodities, and other non-U.S. stock asset classes as they are investing in the S&P 500. U.S. stocks are merely one part of a large universe of investment and risk opportunities. Many investors believe that foreign markets pose too much risk to include as part of their portfolios. But investors who believe that, and who invest only in U.S. common stocks, actually face more risk than investors who include foreign securities in their portfolios. Many foreign stock exchanges are weakly correlated to the U.S. stock market. And, as we learned in our chapters on fundamental stock analysis techniques, research shows that many of our contrarian indicators are as effective ferreting out foreign stocks as they are shares in U.S. companies.

■ NOTES FROM A CONTRARIAN PORTFOLIO MANAGER

One of the strategies I find most difficult to explain to our clients is the idea that, if we diversify in this fashion, it's almost certain that at any one time, some of our investments won't be doing well. We manage risk in clients' portfolios by looking for investments that are not correlated, or are negatively correlated. However, in doing so, we create portfolios that we know won't have all cylinders firing at any one time. Many people struggle with this concept, asking: "Shouldn't we be working to have every investment be a winner all the time?" Perhaps, but if we have that type of portfolio, it will be highly volatile. If we can make money on everything all at once, the opposite can also be true: We can lose money on everything all at once. And with those magnified up-and-down swings, my concern is that the increased risk will drive my client out of the market. If I can find two different investments that will make 12 percent, I'd just as soon have them do so at different times, dampening the volatility.

While this isn't, in the strictest sense, a contrarian philosophy, it does tend to reduce that wrenching volatility over time. And since a lot of our clients tend to be within eyeshot of retirement, they are much more comfortable with more predictable, consistent returns. ■

From time to time, it does happen that an entire asset class is a true contrarian play. Values are compelling and a long stretch of languishing prices begs for us to overweight that asset in a portfolio. Gold stocks in 1992 come to mind as an example, as do U.S. common stocks in 1981, and Japanese stocks in 1994. Contrarians can certainly take a 100-percent position in an asset class, but if they make this kind of move, they should understand the huge risks.*

Cash Is Not Trash

Cash is an overlooked—but extremely important—asset class for an investor who wants to reduce risk.† For instance, after a long bull market, market timing usually has a bad name and many market seers extol the virtues of remaining fully invested in stocks at all times.‡ Also, investors find little appeal in an investment like cash that has a low-but-predictable rate of return. However, cash as an investment has some alluring characteristics.

Always remember that when you have cash to invest, you are weighing the potential returns of other investments against those for a block of cash. In other words, you ask: "Will this investment outperform cash?" Put another way, since cash almost always earns interest, other investments such as stocks must offer enough of an incremental return to justify taking on the extra risk: "Is the potential higher return I can earn on this stock worth the risk of losing money?" Let's consider this concept more closely.

First, cash is noncorrelated to any other risk-based investment. Since cash nearly always has a positive return, it has no correlation to other classes of assets that may or may not show a positive return. For instance, if we assume the stock market notches losses in one year out of three, or one year out of four, we can safely say that cash

---

* Most investors fail to see U.S. common stocks as a single asset class, just one opportunity among many investment possibilities. We can't emphasize enough that a portfolio of 20 U.S. stocks, while diversified enough to protect against a big loss caused by one of the companies coming out with stock-punishing bad news, is not diversified against the risk of the broader U.S. market. For instance, a bear market caused by a U.S. economic recession will do great damage to any U.S. stock portfolio, no matter how well diversified between industries, or how carefully selected the stocks are.

† When we discuss cash, we are referring to short-term, interest-bearing instruments: money market funds, certificates of deposit (CDs), Treasury bills, commercial paper, etc.

‡ The authors can assure the reader that this is not a pervasive feeling among investors at market bottoms.

will outperform stocks roughly 25 to 33 percent of the time. This alone makes it worth considering as part of your portfolio plan.

Second, cash investments such as money-market funds or certificates of deposit exhibit very low volatility, diminishing a portfolio's risk.

Finally, cash can easily be included in any contrarian strategy. Any time that cash has underperformed stocks and bonds for a long period, contrarians can consider cash a legitimate investment choice. Returns on cash won't necessarily increase per se. But when the stock and bond markets have strong returns for several years in a row, meaning cash has underperformed, the odds are that stocks and bonds are due for a tough year. That makes cash a possible contrarian play.

Raising cash in a portfolio that's fully invested in stocks or bonds is the same as investing in cash. You don't have to do it all at once. If you usually buy 5 percent positions in each new contrarian stock, as you sell some of your holdings, limit each new buy to 3 to 4 percent of the account's value (leaving the other 1 to 2 percent in cash).

Many investors disdain cash because they see the return on a certificate of deposit or money market fund as inadequate compared to what they hope to earn in the stock market. True, cash offers lower returns, on average, over time. But if a money market is paying 3 percent, and the stock market drops 15 percent, cash has an effective return of 18 percent. That can have a big impact on the returns of your portfolio.

In addition, cash has an important place in a portfolio that has above-average volatility. Consider a portfolio of one stock. The stock has a beta of 1.20, meaning that it will move 20 percent more than the stock market and in the same direction. If the investor wishes to maintain a rough parity with stock market volatility, a portfolio of 20 percent cash and 80 percent in that stock will do the trick .

Cash can help dampen overall portfolio risk and volatility. At times, contrarians will find themselves holding very volatile stocks, bonds or funds, and will need to add some cash to reduce risk.

Contrarians should get in the habit of comparing the possible returns of a stock against the nearly guaranteed return from cash. If you're looking at a stock that offers a possible 11-percent return, and cash pays 5 percent, a contrarian should understand the stock will have an excess return of 6 percent. Knowing that 5 percent is in the bag by staying in cash, the contrarian needs to ask: "Should I buy the stock?"

If the stock poses a possible loss of 20 percent (fairly common in a bear market year), this compares to zero risk for cash. The contrarian must decide whether the possible extra return of 6 percent is worth risking the 20-percent loss.

SUMMARY

In general, investors do not adequately assess risk as they build their portfolios. They often try to diversify, but only swap the risk of an individual stock for the risk of the U.S. stock market as a whole. Contrarians, often investing in distressed securities, need to make sure each stock accounts for no more than 3 to 5 percent of the entire portfolio value. Investors also must preserve their capital by using strict loss parameters.

Our recommendations:

1. Limit purchases of each stock to 5 percent (and preferably less), of the portfolio's value.

2. Limit industry exposure, or theme exposure, to 20 percent of the portfolio, and preferably less.

3. Use a stop loss of 25 percent on any one stock.

4. Seek noncorrelated investments.

5. Don't overlook the risk diversification benefits of international stocks.

6. Always compare an investment's risk and return to cash.

By paying particular attention to risk, the investor can give the contrarian strategy enough time to work. Contrarians can never spend enough time looking at risk. Since risk can't be eliminated if higher returns are sought, minimizing the effects of risk becomes central to successful investing.

CHAPTER 13

CONTRARIAN SELLING: FOLLOW THE RULES

*A*t *the beginning of a cask and at the end
take your fill; in the middle be sparing.*

—Hesiod

In the stock-market game, knowing when to sell may be the most difficult skill to master. Buying is easy by comparison: You set certain guidelines, and when they are met, you buy the stock. But selling is charged with emotion.

HARD SELL

It's easy to see why selling is so tough. When a position is profitable, we fear losing those profits, yet can't bring ourselves to sell because we are greedy for more.

When we have a stock that's a loser, we fear further losses. But we don't want to sell, hoping the stock will rebound and give us the profits we hoped for when we bought it. Wanting to be proved right, we stand pat or even buy more.

With stocks, then, we face two tough selling decisions:

- With a stock that's been a winner, when to sell and keep your profit
- With a loser, when to admit we made a bad choice, sell it and move on to better opportunities

In this chapter, we're going to show you how to protect those profits and cut loose those losers, skills that will lead to long-term profits for your contrarian stock portfolio.

SELLING: RULES OF THE ROAD

Since selling is so difficult, particularly with contrarian stocks, we've established some rules to guide us along:

1. *When you buy a stock, put in place a stop-loss order 25 percent below a stock's purchase price. The order should be good until canceled.*

A stop-loss order is simply a standing order to liquidate at a specific price. The order can be a mental one, or can be actually entered with your broker to be kept in place until you say otherwise.*

With a 25-percent stop loss, a stock you bought for $16 will automatically be sold if the price falls to $12 ($16 purchase price − 25 percent loss = $12 stop-loss price). You should place this order as soon as your purchase is confirmed.

By limiting your loss on any stock to 25 percent of its purchase price, and limiting each stock to a maximum of 5 percent of your portfolio's total value, the most you can lose on any one stock is a bit more than 1 percent of your portfolio's total value. This first selling rule is aimed at reducing your overall risk.

2. *Sell your winners after a 50-percent profit, or after three years, whichever comes first.*

This rule forces you to refresh your portfolio with better opportunities, but not so often that you are trading constantly.

There are some exceptions to this rule. For instance, when a company's prospects have clearly improved since you bought its stock, you may want to hold on to it longer.

---

*Note that once the stop-loss order is entered, it will be adjusted as a stock reaches ex-dividend. For instance a $25 stop loss will be automatically changed to $24.75 when the stock goes ex-dividend by 25 cents.

3. *With a stock that's a winner, but isn't yet set to be sold, establish a stop loss that guarantees you a profit of 30 percent or more.*

This rule is designed to guarantee at least part of your profits. For instance, a stock you bought for $10 runs up to $15 in eight months. You want to hold on, but are uncertain what's in store for the market. So you set a stop loss of $13 (a 30 percent profit over the $10 purchase price). As a stock climbs higher, so does the stop-loss point. The stop-loss trigger guarantees you a profit, but also allows for the normal fluctuations of the market.

Taking Stock of a Stop Loss

Most investors see the benefits of stop-loss orders, but few use them. Typically, a well-meaning investor owns a stock, sees its value increase, and then sets a stop-loss order that's 10 to 20 percent below the stock's now-higher price. The stock drops to the stop-loss level, the investor is sold out and the shares reverse course and go on to double.

The now-angry investor decides never to use a stop-loss order again.

■ *NOTES FROM A CONTRARIAN PORTFOLIO MANAGER*

Every investor, at one time or another, tries a stop-loss order. They may even try two or three. But the first time a big gainer gets away because the stock drops to its stop-loss point before reversing and making its big jump, the investor vows to never use one again. That's unfortunate since a stop loss is likely the only disciplined selling rule an investor can have. It's not perfect, but it sure beats riding a stock into the ground. Anytime I've taken a big loss on a stock, I look back and realize that a stop loss would have saved me much grief. ■

We believe the general distaste for stop losses has two causes:

• Investors don't know how to properly set them.
• They forget the purpose of stop losses is to actually stop the bleeding.

The second is the easier to discuss. A stop loss gets an investor out of a stock at a specific point. We use them because we know that it's nearly impossible to predict how the market will move, or to anticipate information that unexpectedly changes a stock's prospects. Events such as a war, the assassination of an important political figure, or the league affiliation of the winner of the Super Bowl can have an impact on your stock that wasn't in your thesis when you bought it.* The stop loss slashes the risk that you'll take a very big loss.

On each stock you buy, set the stop-loss trigger at 75 percent of your purchase price. By doing this, and keeping each stock to 5 percent of your portfolio or less, no single stock can steal away more than 1.25 percent of your total holdings (25-percent fall in a 5-percent stock position = 1.25 percent of the total portfolio value).

The stop loss allows for plenty of movement (especially when you buy a stock *before* all the bad news is out), but still protects your capital. Sometimes contrarian plays just don't work out—the stock falls still more because the company has deep problems. If a stock falls 50 percent from its high (our initial contrarian "buy" trigger), and tacks on another 25-percent drop besides, the shares are now down by two-thirds from its high-water mark. Stocks that give back two-thirds of an upward move have higher-than-normal prospects of going still lower.

With a stop loss, you eliminate the chance for a small loss to turn into a big one. Therefore, every stop-loss order triggered is a successful one. If your portfolio strategy eliminates the possibility of a big, crushing loss, you have a tremendous advantage over other investors. Don't worry about the loss. There are plenty of other contrarian stocks to buy.

When a stop loss is triggered, all that means is you won't make your money back on that particular stock. You will make it back, just on a different pick. Investors seem to believe (irrationally) that if the stock isn't sold, the loss isn't real. We all cling to hope, and when we sell, we abandon hope.† With a loser, however, clinging to hope can extract a terrible price on our investment return.

---

*Historically, when the Super Bowl is won by an old National Football League team, the market has been bullish. After an AFL win, the market has been bearish. The authors, living in Upstate New York and fans of the AFL Buffalo Bills and the old NFL Pittsburgh Steelers, are torn in their affections.
†This reminds us of the chilling words that mark the gates of Hell in Dante's *Inferno:* "Abandon hope, all ye who enter here."

■ *NOTES FROM A CONTRARIAN PORTFOLIO MANAGER*

As a professional investor, I accept that being wrong sometimes is just part of the business. You must understand that, too. Your losses, commissions, fees, and taxes are simply your overhead. You will always have losses tucked in among your winners and just need to accept that. *   ■

Mastering stop losses takes time. That's particularly true when you're trying to protect your profits by setting them on stocks that have moved higher.

Limiting Losses

Let's study our suggestion that you put in place a mechanical, 25-percent stop loss on every stock you buy. In commodities trading, every position should have a stop loss from inception. Ditto for a contrarian portfolio.

Assuming an investor places only 3 percent† of his portfolio in each contrarian stock, a 25-percent stop loss means each position risks only 0.75 percent (3 percent multiplied by 25 percent) of the total portfolio.

Example

- $100,000 account
- $3,000 purchase (3 percent limit)
- 25-percent stop loss equals $750 potential loss
- $750 = 0.75 percent of the entire $100,000 portfolio

By limiting losses on each position, contrarians guarantee their long-term survival. Remember, contrarian picks are often the shares of distressed companies. Some won't make it.

---

* Investment "systems" disciple Larry Williams actually says investors should go to a casino and play a game that results in hundreds of small losses. By doing this, he believes, investors can get used to taking losses on a regular basis. (*The Definitive Guide To Futures Trading*, Volume II, Windsor Books, Brightwater, NY, 1989, p. 264.)
† We've said no single stock should constitute more than 5 percent of your portfolio when you buy it, although 3 percent is probably even better. In this example, we're using the more-conservative 3 percent figure.

The first thing you should decide is whether to use a "mental" stop loss or a "mechanical" one that you place with your broker as "good until canceled." Some big-name investors might avoid setting actual stops so they don't tip their hands to other traders. Most investors, however, don't actually set them because they don't want to commit themselves to selling a stock automatically. That's a mistake.

Sure, some stocks that are losers will eventually move back into the black, and your stop-loss order will leave some profits on the table. But the bigger risk is in ignoring your mental stop-loss point, and watching the stock drop still deeper into the red. You're frozen at the switch.

Investors seem to have a selective memory about stop-loss orders. They can set and adjust a stop loss six times, and when whipsawed out the seventh, they seem to forget that their stop-loss technique worked six times in a row.*

Stops on Your Winners

You have a stock that's trending beautifully as it moves higher (the price rise is persistent, meaning it continues to hit higher lows and higher highs).You want to stay with the stock, but also want to make sure you keep some of your profits. So you set a stop loss. The question: *when* to set the stop and *where* to put it.

Chart analysis is one tool that can help us understand how we set our stop-loss triggers.

In chart analysis, you study a stock's price chart and look for price action that defines near-term peaks or troughs. It's likely those peaks and troughs exist because stop-loss orders have accumulated around those areas. We'll begin to see how the "support" and "resistance" levels referred to by technical analysts are formed.

Consider the price chart in Figure 13.1. Point #1 stands out as an area where stop-loss orders will accumulate. Should the stock break down through this point, it would probably signal a new downtrend. The stock rallies to a peak at #2, where again, new stop orders will accumulate. Note that at #2, some orders will be orders to sell by

---

*In a whipsaw, the investor has the frustration of making bad call after bad call. For instance, the investor may buy a stock at $25, sell it at $20, watch it go to $30, purchase again, only to see it drop back to $25.

Figure 13.1

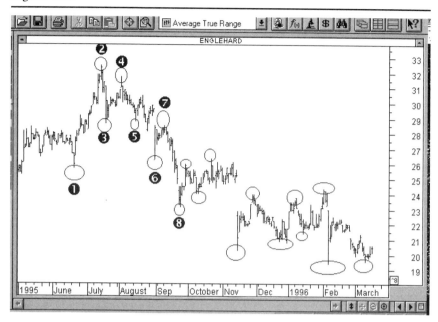

those who missed the top, and some will be buy-stops for those who are short on the stock.

A decline to #3 keeps #2 intact, but new stops (generally sells) will accumulate there as well. A rally to #4 does not break the stops at #2, so few new stops will be set there. The decline to #5 does not violate stops at #3.

The move down between #5 and #6 now takes out the stops at #3, but those set at #1 are still good, if they haven't been changed since. The rally to #7 attempts to fill a gap, and it fails. The decline to #8 now takes out all the sell stops that have accumulated from point #1.

This is a fairly typical chart of a stock's price movement. Setting proper stop-loss orders with price movements this erratic is difficult, if not impossible. One problem is that, if the stock was bought somewhere around #1, the investor could not know the stock was poised to run up to a new high, only to collapse by one-third after the highs were made. Of course, a contrarian would not have purchased this stock in the first place, since it fails to meet guidelines for contrarian investing.

Nonetheless, assuming you bought in at #1 around $26 per share, a stop loss in the vicinity of $23 was a reasonable one to set. This allowed for a 10-percent correction (to $23.50) without triggering a sale. Using 10 percent as a stop-loss trigger creates too narrow a margin, however. It is not unusual for contrarian stocks to experience sharp—but temporary—10-percent drops.

There is no easy rule for setting stop losses on a stock that's already shown a good return. The challenge is balancing risk and reward. If we set our stops too tightly, we'll be shaken out by a normal correction. If we set the stops too loosely, we could give up too much of our profit.

WHEN TO HOLD 'EM, WHEN TO FOLD 'EM

With stocks that don't hit either of the stop-losses, contrarians should expect to hold them three years, or until a 50-percent profit is realized, whichever comes first. Let's look at each piece of that selling rule.

Ben Graham felt that a position should be liquidated after a 50-percent profit, or 24 to 36 months from purchase, whichever came first. This would seem to be overly simplistic, and would leave a lot of profit on the table. However, broken into its two components, price and time, analysis shows that Graham's selling rule is a pretty good starting point for study.

Academic research we've reviewed underscores the validity of holding contrarian stocks for two to three years.* In addition, John Howe's work shows that stocks with a 50-percent appreciation (his "good news" stocks) underperformed a broad market index after the 50 percent threshold was reached. In other words, once a stock has risen 50 percent, the stock tends to underperform the market, meaning better opportunities lay elsewhere.

Thus, selling a stock after three years or a 50-percent increase has a proven basis. These two simple guidelines offer several benefits:

1. They are objective and not subject to interpretation. Contrarians can spend more time looking for good stocks, and less time fretting about when to sell.

---

*Studies by Henry Oppenheimer, Werner DeBondt, Richard Thaler, Gregg Jahnke, and Stephen Klaffke are cited throughout this book.

2. They force you to refresh your portfolio, picking up stocks with potential for higher returns. Once a stock has been held for 36 months, you automatically replace it.

3. They help maintain your contrarian viewpoint; for a beaten-down stock to rise 50 percent, investors clearly had to change their opinion from bearish to bullish.

Exceptions to the Rule

We admit our "up-by-half rule" will occasionally leave a lot of money on the table. You will, from time to time, lose those extra profits on a stock that you sell at $25 after a 50-percent jump, if it then zooms to $150. Sometimes there is merit in holding a stock that has risen 50 percent. A return of 100, 200, or 300 percent on a stock can really put a lot of sock in your portfolio.

Following are four rules to help you decide when it's worth holding on longer. Hold the stock:

1. If it is *obvious* that the company's prospects are continuing to improve. Contrarians often buy a stock just as a turnaround begins, and get a 50-percent profit in short order. Perhaps it's clear that the 50-percent jump is just the beginning. To protect yourself, raise the initial stop-loss order to guarantee a 30-percent profit on the position, should the stock fall back. As you continue to hold, adjust your stops to assure that you'll keep from 60 to 70 percent of the gain you've made to that point. If the stock reaches a 100-percent profit, put in a new stop loss that guarantees, at minimum, a 60-percent profit.*

2. If new insider buying emerges.† If the position increases 50 percent, and insiders are buying the stock (more than $120,000), hold on. Remember, insider accumulation is our

---

* A $10 stock that has risen to $15 and is held, would require replacing the initial stop-loss order of $7.50 with one at $13. The $13 level guarantees at least a 30 percent profit. If that same stock zooms to $20, replace your $13 stop-loss with one at $16. That guarantees a 60% profit.

† As we discussed in our chapter on insiders, insider selling is not a valid sell signal. Insiders may sell for reasons having more to do with personal financial needs than prospects for the stock. However, if a stock has risen more than 50 percent and multiple insider sales emerge, a sale would be warranted since the basic 50 percent profit rule has been met.

most bullish "buy" indicator. Remember to use a stop-loss to keep most of your profits.

3. If it continues to climb the proverbial "wall of worry." If you are bullish and long a stock, and the price climbs while the crowd continues to be bearish, you have a true contrarian play on your hands and might want to hold it. The longer it takes for people to come around, the bigger the profit potential.*

4. If you get continuous, positive feedback. It seems obvious, but it must be said: The fact that you have a profit is a good reason to stay in. The market is endorsing your judgment and you are on the right side of the stock. If your profit on the position is higher now than last month, and that was higher than at the beginning of the year, the upward trend is persistent and in your favor and you can run with the position a bit longer. If you find your profit at the end of the month has dropped from the prior month, it may be a correction or it may be a peak. If you find yourself on the fence trying to figure out which, sell and pocket your profits.

Employ these exceptions with extreme caution. Often, greed blinds us to the wisdom of selling a stock. Once a stock has moved your way, sometimes it's hard to let go. Absent strong reasons to the contrary, sell the stock after a 50-percent profit, or 3 years.

Wisdom to Sell By

Since selling decisions are so difficult, there are a few other maxims worth keeping in mind.

Contrarians don't try to predict prices. No one knows where a stock's price is going to go. Once a price trend is under way, no investor knows how long it will last, or how far it will run.

---

* It bears repeating: When the stock market bottoms and begins to rise, most people simply don't believe it. They are slow to realize that something has changed, and they're still operating based on the losses they have had, or a set of now outdated assumptions. Eventually, they see the light. If people are bearish on a stock that you hold, new money can be brought in by other investors to drive your stock higher.

Even some of the analysis tools we've discussed in this book cannot predict an irrational market move.*

You may buy a stock at $16 and see it surge to $35, where by all rational measures it is fully priced. It can just as easily go to $80 as a speculative frenzy takes hold. We would love to catch that move from $35 to $80, but we'll find that even proven fundamental- and technical-analysis tools will not let us do so consistently. Let's consider a few examples.

Some tools of technical analysis, so useful for buying stocks, can fall short under our contrarian system. To see what we mean, consider the "moving average," a favorite tool of the technical analyst. A moving average is the average closing price of a stock over a set number of days (100- and 200-day averages are among the most commonly used). In a 50-day moving average, we compute the average closing price of a stock over 50 days. We begin by calculating the average from days 1 to 50. On day 51, the average is computed from days 2 to 51, and so on. By doing this, we get a "moving" average.

In a moving-average system, the investor buys a stock when its price crosses above the moving average price, and sells when the share price falls beneath the moving average price.

When using a moving-average system, it isn't unusual to be "stopped out" by a temporary price reversal—only to see the trend resume its upward march, stronger than before.

Take a look at the upward trend of Coca Cola shown in Figure 13.2. With about a dozen chances to be whipsawed out of this stock in the $40 range from mid-1992 to mid-1994, few investors would have been left to catch the stock and stay with it to its peak in the mid-$80s.

We could illustrate dozens of other examples. The fact is that it is impossible to use technical analysis to correctly measure a trend often enough to apply it as a contrarian system for selling stocks.

Fundamental measures, while helpful, often just don't work. For many years, investors believed that once the dividend yield on the S&P 500 dropped below 3 percent, stocks were overvalued. By 1996,

---

*Ironically, *irrational* market moves are terrific when it comes to buying. A stock gets pounded down well below fair value as the crowd overreacts to some piece of news. Contrarians can pounce on those stocks as buys. It's much more difficult to use irrational exuberance as a selling technique.

Figure 13.2

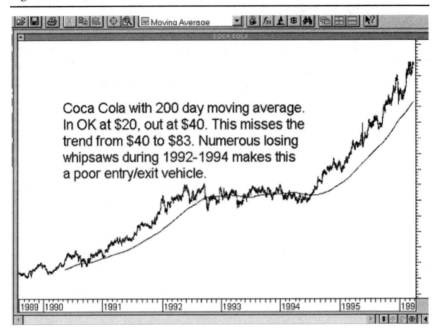

Coca Cola with 200 day moving average.
In OK at $20, out at $40. This misses the
trend from $40 to $83. Numerous losing
whipsaws during 1992-1994 makes this
a poor entry/exit vehicle.

investors who sold stocks on this signal sat by and watched the Dow march more than 2,000 points.

Other investments are measured more along psychological guidelines. Gold, for instance, is most profitable when the markets are least rational—times of panic. It matters not that fundamental analysis shows that industrial supply and demand are in balance. If people want to own gold, fundamental analysis won't measure the irrational need of investors to find gold's perceived safe harbor.

When a stock has a large short interest, and begins to move higher, a short squeeze can occur.* In that situation, the price of the stock exceeds any rational measure of valuation. Investors caught short, in a desperate need to cover, will pay almost any price for the stock. Once again, valuation is driven by needs having nothing

---

*In a short squeeze, a stock rises rapidly, forcing those who sold "short" using borrowed stock, to go out into the market to replace the shares—often at almost any price. On a stock that has attracted a lot of short sellers, the rapid rise accelerates as many short-sellers find themselves in this tight spot. Such stocks are often marked by a price jump that accelerates.

to do with earnings, book value, or other traditional, rational value measurements.

Since no one knows where prices are going to go, price targets or analysis tools can be of limited value. That leads directly to our next maxim.

Don't waste time second-guessing yourself for poor or untimely selling decisions.

Like all other investors, contrarians sometimes make mistakes. We sell too early, missing a huge price jump. Or we ignore our proven rules for selling, and take a huge loss as a result. Our rules for selling are designed to take a lot of the guesswork out of the process—reducing the number of times we'll engage in self-doubt.

When you do make a mistake, however, learn from it, forgive yourself, and move on.

■ *NOTES FROM A CONTRARIAN PORTFOLIO MANAGER*

Sometimes our stop-loss system works very well, allowing us to protect our profits. Remember Read-Rite, the maker of disk-drive components? After buying RDRT shares in September 1996 at $16 each, we set our 25-percent stop loss. As it turns out, we didn't need it. But once the stock climbed past $24, and we had our 50-percent profit (which happened in a matter of weeks), we placed a sliding stop loss 20 percent below the stock's high. That stop loss would let us keep at least a 30-percent profit.

The stock spiked to $33 in January 1997, the stock fell back and we sold at $28, locking in a 75 percent profit.

A couple of rallies in February and April pushed the stock back to $33, and had us wondering if we'd gotten out too early.

By May, the stock had fallen all the way back to $20, underscoring the value of sticking with our trading rules. Had we held on, we would have given back two-thirds of our gain.

At times, we'll concede, our stop-loss triggers will leave some profits on the table. Take our experience with Timberland, which makes and sells footwear. The stock had tumbled and we picked up a 3 percent position at $18 in August 1996. It was our kind of stock, smacked downward on earnings worries with an easy-to-understand business.

By February, the stock had risen, and then fell, triggering our profit-protecting stop loss. We were out at $38—better than a double. Were we pleased with ourselves!

Unfortunately, that drop to $38 proved a short-term correction. Timberland shares resumed their advance, tacking on another 30 points in a near-vertical ascent over the next six months.

Did this cause us to question our discipline? You bet. Did we change it? Not a chance.   ■

Summary

While investors overwhelmingly concentrate on picking out stocks to buy, we take the contrary view (naturally) that knowing how to sell is the most important skill an investor can develop. Our selling rules help you maximize profits while keeping losses to a minimum.

1. When you buy a stock, establish a stop loss that will get you out of a stock if it drops 25 percent from its purchase price.

2. Sell your winners after a 50-percent profit, or after three years, whichever comes first. There are exceptions: For instance, if a company clearly has brighter prospects going forward, you can hold on.

3. On a stock that's up 50 percent, set up a stop-loss that lets you keep at least a 30-percent profit. On stocks that are up even more, it's worth considering stop-losses that let you keep 70 percent of your profits. The stop losses allow for normal volatility, but are strict enough to keep you from losing your gains.

With a system that requires discipline, contrarians can eliminate moves made on gut instinct, those most likely to lead to inconsistent—or even disappointing—results.

CHAPTER 14

PLANNING TO WIN: CREATING YOUR CONTRARIAN STRATEGY

The secret of success is constancy to purpose.

—Benjamin Disraeli

We have found that all successful investors, without exception, share two defining characteristics:

1. They have a plan.
2. They follow that plan with unwavering discipline.

There is an old saying in the commodity pits: "Plan your work and work your plan." Hammer out a strategy for investing, and then follow that strategy. Successful investors don't fly by the seat of their pants. Some people seem to think that real pros leap into the markets each day, react instinctively and with dispatch, plunge through a day's trading with style and aplomb, and end each day with a pocketful of profits.

Successful investors build their styles over a period of years. They hit dead ends, have a cold hand for long stretches, and at times notch losses. But they persevere. Eventually, their discipline, and their willingness to stay with what they know, pays off. The approach they've developed through the years lets them ring up solid profits over time.

Unfortunately, that simple path to success eludes most investors. They confuse brains with a bull market, or constantly change their investing style, too happy to embrace the *theory du jour*.

Some investors, victims of their own inexperience, come to believe the markets are rigged, that insiders and other mysterious groups control the market to the detriment of individual investors. These investors would never concede that their own lack of ability is the source of their problems.

While we do believe that buying and selling by insiders at a particular company is often a good indicator of that firm's future prospects, buying is more predictive than selling. And, sometimes, even these insiders can be wrong.

Some technophiles believe the true path to wealth is found in the computer. They spend their days and nights in a search for the perfect trading system, one that makes profitable investing as simple as pushing a button and printing the results. When something appears promising (buy stocks on a day when the temperature in Chicago is 20 degrees higher than New York, then sell when the temperature in Chicago drops 10 degrees from its high), they embrace it—only to see it fail. They return to their computers to tweak their formulas and try again.

Eventually, they lose all their interest—or all their money.

Other investors personalize the entire process. In moments of paranoia, they believe that the market is out to *get them*. When that stock they bought dropped to their stop-loss point, took them out, and then rallied 20 points, it was because *"they were out to get me."*

■ *NOTES FROM A CONTRARIAN PORTFOLIO MANAGER*

I bought shares in a fertilizer company for our portfolios. The industry was depressed, nobody cared, and admittedly, fertilizer production isn't very sexy; perfect for the contrarian. I bought the stock for discretionary accounts in a high-yield stock portfolio. As a limited partnership trading on the NYSE, the stock was throwing off a 20-percent yield, (all its earnings) and the price doubled over the three years we owned it as the shortage of grain sparked fence-to-fence crop planting and a huge demand for fertilizer.

The company was scheduled to change into a corporation from a partnership and would no longer be required to pay out all its earnings as dividends to its unit holders. The dividend would certainly be cut to something around a 1 to 2 percent yield. That change was to occur 10 months in the future. Concerned the price would drop as the date of incorporation neared, I sold a 30,000-share position at $36. Two days later, a newsletter writer on a national financial news program mentioned the company as an excellent buy because of its yield. The shares rocketed $9 to $45 (even though the writer had his facts all wrong!). A client called and questioned the sale. He asked: "Why didn't we wait?"

My response: I felt lucky to have bought the stock in the first place, because the subsequent grain shortage couldn't have been foreseen. But, I was unlucky to have sold the stock before the TV interview.

I didn't blame myself, I didn't blame the newsletter writer, I didn't curse the network. I was too busy thinking about what I would buy next. ∎

Successful investing comes down to this: Work hard to formulate an opinion, then have the conviction to act on that opinion. The results depend on the soundness of the technique. In a few cases, bad luck overwhelms good judgment or sound reasoning. We are tempted to say the resulting losses are "unfair." But in the market, there is no fair or unfair. You have a profit, or you have a loss. What you shouldn't have is anger, hysteria, paranoia, myopia, hair loss, or a dozen other things that personalize the experience. All this can be avoided by having a sound investment plan and the discipline to follow it long-term.

UNDERSTAND YOURSELF: ARE YOU A CONTRARIAN?

When you start developing your plan, begin by analyzing yourself. This analysis should be an honest assessment of who you are, and *not what you would like to be*. We'd all like to be that fearless, take-no-prisoners trader who everyday rips out the hearts of the opposition and takes home the big bucks.

The truth is we're a sales rep in Topeka, an insurance adjuster in Eugene, a corporate staffer in Houston, or a software writer in

Baltimore. We have a family, a mortgage, car payments, aging parents, and worries that our savings won't reach what we'll need for retirement. We can't bet the ranch on any particular idea, but we also can't afford to settle for the meager returns of a bank CD. We're willing to take on some risk for higher returns. In fact, we need to.

We also need to understand our own personalities. Since successful contrarian investing is all about going against the crowd, you must be an independent thinker. Can you do this? Or are you comfortable only as a follower?

Successful investing requires discipline. Can you stick with your game plan through good times and bad? Do you have enough confidence in your methods and strategies to apply them time after time?

How comfortable are you with risk? Contrarians often buy stocks or invest in sectors or markets that are perceived as highly risky. Can you follow such a strategy without losing your nerve before your plan has a chance to work?

In short, do you have the focus, patience, independence, discipline, and nerve to be a contrarian investor?

■ *NOTES FROM A CONTRARIAN PORTFOLIO MANAGER*

Compatibility between investor and investment style is one of the most overlooked concepts in the investing field. What works very well for one investor may be disastrous for another. I think that's why a lot of investors fail. They may have a good investment strategy or technique, but they're not comfortable with it because it's not compatible with their natures. The result: They don't stick with it.

For instance, I learned over the years that the only way I could control my anxiety about risk was to set very strict stop-loss orders on my stock positions. I found that I had a tough time deciding when to sell a high-risk position. The automatic stop loss takes that decision out of my hands, and has worked very well for me. When I trade for my own account, every single position has a good-until-canceled, stop-loss order attached to it. When I do get stopped out of a stock or other investment, I never look back in regret or second-guess myself. In fact, I congratulate myself for showing the discipline to stay with my strategy. ■

Consider Time: Do You Have the Discipline?

How much time can you devote to your investment plan? Be realistic. If you have five kids, and two play soccer on a travel team, and you have a big lawn and do your own yard work on weekends, you can't spend the hours each week that a lot of strategies demand. You can't do detailed, fundamental and technical analysis on the top five stocks in an industry that interests you—you just don't have the time (or, probably, the peace and quiet) needed to think through your plan, to read the footnotes in five different annual reports and to crunch the numbers to zero in on the best investment.

Discipline is important. You need to schedule time to stay on top of your plan. Perhaps you have an hour a day to devote to your investments. Others may have a three-hour block once every week. You need to make sure that your plan fits the amount and type of time available. If you have one evening each week, a strategy that demands daily attention isn't going to work. On the other hand, if you only get 30 minutes each day, you've got to be very stingy with what you allow into that 30 minutes.

■ *NOTES FROM A CONTRARIAN PORTFOLIO MANAGER*

Since I have an entire work week to devote to investing, I have a lot of choices. I find that I use different time frames for different investments, depending on what I am doing.

I analyze the investments in my children's accounts on an annual basis. They have many years for their money to grow, so I tend to choose a country, or an area of the world (Europe, Asia, etc.) as an investment theme, and then let the money I've invested for them accumulate over a period of years. But in my personal accounts, when I trade commodities, I spend an hour each evening and another two or three over the weekend formulating strategy. Commodity trading demands very close stewardship.*

---

*It's instructive that I suspended my commodity trading while writing this book. Since I couldn't devote the proper amount of time to my clients, this book, and my trading, I gave up the trading. I didn't want to put my clients at risk by spreading myself too thin, or run the risk of poor investment results. So, my own commodity trading had to go.

Client portfolios, while a daily duty, usually demand a weekly review. While I have to monitor their positions constantly, I tend to make adjustments week by week, as opposed to daily or monthly.

The method I use is a direct reflection of the appropriate strategies to follow for each investment task. Each is legitimate in its own use. I would be foolish to analyze my kids' accounts every day, and just as foolish to let my clients' portfolios lie unattended for a month at a time. ■

RESEARCH RESOURCES: ARE YOU WILLING TO DO YOUR HOMEWORK?

Research gives you the knowledge you need to form opinions. For your plan to work, the research must be available consistently. You need to be able to see the same magazines, newspapers, research reports, newsletters, or investment programs week after week, month after month, or quarter after quarter. If the information is something you see only sporadically, you might not want to use it as a basis for investment decisions.

If you buy stocks based on tips you got from some guy you sat next to at the corner bar, or based on an interview you saw on cable TV, you probably don't have a consistent investment plan at work. You watched the interview, it sounded good, you invested. Is that really a discipline? What if the source changed his opinion the next day? Would you know about it? If he did change his opinion, and you missed it, wouldn't you also miss your "sell" signal?

It's better to identify the resources you can get consistently. A good example would be the Value Line Investment Survey. If you can't afford the annual subscription, don't worry. Your library probably carries it. Other sources can also work well: Your broker's weekly research summary, or a computerized subscription to a monthly mutual-fund rating service.

We're not saying to use these resources to make your buying decisions for you. Remember, as contrarians, we must be independent thinkers. But these magazines, newsletters, or newspapers can help you pick out stocks that everyone else seems to hate, or help you decide which stock to buy once you've identified some contrarian candidates from one market or industry.

Any reputable source of information that *is consistently accessible* is acceptable. You want a clear understanding of the source: how it works, what it means, how it changes from time to time. You need consistency in your research materials in order to be consistent in your discipline. If the input is haphazard, so will be the result.

Remember, the source must offer information that allows you to both buy and sell. If you come across an intriguing contrarian stock mentioned in a monthly magazine, you must consider how you are going to get the information you need to know when to sell. For instance, you may read about a labor disaster plaguing a New Guinea mining company. Bullish on gold, you'd like to buy on this bad news, capitalizing on the depressed price. Fair enough. But how will you monitor the investment? Where are you going to get more news once you own it?

Our rule that you sell after a 50-percent profit can be used as a proxy for this kind of information. However, you will obviously violate that rule at times because of unexpected bad news that changes your whole investment thesis. You can't be asleep at the switch, and your sources should keep you updated on each position you hold.

We can group these resources into several classes.

Excellent Core Sources for Building a Discipline
- The Value Line Investment Survey
- Morningstar
- Lipper
- Weekly Research From Your Broker*
- Standard and Poor's Research
- Knight Ridder Commodity Research

All of these offer regular and detailed reports of facts, figures, and opinions on a wide variety of investments. Since each offers regular follow-up analysis, they are good starting points for investment

---

* Most brokerage houses publish a weekly book that attempts to cover, in a comprehensive way, the meaningful research published that week by the company's analysts. In addition, more detailed individual reports are also issued. Typically, these weekly publications run 25 to 100 pages.

selection and offer enough variety to satisfy the needs of most investors.

Good Sources for New Ideas
- *Barron's* (The contrarian's favorite weekly)
- *The Wall Street Journal*
- *Investor's Business Daily*
- *The Economist*
- *The Financial Times*

General Circulation Magazines for In-Depth Articles to Learn New Things
- *Kiplinger's*
- *Money*
- *Fortune*
- *Forbes*
- *Worth*
- *Smart Money*
- *Business Week*
- *The Economist*

Your local library will probably carry most of these resources. If not, you need to buy them yourself, or eliminate them as a resource.

If you have to pick only one or two, we would suggest a subscription to one of the business dailies (*The Wall Street Journal* or *Investor's Business Daily*) and the use of the Value Line Investment Survey (many people don't use full-service brokers and, therefore, don't have access to weekly analyst research). We prefer *The Wall Street Journal* for its more comprehensive look at business, but believe that *Investor's Business Daily* has more information for the trader.

The weekly Saturday trek to the newsstand to pick up *Barron's* is always enjoyed by the contrarian.* Reading *Barron's* over the

---

* *Barron's* is now available over the Internet on Saturday morning via subscription, but it just doesn't feel the same as going to the newsstand to pick it up.

weekend is a good way for contrarians to refocus, reflect on their investments, and formulate new ideas. It's stimulating intellectually, besides. *Barron's* offers data on the week's trading in nearly all markets, including a lot of data that's nearly impossible to find anywhere else. *Barron's* is worthy reading for any contrarian.

Generally overlooked by American readers is the *Financial Times*. This business daily, published in London, provides excellent perspective on the world's markets, especially since it gives a global view that myopic U.S. investors too often lack. For anyone pursuing contrarian investments abroad, the *Financial Times* is must reading. It costs about the same as *The Wall Street Journal*, so is a luxury for many. Many libraries carry it, especially those in larger cities. Most newsstands have it as well.

Many investors believe that original research is the best. Securing annual reports, 10-K filings, and other direct-source material is a time-honored methodology. However, we believe there is so much good thinking and well-reasoned commentary available, that the contrarian's time is better spent on larger ideas rather than reading footnotes buried in the back of annual reports. We believe the technical, financial and accounting knowledge needed to decipher these reports is beyond the ability of most investors.

Remember, true contrarian ideas are not all that common, so contrarians must cast a wide net. You can't afford to be a specialist. You may find an opportunity today in Latin America, tomorrow in France, next week in gold, and a month from now in auto-parts suppliers. It may be an industry in the United Kingdom, or a company in Alabama. You must be willing to rely on the detail work done by others, if you are to be a successful contrarian.

What we're advocating is to use your time where it will do the most good. If it's clear to you that trucking stocks have been beaten down and left for dead, there's nothing wrong with using analysts' reports to decide which one of the pack is the strongest financially. As a contrarian, you might be buying these trucking companies even though analysts rate the group as a "hold" (which, as you no doubt know, is often Wall Street parlance for "sell").

New York, Boston, San Francisco, and even St. Louis are well-populated with analysts whose function it is to read this stuff and make sense of it. While we readily admit that there are a certain number of good investments that will slip by because your head isn't buried in the back of an annual report, you will also find that you'll pick plenty of winners because you were able to think independently about the big picture.

■ *NOTES FROM A CONTRARIAN PORTFOLIO MANAGER*

Investors seem to like pointing out all the bad ideas analysts have as if it's some kind of sport. When I find what I believe to be is a good contrarian theme, I'm always happy to let the analyst do the detailed analysis.

For instance, when I decided that electric utility stocks were too cheap to be ignored, I didn't spend any time at all analyzing financial statements. I was looking for electric utilities with a low cost structure. I could have ordered a hundred annual reports and pored through them. Utility analysts do a much better job of figuring that all out. I looked at the analysts' work and bought four stocks that met my needs.

Sometimes I spend my time on the larger themes, and leave the detail work to others. I only have so many hours that I can devote to the work, and I have to be very careful how I spend them.   ■

COUNT YOUR MONEY: HOW MUCH CAN YOU INVEST?

How much money you have to invest determines, to a large extent, your contrarian investment plan.

If you have $10,000 to commit, you will find country, industry, and index ideas easiest to work with since they provide broad diversification in a single investment. The need to diversify will force you mostly into themes rather than individual stocks. Therefore, mutual funds, closed-end funds, and country funds will be your investments of choice. In addition, your research will be limited to larger ideas. Since you have a limited budget, you must look for a handful of strong ideas, rejecting most after a rigorous review. You can, however, begin your individual stock selection by trying a couple of contrarian stocks. It's never too early to begin.

Once you have accumulated $25,000 or more, individual stock picks will be more prevalent, with a smattering still of funds and fund groups.

At $50,000 or more, individual stocks should form the bulk of your portfolio. You might have an account with a large mutual fund family (make sure it's a family that lets you switch easily between funds as your ideas change), as well as a brokerage account for your stock picks. Your need for research might place you with a full-service firm, but a discount broker is adequate if you have other research sources. The approach to contrarian investing we outline in this book involves fairly low portfolio turnover, so commission levels may be less of an issue than access to information and research.*

Contrarians investing $200,000, $300,000, or more have a nearly limitless menu. Accounts managed by professional portfolio managers, commodity exposure, funds, stocks, and options are all acceptable. Nearly any idea, large or small, can be accommodated. The challenge becomes rejecting all but the best ideas; when you have cash to invest, it's easy to rationalize an investment by telling yourself that you'll only risk "a little bit" of money. What you'll discover is that you have more money than you do great contrarian ideas.

Just because you invest a lot of money doesn't mean that you have to spend a comparably greater amount of time with your plan. Once you've analyzed an opportunity, you should be putting a specific percentage of your portfolio into that idea. It doesn't take more time to analyze simply because you'll be investing $50,000 instead of $5,000. You may be more careful as the amount of each single investment grows, but a $50,000 investment doesn't take 10 times as much time to figure out as a $5,000 one. As you increase the number of positions, not the amount of money invested in each, you're increasing your work load. You need to be aware of that. That may curtail the number of ideas you can use if your time is limited.

If you are nervous about risk, you should diversify as much as possible in your portfolio, and spend your time making sure you are buying the best-quality contrarian investments. If you like individual stocks, you might restrict yourself to stocks in the S&P 500 (bearing in mind that they will be highly correlated), companies with big market capitalizations, or companies followed by a consistent research source, like Value Line.

---

* As the battle for the investor's commission dollar continues, new and innovative ideas are coming to the fore. Full service brokerages, for instance, are offering flat-fee accounts, instead of commissions on each trade. Internet brokerage-house providers are slashing per-ticket minimums. Explore thoroughly to find the service most compatible with your investment plan.

WORK YOUR PLAN: CAN YOU STICK WITH THE PROGRAM?

Many investors craft an excellent strategy but then fail because they don't apply it. Ironically, investors then often blame their failure on their plan, not recognizing that they didn't actually use it long enough to gauge its value.

Investing styles, fads, and interests change over time. What worked last year, or for the past five years, will probably not generate the same excellent results in the five years ahead. Therefore, a sound strategy should not be abandoned simply because results have been unsatisfactory. Often, investors will change direction just before their plan would have started to work. That's why long-term commitment is needed. The lack of confidence in a strategy usually means the investor really didn't understand the strategy in the first place.

It's simply not enough to read about a successful investment strategy and then, in a rush of enthusiasm (Holy Grail found!), begin to apply it. Investors haven't looked to see if that approach is consistent with their personality. They probably don't understand it. And they will probably discard it as soon as it generates losses.

The most important rule in working the plan is to thoroughly understand the strategy, both in its larger themes and in its details. While a cursory understanding will allow you to implement the strategy and run it, a superficial knowledge will not give you the confidence to stick with it through tough times. Doubts will creep in when losses mount. Periods of poor performance will cause impatience.

There is only one way to thoroughly understand your strategy. You must be a student of it. It is not enough to go down a checklist, whether ours or someone else's. You need to study the strategy, explore its nuances, think about it. Read all you can find about the various aspects of your strategy.

For instance, before you adopt our idea for a 25-percent stop-loss, find out all you can about stop-loss orders. Study what others have done with stop-loss orders and what they recommend. Your goal is to know so much about stop losses that you have proven to yourself they are necessary and that the technique you put in place is the best available.

As your knowledge about each facet of your plan increases, so will your confidence. And with confidence, will come the ability to stick with your plan to let it work.

Accept the Failures

No strategy will work all the time. They all make compromises that generate excellent performance sometimes and poor performance at others. You must understand that, no matter how much you tinker with your system, it will not succeed each and every time you use it.* If you expect big returns, year after year, you'll become frustrated and never have the conviction to stay with your strategy long enough to make money with it. Your strategy must simply work well enough, often enough, to build profits over time.

■ NOTES FROM A CONTRARIAN PORTFOLIO MANAGER

When I trade commodities, I expect to lose money on 65 to 70 percent of my trades. This has proved a remarkably consistent number over the years. I lose that often because I take a lot of buy and sell signals. I set fairly tight stop-loss orders to limit my risk and, as a result, get beat up a lot. But those tight stop-loss parameters cut my losses before they can run. And I make enough money on the other 30 percent of my trades to more than overcome the losses and to leave me with a profit that's well worth the time I've invested.

I've found that, if I try to reduce the number of losing trades, I wind up missing some big moves. If I shoot for too many big winners, the percentage of losses on each trade increases. I am content to take the losses I do because I know that no system is perfect, and that my system is no exception to that rule. Sometimes, I just remind myself that a .300 hitter in the American League can make the All Star team. ■

---

*It is well-known among those who trade commodities that a system with *too high* a success rate is probably doomed to failure. Systems that show profitable trades 35 to 55 percent of the time tend to be the most robust and dependable. Higher levels of success probably point to a system curve-fitted to past market history—a history that won't repeat.

Be Patient

An effective investment strategy requires a lot of patience. If your strategy is sound, its value will increase the more you use it. Understand that you'll hit rough spots now and then; it's part of the investing game.

Think in terms of the stock market. We all know the market may or may not go up tomorrow. It may or may not go up this quarter, or this year. But we also know that, the longer we measure, the more likely it is the market will go up. We can speak of the upward bias of the market with more confidence if we look out over a five-year, 10-year or 20-year period.

If the strategy is to buy common stocks, just accept that you will having losing years. Does it make sense to abandon stocks after one bad year? Of course not. The same logic applies to your contrarian stock-picking system.

Be Consistent

For maximum effect, you need to be consistent. If you want to review and adjust your portfolio quarterly, you must do your work every quarter, without fail. You can't be haphazard. Sometimes a portfolio's return is based on one or two ideas that notch huge gains. If you aren't diligent, you could easily miss those ideas.

If you find it difficult to do this, it simply means that you have the wrong system. You've applied a strategy that your limited time cannot accommodate. It's a common error. Make the necessary adjustments.

While no investment approach works *every* time, there are a number of constants that work *over* time. For instance, buying good value is a consistent, long-term winner. Experts will disagree on just what constitutes value. The momentum investor will say he sees value in a little software startup whose shares are trading at 80 times next year's projected earnings (because earnings are expected to grow 120 percent). But, as a contrarian, you're looking for bargains, classically defined. You want to pay 50 cents for $1 worth of assets, or 75 cents for $1 in sales per share. Our research shows that, over time, using these contrarian indicators as part of your plan will generate long-term profits. You can build your strategy around the very simple ideas we outline for you, knowing that—50 years from now—these same concepts will still work.

Creating a strategy based on the semiconductor book-to-bill ratio is not an enduring market concept. It is a temporary market measure that will change radically as technology changes (or as the industry changes the way it measures monthly chip sales). Already, the book-to-bill ratio has been shown to be very prone to interpretive bias in a volatile market sector.

Ignore Popular Opinion

You can't ignore popular opinion. After all, as a contrarian knows, the crowd is right most of the time. Respect popular opinion, but do not let it sway your basic convictions. If your strategy focuses on assets at a discount, don't let pronouncements by market mavens that "value is dead" take you off your game. Stick with it.

■ NOTES FROM A CONTRARIAN PORTFOLIO MANAGER

The ability to anticipate the market—instead of reacting to it—is the most important attribute that separates the consummate investor from the rest of the investing crowd. We find value in investments that are eschewed by the crowd. We believe the crowd will eventually see that value; the crowd will come around to our way of thinking and prove us right. To succeed in this manner, contrarians must formulate an investment strategy based on this philosophy and then stay with that strategy through thick and thin.

Most investors quickly lose heart if a stock or a market goes against them. They place the blame on their strategy and vow never to follow it again. They lurch from one concept to another, always seeking the key to the market. But they'll never find it that way.

Look. Investing, like any other business, has overhead. The investor has no payroll, but he does pay fees and commissions. There is no inventory to count, but losses, like bad inventory, sap profits. And, of course, taxes must be paid. The investor can control expenses and can reduce taxes by not trading too much, and by taking mostly long-term gains. But, the investor cannot control the market and, so, losses will at times accrue.

Get used to them. They are inevitable; and no strategy, no system, can eliminate them. If your strategy is sound, it will show reasonable profit over time for the risk you run. This is all you can ask of it.   ■

SUMMARY

To succeed as a contrarian demands a well-reasoned plan that can be adhered to consistently over time. Contrarians need to know how much time and how much money they can devote to their stock-picking strategy. Any discussion about forming and sticking with a good investment strategy inevitably comes back to basics. Discipline, organization, patience, and persistence all play a part. Acting against popular opinion is never easy, and often is difficult. But, like any other enterprise, sound thought, consistently applied, can win the day. Formulating a plan, and then applying that plan, are absolute and basic ingredients to a profitable investment experience.

CHAPTER 15

SUMMARY: THE RULES OF THE CONTRARIAN SYSTEM

The easiest job I have ever tackled in this world is that of making money. It is, in fact, almost as easy as losing it. Almost, but not quite.

—H.L. Mencken

Listen to some of the big-name contrarians outline their latest ideas and you might well conclude that succeeding as a contrarian depends more on gut instinct than on quantifiable facts. Some of the better-known contrarians seem to have the instinct to zig when all other investors are in an irrationally exuberant zag. A contrarian sees that gold has fallen completely off investors' radar screens, buys gold, and profits handsomely when the rest of the market (much later) realizes the same thing.

Successful contrarians have honed the instinct to zero in on that unloved specialty-chemical company when other investors are still fuming about disappointing earnings. What the contrarians have done is to process a hodgepodge of information from sundry sources to correctly predict that chemical company stock will generate a double-digit return during the next 12 months. Those sources include the financial statements that demonstrate the company's strength, and articles in academic economic journals detailing the growing demand for chemicals in new economies such as China and India.

The trouble is that most investors don't have the time, information, and specialized knowledge this process demands. And that "instinct" can desert you just when you depend on it most. Our goal for this book was to develop a clear and easy-to-use set of rules for buying and selling contrarian stocks. We believe all investors can significantly boost returns without having to rely on instinct. The fact is, both you and that big-name investor will be using the same approach to buy out-of-favor stocks. It's just that our rules serve as a quantifiable *proxy* for that instinct. And, unlike gut instinct, rules won't leave you just when you need them most.

You will find our guidelines simple to use, particularly those that reduce the buying or selling decision to a single number or ratio. We believe the rules we outline, if followed, will set you on a profitable path by creating in you the contrarian mindset.

The rules we have compiled might strike the reader as overly simple. Investors too often believe that only sophisticated systems will generate profits. Quite the opposite. The simpler the system, the more successful it's likely to be. The fewer the moving parts, the fewer the things that can break.

Note: Not one of these rules is arbitrary. Each has been proven to work by the academic research cited in this book. What we've done is survey the relevant work done during the past 20 years, decipher and organize it, and create a set of investment rules that, taken together, create a contrarian investment discipline.

THE BUY RULES

The Initial Trigger: "Down-By-Half Rule"

A stock must be down in price by at least 50 percent from its 52-week high to be considered for purchase (for instance, a stock with a 52-week high of $50 must fall to $25 or less before you can consider it a "buy"). This is the most important rule, and under no circumstances must you violate it. The stock must still be down at least 50 percent when you actually purchase it. A $50 stock that drops to $22 cannot be purchased when it later rises to $28.*

The "down-by-half rule" defines a contrarian stock. It serves as an objective proxy for the psychology of the crowd. A stock that has dropped in price by 50 percent or more is deemed a contrarian play—despised by the crowd, shunned by investors, unloved. It is the best, objective measure we could find to define a contrarian investment.

Research shows that stocks down 50 percent or more tend to outperform the broad market averages for up to three years after the shares first fall. Investors wooed by good news can be a fickle lot, and are quick to dump shares when bad news surfaces. Stocks that have been hammered, by contrast, tend to have much less downside risk, and are prone to big price jumps when prospects improve.

Just because a stock is trading at less than 50 percent of its high doesn't automatically make it a buy. It only means the stock is worth examining as a potential contrarian play.

The Confirming Indicators

In addition to being down by half, a stock must meet one of two confirming indicators: Either show major insider buying, or meet two of four fundamental indicators.

1. *Major stock purchases by insiders or knowledgeable outsiders.* With a stock that's down 50 percent, insider buying within the prior six months makes a stock an almost automatic buy. The purchases should be for cash by corporate officers or company directors, although the exercise of nonqualified stock options, where the stock is held and not sold, is also a good sign.

Research shows that the average insider purchase is $59,000. We've doubled that number, meaning insider purchases are not statistically meaningful unless they total at least $120,000. Obviously, the higher the value of the purchases, the better it is. The $120,000 threshold does not have to be met by a single investor. Several insiders

---

*Buying at $28 in this case is tantamount to waiting for the crowd to push the price higher before moving in. This contradicts the contrarian philosophy and, if practiced enough, will nurture the wrong behavior.

purchasing an aggregate of $120,000 or more trips the trigger, even though each insider individually purchased less than that amount.

Insiders are required by law to disclose their purchases and sales of company stock in a timely manner, generally, the tenth day of the month following the purchase or sale.

Indeed, we view multiple purchases as multiple votes of confidence.

We think it's significant when insiders are willing to pony up their own money to buy stock down by 50 percent or more. In our experience, that's an indicator of better times to come.

In addition, we don't want to see sales of the stock during the prior six months. Sales, in addition to purchases, indicates a split view of the company's prospects and not a strong enough vote of confidence.

Research shows that insider buying is a valid "buy" signal, though the use of insider selling as a "sell" signal is less conclusive.

Similar logic applies to knowledgeable outsiders—well-known investors like a Warren Buffett or a Michael Price. When big-money investors see enough opportunity in a problem company to take a big position, we view that as a positive signal for purchase. Outsiders who go over 5 percent of a company's shares have to file a form called a Schedule 13D with the Securities and Exchange Commission in Washington. When an outside investor purchases enough of a stock that's down by half to trigger this SEC regulation, it becomes a "buy" in our book.

And since the investor must state the reason for purchasing the shares, we can get some additional insight on the company's prospects by reading a 13D filing.

If the knowledgeable outsider already owns 5 percent of the stock, he must add to his position by 10 percent or more to make the beaten-down stock a buy.

If purchases by insiders, or knowledgeable outsiders are not evident, we must turn to our fundamental indicators to confirm the stock as a buy.

2. *Must meet at least two of the following four fundamental analysis indicators.* These indicators help us avoid stocks in companies that are merely concepts and not real businesses. The four ratios help establish that the ingredients for a turnaround (sales, profits, cash flow, and assets) are present behind the stock.

• *Price/Earnings (P/E) Ratio of Less Than 12.* We define *earnings* as trailing 12-month earnings, not forecasted earnings. We recognize that a stock that has tanked by half is, in most cases, expected to post future earnings below past earnings, meaning the "leading" P/E is not as reliable.* However, these past earnings also illustrate the company's potential for earning money. A P/E of less than 12 means you are buying a stock trading at a discount to its potential earnings power.

Stocks trading at low multiples of trailing earnings per share are typically companies facing some kind of problem. The company may have had a bad quarter, or might be a cyclical company like an auto maker whose shares tend to trade at low P/E ratios toward the end of an economic cycle. (Investors fear that fewer cars will be sold when the economy slows, slowing the carmakers' profits.)

Research shows that portfolios of low P/E stocks tend to outperform high P/E stocks, while also posing less risk.

• *Price/Free Cash Flow (P/FCF) Ratio of Less Than 10.* Stocks trading at low multiples of price/free cash flow per share also tend to outperform high P/FCF stocks, research shows. Free cash flow is money left over after the company pays its bills, which is available to buy back stock or boost dividends. Investors who buy low P/FCF shares are buying cash flow on sale.

• *Price/Book Value (P/BV) Ratio of Less Than 1.0.* Book value is simply the residual value of the company; the value of its assets. Whenever you can assemble a portfolio of stocks where you can pay 60, 70, or 80 cents for $1 worth of book value, do so. Research demonstrates that this is far better than paying $2, $3, or $4 for $1 in book value.

• *Price/Sales (P/S) Ratio of Less Than 1.0.* Sales are the raw materials for profits. Sales supply the cash necessary to create a turnaround. Investors who key on this ratio note that management has a toolbox of techniques available to skew a company's reported profits. These techniques include, but are not limited to, the timing of restructuring charges, depreciation, and tax losses. But sales are essentially sales. Buying a company whose stock price is less than one times its sales per

---

*The P/E ratio is derived by dividing the price of the stock by the trailing 12 months' earnings per share. A $12 stock with a trailing earnings of $2 per share is trading at a P/E of 6.

share can be viewed as a bargain. And, like low P/Es, P/BV and P/FCF, a low price/sales ratio is further evidence that a company is out of favor.

Warning! Examine closely any company that meets three or all four of these ratio requirements. A company meeting all four may do so because it is too weak to survive. If a company meets three or four of our fundamental guidelines, it's worth looking for insider buying to confirm the firm isn't headed out of business.

The Minor Rules

Stocks must be at least $5 per share. Many institutions won't buy low-priced stocks. You need some kind of institutional ownership or analyst recommendations to help move the stock. Below $5, analysts and institutions are generally not interested. This rule helps you avoid penny stocks. Also, you avoid a $4 stock dropping 50 percent to $2. A $4 high would hardly be considered a great company with a great history.

You're better off buying fewer shares of a higher-priced stock than many shares of a lower-priced one. While many investors believe that more shares give more leverage, it is also true that lower-priced stocks are usually of lower quality. You're already investing in distressed securities. Don't compound the risk by buying even more speculative issues.

Look for companies with market capitalizations greater than $150 million. A company's market cap is the value of the entire business. Since larger companies rarely descend into bankruptcy, the market cap rule can keep you away from very weak companies with poor prospects. Smaller companies also pose problems for institutions because the public float of shares can be too small to make for easy buying or selling.

A too-small market cap might scare away the institutional sponsorship that you'll need later on.

Consider a change in top management as a positive in a company with problems. A company in difficulty will sometimes bring in a new CEO or management team. This is a signal that the tide may turn. At the very least the stock price will usually stabilize as investors take a fresh, wait-and-see attitude.

In a situation that's a close call, don't be afraid to consider qualitative factors such as brand names, a company's big size, or proprietary product po-

sition. For instance, any time you can buy an industry leader, it's a good idea. For that company to fail, you would almost need the entire industry to go out of business—hardly likely.

Look for the "one-timers." In a one-timer, a company's stock is hammered as a one-time event drives down the price of the stock. It may be a canceled order, an accident, or an earnings adjustment for obsolete inventory. Whatever the source, the event is a one-time affair in the operation of an otherwise healthy company. Once the dust settles from the one-timer, the solid fundamentals will reassert themselves and nudge the stock higher. One-timers are excellent contrarian opportunities.

THE SELLING RULES

Knowing when to sell is a much greater challenge then knowing when to buy. And selling is even more important; it's selling that lets you lock in your profit, or keeps you from losing too much money on a bad pick. We believe that a mechanical selling strategy is preferable to one based on judgment. We believe this for two reasons:

- Once investors have a profit, emotions often overcome good judgment. Automatic rules that dictate when to sell eliminate this possibility.

- Without a mechanical selling technique, contrarians will spend too much time analyzing every little wiggle in the price of each stock they own. Contrarians should spend time finding new opportunities, not fretting over old ones.

Our selling guidelines help achieve those two objectives. The guidelines:

Put in Place a 25-Percent "Stop Loss"

When you buy a stock, immediately enter a stop-loss order 25 percent below your purchase price and tell your broker that it's good-until-canceled. If you buy a stock at $10, and it slides to $7.50, you're out. This rule sets a strict risk control on each position. You cut your losses and can look for your next play, yet you allow for normal volatility (you'll rarely pick the bottom on any stock).

All stock-picking disciplines are imperfect and occasionally will cause losses. The essence of contrarian investing is buying shares in distressed companies; some will not make it. Too many investors freeze at the switch and can't bear to admit a mistake. Some even make the mistake of doubling up. The 25 percent rule protects you from debilitating losses that sap your strength, confidence, and capital.

A stop loss is an excellent insurance policy.

Sell After a 50-Percent Gain or Three Years

Sell once the stock shows a 50-percent profit, or three years have passed since purchase, whichever comes first. Much of the research on contrarian investing shows that investors won't see their biggest gains until the second or third year after buying a stock. Other research shows that stocks tend to cool off after a 50-percent gain. We suggest that with most stocks, selling after a 50-percent jump, or three years after making the first buy, is a structured way to lock in profits and move on to the next contrarian play. A 50-percent return is a marked success, and 36 months is long enough to give the idea time to work out.*

The Exception to the 50-Percent Rule

With some contrarian companies, prospects for better profits are so clear that it's worthwhile to stay on board for the ride. For instance, if a transportation stock has been pounded down for months because of high fuel prices, a fall in prices at the pump might dictate holding on even after a 50-percent gain. But the exception has to be a near certainty. Otherwise sell and move on.

If you do hold on beyond that 50-percent profit, you must move your stop loss upward to guarantee a 30-percent profit. For instance, if a $10 stock has risen to $15 and is held, we enter a stop loss at $13 and cancel the initial $7.50 stop loss.

When your gain reaches 100 percent, we suggest you set a stop loss guaranteeing a 70-percent profit. If that same $10 stock rises to $20, set a stop loss at $17 to lock in a 70-percent profit.

---

*As a flip side to the "down-by-half rule," research shows that stocks that have appreciated 50 percent in price tend to underperform the broad market averages.

THE RISK DIVERSIFICATION RULES

Stop-loss orders help reduce risk. But they don't do enough. If you own only two stocks, and they both trigger their stop losses, your portfolio would experience a heart-pounding drop of 25 percent. While we can't eliminate the risk of a general market decline touching off stop-losses on all our stocks, we can minimize that risk through careful diversification. Following are our risk-reduction rules.

The 5-Percent Purchase Rule

No stock, at its time of purchase, can account for more than 5 percent of the portfolio's value. Indeed, 3 percent is even better. This implies a portfolio of at least 20 different stocks. With a $100,000 account, each stock can account for no more than $5,000 at the time the position is purchased. This makes for very prudent diversification in a portfolio that often holds stocks in troubled companies. Along with the stop losses, the 5-percent purchase rule means the maximum you can lose from a drop in one stock is an amount equal to 1.25 percent of the portfolio's total value (5-percent position × 25-percent stop loss = 1.25 percent maximum loss from one stock triggering the stop loss).

The 20-Percent Industry Rule

No more than 20 percent of the portfolio's total value can be held in any one theme or industry. Since stocks within the same industry tend to move in tandem, this rule reduces the potential impact of "industry-specific" risk; in other words, the risk that a single event hits all the companies in that one industry at the same time, causing a big loss in all of them.

The High-Tech Rule

High technology stocks are generally not suitable for contrarian portfolios. We say this because high-tech companies are tough to analyze and demand a special expertise to understand.

High-tech stocks also typically lack the value characteristics defined by our four fundamental "P" ratios. The stocks rarely sell at book value, or at low P/Es. Therefore, contrarians must almost exclusively rely on the "down-by-half rule" and insider purchasing.

However, we also recognize that high tech stocks are particularly vulnerable to breath-taking drops and constitute fertile ground for contrarians. If you choose to purchase high-tech stocks, we suggest you supplement your work with fundamental analysis from a respected research source for details on the outlook for the company's product lines.

The Common Sense Rule

Remember, one of the most attractive points about contrarian investing is that there will always be enough stocks available to buy.* You'll never run out of ideas or opportunities. Every bull market has its losers, and a bear market is a contrarian's playground, since so many companies fall as investor sentiment turns negative.

By remembering this, you'll find it easier to pass up stock that you have mixed feelings about. Always ask yourself a simple question: Does this investment make sense?

The worst thing that can happen is that you miss a profitable opportunity. There will always be others.

Summary

These rules comprise our contrarian investment discipline. Each is based on sound research by academics or on the time-tested work of respected investors. Our guidelines are meant to put the contrarian viewpoint to work on your behalf. Over time, as your experience grows, you'll begin to think like a contrarian and you will no doubt massage these rules a bit to suit your personality. This is all to the good; it puts your portfolio selection process more in harmony with your sense of risk and expectations for reward. However, we can't emphasize too strongly that these rules, followed on their own, should lead to success over time, so any deviation from them should be the exception, and not the rule.

---

*The authors conducted a computer screening of 5,000 stocks in September 1996. This showed no less than 244 that met our three basic rules: Down 50 percent, market cap greater than $150 million, and stock price above $5. When we applied our confirming indicators, however, that list was narrowed to just a handful.

CONTRARIAN MATH

CORRELATION OF RETURNS

Computing correlations of returns is quite simple with today's sophisticated spreadsheet programs. Just enter the comparable numbers on two investments in two columns on a spreadsheet, and then use the built-in correlation function. It doesn't matter if you enter percentage returns, or the actual index or stock values. Assume you have the daily close of one stock in cells B1 to B100, and the second in C1 to C100. The following will compute correlation:

Excel

Use the CORREL function: CORREL(B1:B100,C1:C100)

Lotus 123

Use the CORREL function: CORREL(B1..B100, C1..C100)

A perfect correlation will generate a value of 1.00, and a perfectly negative correlation, –1.00.

VOLATILITY

Computing volatility can be done using the Standard Deviation of Return. The higher the value, the higher the volatility. The value returned will give the typical volatility of the investment for the timeframe expressed in the calculation. Assume you have the daily close of a stock in cells B1:B100.

Excel

Use the STDEV function: STDEV(B1:B100)

Lotus 123

Use the STD function: STD(B1..B100)

If, on a $40 stock, the value given is .52, this means that you can expect the stock to move, up or down, 52 cents two out of three times (an approximation of the first standard deviation) and $1.04 one time in nine (an approximation of the second deviation).

THE CONTRARIAN'S LIBRARY

This book should be considered only as a starting point for the contrarian. We have brought together, in one volume, much of the work done by many great investors and thinkers over many years. However, this telling of the tale can only touch on the high points of the research and labor done during the modern investment era. We encourage readers to become students of contrarian investing. And, the best way to do so is to engage in study of the works of the past.

We present a partial list of what we call The Contrarian's Library. Not every book is on the subject of contrarian investing, but each lends, in its own way, a bit of illumination on the subject.

We list our selections in random order.

> *Extraordinary Popular Delusions and the Madness of Crowds*, by Charles MacKay; originally published in 1841, many versions available in print (we used the Crown Paperback version, Crown Trade Paperbacks, New York, New York, 1980). To put it bluntly, you can't call yourself a contrarian until you've read this book. The first comprehensive chronicling of history's greatest manias is as entertaining today as it was 150 years ago.

> *Crashes, Why They Happen—What To Do*, by Robert Beckman; Sidgwick & Jackson, London, 1988. One of Europe's best known financial commentators offers an enjoyable history of market mayhem.

> *Great Crash, 1929, The*, by John Kenneth Galbraith; Houghton Mifflin, Boston, 1954. The classic recounting of the 1929 Crash has been reprinted numerous times and should be in print in your bookstore. For any contrarian, a poignant reminder of psychology gone awry.

> *New Contrarian Investment Strategy, The*, by David Dreman; Random House, New York, New York, 1982. The benefits of

low P/E investing are thoroughly explored by the acknowledged master of the subject.

A Random Walk Down Wall Street, by Burton G. Malkiel; W.W. Norton and Company, New York, New York 1996. Malkiel's book has created more controversy than any other work in our time. Whether or not you believe that prices move randomly, you need to know the argument.

Reminiscences of a Stock Operator, by Edwin Lefevre; John Wiley and Sons, New York, New York, 1994. Lefevre's book is widely reputed to be the chronicles of the notorious speculator Jesse Livermore. Said to be read by more professional traders than any other book. Great fun and great insights.

Security Analysis, by Benjamin Graham and David Dodd; McGraw-Hill, New York, 1988. The single greatest book on analyzing stock value. We don't know anyone who has read the entire book, but any time spent with *Security Analysis* can give you the flavor of what thoughtful, insightful analysis entails.

What Works On Wall Street, by James P. O'Shaughnessy; McGraw-Hill, New York, 1996. O'Shaughnessy has written a classic, detailing dozens of studies done on all types of investment strategies and tactics to find out what does and does not work.

Encyclopedia of Technical Market Indicators, by Robert W. Colby and Thomas A. Meyers; Business One Irwin, 1988, Homewood, Illinois and *New Science of Technical Analysis*, by Thomas R. De-Mark; John Wiley and Sons, 1994, New York. Both give good overviews of technical analysis. Also, we highly recommend any books by John R. Murphy.

INDEX

The authors are interested in
the readers' questions and comments:

Anthony Gallea
William Patalon III
P.O. Box 38
Pittsford, New York 14534

E-Mail to: GALLEA@MSN.COM